Child Welfare

Fields of Practice Series

Francis J. Turner and Herbert S. Strean, Editors

Child Welfare

Erva Zuckerman

82-4602

FP

THE FREE PRESS
A Division of Macmillan Publishing Co., Inc.
NEW YORK

Collier Macmillan Publishers
LONDON

The Free Press
A Division of Macmillan Publishing Co., Inc.
866 Third Avenue, New York, N.Y. 10022

Collier Macmillan Canada, Inc.

Printed in the United States of America

printing number

1 2 3 4 5 6 7 8 9 10

Library of Congress Cataloging in Publication Data

Zuckerman, Erva.
  Child welfare.

  (Fields of practice series)
  Bibliography: p.
  1. Child welfare—United States. 2. Social work with children—United States. I. Title. II. Series.
HV741.Z82   1982   362.7'95   82-71569
ISBN 0-02-935900-7

Copyright Acknowledgments

Excerpts from *Unplanned Parenthood* by Frank E. Furstenberg, Jr., 1976, pp. 217–219. Copyright © 1976 by The Free Press, a Division of Macmillan Publishing Co., Inc. Reprinted with permission of Macmillan Publishing Co., Inc. See pp. 141–142.

Excerpts from *Beyond the Best Interests of the Child* by Joseph Goldstein, Anna Freud, and Albert J. Solnit, 1973, pp. 32–34. Copyright © 1973 by The Free Press, a Division of Macmillan Publishing Co., Inc. Reprinted with permission of Macmillan Publishing Co., Inc. See p. 121.

Excerpts from "Family Union Keeps Families Together," by M. Dunu and M. Clay, in *Practice Digest*, vol. 1, no. 1 (June 1978), p. 23. Copyright 1978, National Association of Social Workers, Inc. Reprinted with permission. See p. 103.

Excerpts from "The Stresses of Treating Child Abuse," by Stuart Copans, Helen Krell, John H. Gundy, Janet Rogan, and Frances Field, in *Children Today*, vol. 8, no. 1 (January–February 1979), pp. 22–35. Reprinted with permission. Reprints of this article may be obtained by writing to Dr. Stuart Copans, Medical Director, Adolescent Alcohol and Substance Abuse Treatment Program, Brattleboro Retreat, Brattleboro, Vermont. See pp. 45–46.

Excerpts from "Specialized Foster Homes for Severely Mistreated Children," by Paul R. Harling, L.C.S.W., and Joan Haines, S.A., in *Children Today*, vol. 9, no. 4 (July–August 1980), pp. 16–18. Reprinted with permission. See pp. 108–109.

Excerpts from "Behavioral Techniques in Foster Care," by Theodore J. Stein and Eileen D. Gambrill, in *Social Work*, vol. 21, no. 1 (January 1976), pp. 35-36. Copyright 1976, National Association of Social Workers, Inc. Reprinted with permission. See pp. 98–99.

Excerpts from "A Family-Help Program That Really Works," by Sherida Bush, in *Psychology Today* (May 1977), pp. 48, 50. Copyright © 1977 Ziff Davis Publishing Co. Reprinted with permission. See pp. 69–70.

Appendix A, The Protective Services Casework Process, from *Helping in Child Protective Services*, Wayne Holder and Cynthia Mohr, eds. Denver, Colorado: The American Humane Association, 1980. Reprinted with permission. See pp. 189–193.

Appendix B, Permanency Planning, from *Permanent Planning Guide for Children and Youth Services*, by M. Jones and J. Biesecker. Millersville, Pa.: Millersville State College, 1977. Reprinted with permission. See pp. 194–199.

Appendix C, Sample Written Agreement, from *Permanent Planning for Children in Foster Care: A Handbook for Social Workers* (OHDS) 77-30124, by Victor Pike, Susan Downs, Arthur Emlen, Glen Downs, and Denise Case. Washington, D.C.: U.S. Government Printing Office, 1977. Reprinted with permission. See pp. 200–201.

*To Judy, Tim, and Sarah—and the rest of
the future generation*

Contents

Foreword

In 1978 The Free Press published the first of a series of books each of which addresses a particular theoretical approach of significance in the helping professions. Once this series was well underway it became evident that a second series was needed, one that differentially examines practice from the dimension of specific fields of practice.

Every profession has to face the complex question of specialization versus generalization. In this regard it has to come to terms with issues related to training and practice, and to make decisions about the relative emphasis given to those matters that are common to all areas of the profession's various fields of practice and those that are specific to each area.

There are of course dangers in emphasizing either extreme. If the generic is overemphasized there is a risk that important aspects of practice will be dealt with at a level of abstraction that bears little immediate relevance to what the worker actually does. If the emphasis is on the particular there is the danger of fragmentation and neglect of the need to search for commonalities and interconnections. Obviously, a balance between these two extremes is desirable.

Many of the human services, and social work in particular, have tended to overemphasize the generic to the detriment of the specific needs of clients with highly specialized needs. The majority of social work literature over the past three decades has focused either on modalities of practice as a single entity or on a specific theoretical basis of practice. This is not to say that there are not practitioners who are highly skilled in working effectively with specialized groups of clients. What is lacking is an organized compilation of the particular practice components of each of these specialized areas of practice in a way that is readily accessible to other practitioners in these areas.

Certainly within the periodical literature of social work there is a rich array of individual articles addressing specific components of practice involving work with particular client target groups. But such articles are scattered and not written from a common perspective and thus are of varying utility to practitioners.

It is the purpose of this new series to move in the direction of tapping this rich wealth of practice wisdom in a way that makes it readily available on a broad basis. To this end a series of specific fields of practice has been identified and known experts in each field have been asked to write about practice in their speciality from a common framework.

The goal of each book is to address not only the therapeutic aspects of practice in these fields but also the range of sociological, policy, administration, and research areas so as to present the reader with an overview of the specific field of practice as well as the specifics about therapy. In addition to helping the individual worker to learn more about a specific field of practice, the series as a whole, it is hoped, will provide an opportunity to make comparisons among fields of practice and thus facilitate the ongoing expansion of general knowledge.

Certainly there is growing awareness of the need for addressing the specific training and practice needs of each field of practice. Many schools of social work now arrange their curricula along the line of fields of practice. The NASW has utilized the notion of fields of practice to relate systematically to how some social workers are employed and to prescribe the roles most appropriate for them.

The fields selected for coverage in this series may or may not represent clearly defined areas of specialization in social work. Rather they are identifiable human needs or problem populations or even settings for which a discrete and identifiable cluster of attitudes, skills, and knowledge is thought to be needed in order to intervene effectively.

We are pleased to welcome Erva Zuckerman's book, *Child Welfare*, to our Fields of Practice Series. Zuckerman's many years of experience in child welfare as a practitioner, supervisor, and administrator are clearly reflected in the ensuing pages. Not only has she fully described the many tasks of the social worker in child welfare, but she has clearly pinpointed the necessary skills, attitudes, and knowledge that are required of the social worker in adoption, foster care, institutional work, and in other facets of child welfare. Zuckerman ably addresses the psychosocial needs of the child. In addition, she is equally attuned to the concerns and anxieties of natural parents, foster parents, and adoptive parents. What they need from the practicing social worker is constantly addressed in this volume.

This book is written for the practitioner and student as well as for the administrator and academician. It surveys the pertinent literature in child welfare, including some of the research, and is an up-to-date book on all facets of child welfare.

Acknowledgments

The purpose of this volume is to bring together, from many different sources, knowledge and experience that will be of value to practitioners and students in the field of child welfare. My debt to those who have been quoted in the text is evident, but there are many others without whose help this book could not have been written.

In addition to my gratitude to the administrators of the Nassau County Department of Social Services for the support they gave me in this undertaking, I would like to thank the following colleagues for graciously sharing with me material used in this volume: Doris Aronson, Noel Burks, Barbara Brandt, Marian Girardin, Anna Gravelli, Arlene Kochman, Jacqueline Lee, Walter Lowden, Gratia Schroeder, Robert Sunley, Sandra Wechsler, and, particularly, Sue Mihalik, who gave freely of her time to review early drafts and to share with me her long experience as a supervisor in child welfare. Thanks are due also to Dr. Catherine Papell of Adelphi University for her assistance in the initial phase of my research. Finally, I wish to thank the editors of this series, Dr. Herbert Strean and Dr. Frank Turner, and the editors at The Free Press for their unfailing encouragement and helpful suggestions, and my husband, Jack, for his endurance throughout the writing of this book.

CHAPTER 1

Every Child Needs a Family

CHILD WELFARE, as a specialized field of social work practice, is concerned with the unique needs of children. What are these needs, apart from those that children share with other human beings?

From the moment of birth, a child requires care in order to survive. Normally, this care is given by the parents or other members of the family. The functions of a family go beyond the essential need to insure the physical survival of its members, especially the most vulnerable member—the newborn baby. A child's first experiences of socialization occur in the family. The emotional bond to another human being that is necessary to emotional growth first develops there. The stimulation an infant receives from a nurturing adult supplies the foundation for later cognitive development.

These functions may be performed by a single parent with some type of support, shared by two parents, or fulfilled by the members of an extended family. The particular form of a family, its defined role, and the support it receives in fulfilling its functions will depend on the larger environment in which it operates.

In many tribal societies, a child may be cared for by any or all of the adults in the tribal group. Raising children is a shared responsibility of the tribe, and there is usually someone familiar to the child who can take over in emergencies.

The traditions of most Eastern cultures are passed on to the children through extended families in stable communities. Respected elders often share the functions of nurturing and socializing the children, while

1

the energies of the parents are engaged in providing for the family's physical needs.

The socialization function is generally the responsibility of child-care specialists in socialist countries. The group care provided for even very young children serves the dual purpose of inculcating the desired values and behavior in children while freeing their parents to work outside the home. By taking over this function from the family, the state can facilitate the transition from one form of society to another.

In contrast, the nuclear family in the United States is expected to be independent and self-sufficient and to raise its children with little support or interference from society. This heritage from the pioneer families who developed the West persists even though an urbanized industrial system has replaced the frontier society.

It is possible for a well-functioning nuclear family to prepare its children to participate competently in an individualistic society, but for society as a whole the price of this freedom and independence has been loss of the supports that an extended family or a small community can provide. The resulting isolation is one factor in a growing problem of child abuse and neglect. As Specht (1981) put it, "Fragmentation of the family and kinship group and alienation and anomie are the bitter fruits of a highly individualistic, mobile, and technically oriented civilization" (p. 9).

Without supports and under pressure, nuclear families have been disintegrating at an alarming rate. The 1980 census figures showed a significant increase in single parent families. More than one sixth of the 58.4 million families were in this category, nearly two million of them headed by males and some eight and a half million headed by females. Between 1970 and 1980 there was a 37.7 percent increase in male head of households and a 52.7 percent increase in female heads of households. Almost a quarter of the sixty-one million children under eighteen were not living with both parents. Less than half the black children were living with both parents. More of them lived with mother only (43.8 percent compared to 13.5 percent for white children) and more lived with neither parent (12 percent compared to 2 percent). The percentage living with father only showed less difference (1.6 percent white children and 2 percent black children). Not all these children needed help from society, of course. Some families have networks of relatives or friends who will come to their aid in a crisis, and others are fortunate in living in supportive neighborhoods.

An extended family has many natural and informal ways of filling gaps in parental care created by death, illness, absence, or incapacity. A grandmother or aunt may care for children when their mother has to work. Relatives may take in a motherless child or help out a widowed mother. A parent unable to cope with a child's behavior can often find respite or support by turning to those who are older, wiser, or more experienced. Among many native American tribes, grandparents play a significant role in raising the children. In a small, closely knit community it is difficult for abuse or neglect to go unnoticed, and social restraints may be applied.

With industrialization and urbanization, many of these informal supports have disappeared and have had to be replaced by more formal arrangements for day-care services, foster care, or adoption. The role of insuring that these institutional supports will be provided has been delegated by our society to the field of social work and within that profession to child welfare services.

The Distinctive Contribution of Social Work: A Historical Perspective

Our views as to what constitutes the welfare of children have changed dramatically in the past century or two, and these changing attitudes have been reflected in our laws. Both the profession of social work and the field of child welfare developed out of the economic and social changes that took place during the nineteenth century.

Child welfare services arose in response to a massive need for substitute care for orphaned and abandoned children. Wars, epidemics, and the industrial revolution had left thousands of these children, roaming the streets of our large cities, surviving as they could. Delinquency and the exploitation of children by unscrupulous adults were an inevitable result.

> Ragged, verminous, barefoot, the vagrant children slept where they could: in doorways, under stairways, in privies, on hay barges, in discarded packing boxes, and on piles of rubbish in alleys and littered back yards. The older boys often became members of street gangs who terrified respectable citizens when they weren't bashing one another's heads in; many of the girls were accomplished streetwalkers by the time they were twelve or thirteen years old. (Fry, 1974, p. 6)

The practices by which some earlier civilizations had solved the problem of unwanted or orphaned children—exposure, infanticide, or selling into slavery—while socially unacceptable, continued to exist.

> Exposure was not uncommon, only now it was called abandonment and was sometimes refined by leaving the baby in a basket at the door of a dwelling or on the steps of a church. As for infanticide, in New York City in the middle years of the last century it was a common occurrence. Scarcely a day passed without the discovery of the body of an unwanted baby, suffocated in an ash can, thrown into a back alley, or floating on one of the rivers. (Fry, 1974, p. 6)

When the Sisters of Charity opened the New York Foundling Hospital in 1869 in a small brownstone, this child murder was greatly reduced as hundreds of children were brought to the orphanage's doors (Fontana, 1976).

Abandoned infants might be cared for by religious societies, but the usual alternatives for children were indenture or the public almshouse. The beginnings of child welfare as a field of social work can be traced back to the mid-1800s, when the special needs of children were recognized by removing them from the almshouses they shared with the "poor, feeble-minded, insane and otherwise dependent persons" and placing them in orphan asylums. One of the earliest child-caring institutions, the House of Refuge, was established in New York in 1825 to care for children who would otherwise have been confined in adult penal institutions, although their only crime might have been vagrancy because they were abandoned (Catalano, Howard, & Ross, 1974).

Prior to the industrial revolution, the almshouse had seldom been needed for children. In an economy based on agriculture and crafts, children began to perform adult functions as soon as they were able and thus to contribute to the financial support of their families. While apprenticeship and indenture were often subject to abuse, they played a constructive role, as well, in preparing children for their place in society as adults.

The rise of factories had an impact on the resources for child care, as well as upon employment available to children and adults. While factories often employed whole families, they could not offer a place in a family, which was the usual arrangement for indentured children. Such opportunities were still available in agriculture, but for city children this meant being transported to a rural area, far from any relatives they might have.

In 1853 a young minister, Charles Loring Brace, undertook to do something about the ten thousand homeless children estimated to be wandering the streets of New York. He founded the Children's Aid Society, which began to send thousands of these children to small towns and farms in rural New York and the expanding Western frontier. The children "were placed with families who would take a child as an act of charity or as a source of free labor" (Catalano, Howard, & Ross, 1974, p. 4). This movement continued for seventy-five years and at its peak was sending three or four thousand children west each year. While the society's founders pointed with pride to many outstanding citizens who had thus been saved from a life of crime or suffering, this experiment left a heritage of dubious worth: the widely held belief that a change of environment or removal from a poorly functioning family is the best solution to meeting a child's needs (Beck, 1979).

Neither the "placing-out system" nor the orphan asylums were able to cope with the number of children in New York State in need of care. In spite of the rapid growth of orphanages, from two in 1825 to over sixty-five in 1866, there were still more than twenty-six thousand children in poorhouses throughout the state. The conditions under which they lived were so deplorable that the Children's Act of 1875 forbade "the retention of children between the ages of 3 and 16 in almshouses" (Report on Provision of Child Welfare Services in New York State, p. 3).

As one state after another passed similar laws, and alternatives were sought for the care of homeless children, controversy between the proponents of foster family care and the supporters of child-caring institutions grew sharper. The orphanages had removed children from the undesirable physical and moral influences of the almshouses, but Brace criticized the impersonal custodial care and regimentation of the institutions for failing to build self-reliance or to prepare children for practical living (Fry, 1974). In turn, others criticized his program for inadequacies in screening and supervising the homes in which he allowed children to be placed.

During the late 1800s and early 1900s, there was considerable movement toward developing free foster homes for children. In the Midwest, another minister, Martin Van Buren Van Ardsdale, established state "children's home societies" whose purpose was

> to find homes . . . in well-to-do families [for] homeless, neglected, and destitute children . . . to look occasionally with discretion into the homes, and thus prevent abuse and neglect, and . . . to make it possible for persons (without children of their own) to adopt a child. (Quoted in Kadushin, 1980, p. 318)

In spite of such efforts, the practical problem of finding free homes for so many children was overwhelming, especially in New York. Many continued to be placed in institutions operated by charitable and religious societies that received a per capita stipend for their charges. This system of reimbursing private agencies for the care of children who are public charges—known as the *New York system*—is still used in New York City (Catalano, Howard, & Ross, 1974).

Older children were often placed in "work homes," such as the one described by James Whitcomb Riley in a well-known verse.

> Little orphant Annie's come to our house to stay,
> To wash the cups and saucers up, an' brush the crumbs away,
> An' shoo the chickens off the porch, an' dust the hearth,
>   an' sweep,
> An' make the fire, and bake the bread,
> An' earn her board an' keep.

This practice of placing out with families was an accepted method by which child-caring institutions prepared their wards for independent living when the time arrived (Kadushin, 1980). Again, there were both problems and advantages. The frequency with which children were exploited led the New York legislature in 1898 to pass yet another law, "an Act to Prevent Evils and Abuses in Connection with the Placing Out of Children" (Catalano, Howard, & Ross, 1974).

Another pioneering approach to foster family care was being developed during this same period by the Boston Children's Aid Society under the leadership of Charles Birtwell. He brought professional standards to the field by individualizing the needs of children and studying and supervising the homes in which they were placed (Kadushin, 1980). Payments to foster families to reimburse them for the costs of caring for the children enabled the agency to exert greater control over the whole process of "boarding out." By the turn of the century, child-caring institutions and boarding out had largely replaced almshouses and indenture as methods of child care, although the last references to indenture and "binding out" were not removed from New York laws until 1923 (Report on Provisions of Child Welfare Services in New York State, p. 4).

The beginning of the twentieth century marked a shift from an adult centered culture to a more child centered view. The first White House Conference on Children in 1909 was followed by the establishment of the U.S. Children's Bureau, the first national public agency devoted to child welfare, and of the Child Welfare League of America, a national organization of child-caring agencies (Fink, 1963). The official statement of the conference stressed that foster homes should be used as a substitute for a child's natural home whenever possible but added that "no child should be removed from his home for reasons of poverty alone" (Turitz & Smith, 1965).

Changing conditions were partly responsible for this new emphasis on strengthening families so that children could be cared for in their own homes. More favorable economic conditions and improved health care had reduced the number of orphaned and abandoned children. The placement agencies found themselves dealing more frequently with children who had at least one parent; the home may have been disrupted by the death, desertion, or chronic illness of the other parent, but ties existed between children and their parents that could not be ignored. One of Birtwell's contributions was to explore foster care as a temporary alternative while a family's problems were being resolved so that the child could be restored to the home.

Allowances known as Mother's Relief had occasionally been given in New York, but the Child Welfare Act of 1915 authorized the granting of allowances to widowed mothers with children under the age of sixteen so that "such children may be suitably cared for in their homes by such mothers." (Report on Provision of Child Welfare Services in New York

State, p. 4). When the Depression brought federal funding to social work in the Social Security Act of 1935, this principle was incorporated into the program of Aid to Dependent Children (ADC), which later became Aid to Families with Dependent Children (AFDC). The change in wording was significant: it signaled the beginning of a trend toward integration in the midst of growing specialization.

Tendencies toward Integration and Specialization

The social work profession has been subject to the same conflicting forces that have impinged on other professions in our society. Just as in medicine the growth of knowledge encouraged specialization, which in turn created a need for integration—represented by the concept of holistic medicine—so in social work the growing trend toward specialization stimulated a search for the generic features that form the common base of the field's specialized branches.

It has been as difficult for the child welfare field to define its activity and set its boundaries as it has been for the social work profession of which it is a part. Both developed out of the activities of a variety of charitable, religious, and humanitarian groups concerned with the conditions of the poor. In the 1800s many of these groups joined forces to form "charity organization societies," whose friendly visitors informed poor families of the many services available for the betterment of their lives. Later, these societies became known as "family welfare societies" and then as "family service" or "community service societies." Their friendly visitors became trained social workers. At the same time, the groups that had been concerned primarily with substitute care for children were reborn as child welfare agencies.

As public support for child welfare services increased through federal funds made available by the Society Security Act, many states established child welfare divisions within their public welfare programs. The historic association of child welfare with child placement was evident in these programs. Home finding, home studies, and the selection and supervision of foster and adoptive homes became their major function. Cases were accepted for intake when there was a need for foster care or adoption. In effect, this meant that children separated from their families were served by child welfare specialists, while a family in need of supportive services to avoid breakdown was more likely to be served by a caseworker in the AFDC program or referred to a family service agency for help. The same was true for an unmarried mother who decided not to give her child up for adoption.

Some effort was made to provide supportive services to AFDC families by the departments that administered this program, but large case-loads and lack of training limited the effectiveness of the services that could be provided. A 1956 amendment to the Social Security Act had required the states to include, within their public assistance programs, services designed to restore families to self-sufficiency. In 1962 another amendment required that these services be provided in the AFDC program and reimbursed states for the administrative expense of providing such services. States were required to develop plans to extend child welfare services, including protective services, to every political subdivision. The definition of child welfare services used in this amendment was broad.

> Child welfare services are those services that supplement, or substitute for, parental care and supervision for the purpose of: protecting the welfare of children and youth; preventing neglect, abuse, and exploitation; helping overcome problems that result in dependency, neglect, or delinquency; and when needed, providing adequate care for children and youth away from their own homes, such as care to be given in foster family homes, adoptive homes, child-caring institutions or other facilities.

The emphasis of this law on programs to supplement parental care, as well as to substitute for it, encouraged the development of *home services to children* under public auspices; preventive and protective services, day care, and homemaker services were included in many of these programs.

The sixties were an era of expansion in social work, particularly in the public sector. With this rapid growth of specialized services, the need for integration began to develop. By the end of the 1960s Congress had acted to separate the provision of services from financial eligibility in public assistance, a move that was supported by the social work profession on the basis that it gave greater professional status to social services and the dignity of choice to clients. This separation left many public welfare agencies with two service divisions, one of which provided general services to individuals and families to assist them toward self-sufficiency; the other provided care primarily to children separated from their families. Frequently, the children's services division had the better trained staff since they were providing a specialized service.

The era of expansion came to an end in 1972, when Congress placed a limit, commonly referred to as the "service ceiling," on federal expenditures for social services. This was followed in 1975 by Title XX of the Social Security Act, which reinforced the trend toward integration. It required a single organizational unit for the provision of all public social services and mandated a planning process that allowed states and localities a limited choice among defined services. Included among the defined services were those traditionally regarded as child welfare services: adoption, foster care for children, and protective services for children.

There was immediate concern in the child welfare field about the effect this integration might have on the gains that had been achieved through specialization. The Children's Bureau, which by now was a part of the Office of Child Development under the Office of Human Development within the Department of Health, Education, and Welfare (HEW), undertook a three-year project, aided by the Child Welfare League of America and a management firm, to determine the impact of this legislation on the delivery of child welfare services and to assist states in increasing the effectiveness of their services.

A preliminary report in 1976 on the first phase of this project revealed that out of twenty-five states surveyed only three maintained a separate administrative division for child welfare services. Most states administered child welfare programs through departments of social services. A few included all social services under umbrella human services agencies. There was some concern that this trend would mean a loss of identity for child welfare needs and dispersal of the highly trained and experienced staff who had provided leadership for child welfare programs. This survey also revealed much variation in the boundaries of child welfare programs. Homemaker services and day care were sometimes a part of child welfare services, but often they were included in family services programs. Day treatment programs were usually classified as mental health services. On the other hand, a growing tendency was noted for children and youth involved with the courts (referred to as Children in Need of Supervision—CHINS) to receive services from child welfare programs (Child Welfare in 25 States). In 1979, in recognition of these varying trends, the name of the Office of Child Development (OCD) was changed to the Administration of Services for Children, Youth, and Their Families (ACYF).

This new emphasis on the integration of services to children with services to their families was the product of many forces. As the federal service ceiling placed more of the financial burden of child welfare services on the states, legislatures became concerned over the rising costs of child care. A number of studies had revealed that many children were, in effect, lost or abandoned in the foster care system, growing up with little, if any, contact with their natural families and no plan for adoption. With fewer orphans coming into care and more children from disturbed or inadequate families, the use of foster care as a solution to many situations began to be questioned. A study in New York that focused on foster care needs and alternatives to placement concluded that in some two thousand cases of children in placement (7 percent of those reviewed), the children belonged at home (Bernstein, Snider, & Meezan, 1975). The case readers judged that many of these children need never have been placed if community resources to support the families had been utilized or available. One of the examples cited in this report will illustrate the basis for these judgments.

> Puerto Rican, male child currently aged 13 was placed in a General Institution two and a half years ago. Placement was precipitated when his mother, who showed some signs of emotional disturbance, was finding it difficult to cope with her large family and was evicted from her apartment. The family is described as closely knit and the five children seemed very well cared for.
>
> The record was not clear as to the reason the family was evicted, since the mother was receiving public assistance. The mother is described as an hysterical character, but was not psychotic and was receiving help from a mental health center. Mother and children were devoted to each other and closely tied. All of the siblings have refused placement to foster homes because of their close ties to mother and longing to be home.
>
> The child's behavior has been described as normal throughout the placement and the psychiatric diagnosis also describes him as normal. The mother's condition during placement has deteriorated somewhat since the placement of the child, apparently as a result of the child's being away from her.
>
> The case reader felt that at the time of placement and currently, the family could have stayed together with the proper supports including assistance with housing, homemaker service, the use of a comprehensive family service center, and perhaps an after-school recreation program. (Pp. 70–71)

Government funding patterns appeared to encourage the placement of children since it was easier for states to obtain reimbursement for foster care costs than for services to support or strengthen a family. Well-publicized investigations in several states (Pisani, 1975) led to demands for child welfare reform and to legislation that provided more funding for services to support families and prevent the need for foster care.

Protective Services: A New Specialization

As the boundaries of the child welfare field were widening to include more services to children in their own homes, a new trend toward specialization within the field was developing. Growing public concern over the extent of child abuse was spurred by the publication of the results of a nationwide survey of hospital and court cases of abuse and neglect (Kempe, 1962). The alarm created by the findings of this survey was so great that by 1968 all fifty states had passed laws requiring the reporting and confirming of suspected cases of abuse and neglect (Radbill, 1968).

The legal basis for social work intervention to protect children was laid in 1874, when the Society for the Prevention of Cruelty to Animals was the only agency willing to petition the courts to remove a maltreated child from her home. The New York Society for the Prevention of Cruelty to Children (SPCC) was organized the following year, and the American Humane Society, which had been established on behalf of animals, opened a division for children. Initially, the emphasis of these societies was on legal action and punishment of the offenders. Later, there was a slow transition from law enforcement to treatment, a shift in focus seen also in the developing practice of social work (Aronson, 1980).

A century later, in 1974, the first national legislation concerned with child abuse, the Child Abuse Prevention and Treatment Act, was passed. The statute set up a National Center on Child Abuse and Neglect within the Department of Health, Education, and Welfare to collect and disseminate information about the causes, incidence, and treatment of abuse and neglect. Millions of dollars have since gone into programs designed to prevent abuse, identify cases, and provide services to alleviate abuse and neglect (Justice and Justice, 1976).

This funding support has tended to develop protective services as a specialized program. Research has focused on identifying the characteristics of families who abuse or neglect their children and on developing appropriate treatment modalities. Legislation intended to improve the reporting of cases and the accountability of the public departments responsible for responding also has fostered the separation of protective services from other programs.

At the same time, the requirement of Title XX that all public social services be coordinated encouraged integration. Recent legislation, including the 1979 New York Child Welfare Reform Act and the 1980 Federal Adoption Assistance and Child Welfare Act, recognized the necessity for special attention to the needs of children but required that specialized children's services be coordinated with all other services affecting families. The use of statewide computerized information systems to provide accountability is another important feature of these laws. The development of these systems has been promoted by federal funding in an effort to improve integration of services.

The need for both specialization and integration must be recognized. Specialization allows us to focus on a particular problem area in an effort to deal with it more effectively, but unless that problem is viewed in relation to all the other areas on which it impinges, the solutions may create more problems than they solve.

Definition of the Field

In this context, child welfare services may be defined as a specialized field of social work practice concerned with assuring children of parental care when the social system that normally provides this care (the family) is unable or unwilling to do so. This definition can encompass the variety of services needed to support, supplement, or substitute for the parental role.

Kadushin (1980) defined the field in a somewhat broader way. In his view, the field is concerned with all aspects of "the parent-child relationship network and the enactment and implementation of parental roles and child roles" (p. 28). This takes the child welfare field into the area it shares with the mental health field—the *child guidance centers* (or clinics, as they were formerly called). Developed as an effort to prevent juvenile delinquency, these centers are an interesting example of the shifting boundaries of the field. While they provide an important supportive service to parents, they have tended, when services are integrated, to be incorporated into comprehensive community health centers or to be funded by departments of mental health. Family service agencies, which provide many similar family counseling services, have remained identified with social services. The emphasis on services to prevent placement has tended to draw family and child welfare services closer together. Substitute care services—such as adoption, foster home care, and institutional care—and protective services for children are the traditional and unique features of the child welfare field (Kahn, 1977). Most of the services provided to children in their own homes—the so-called preventive, or supplementary and supportive, services, such as counseling, homemaker service, and day care—have traditionally been provided by family service agencies. Counseling is shared with the fields of mental health and clinical social work. Day care overlaps with the educational field. Although the specialized character of the child welfare field may be blurred by these shared boundaries, substitute care is rarely the only service needed. Services to children cannot be separated from services to families.

As Kadushin (1980) pointed out, all human services contribute to the welfare of children. When the field is narrowed to assuring children of parental care, many services provided primarily to children are excluded. Even though schools and child health clinics contribute to child development and thus assist parents in performing their roles, they do not have the specific responsibility of insuring that the parental role is performed.

Many social workers who work mainly with children are not included in the child welfare field. School social workers, pediatric social workers in hospital wards, and psychiatric social workers who do play therapy with children in mental health clinics are attached to other specialized fields. In this book the services provided to families and children through these related fields will be dealt with primarily in the area of interdisciplinary relationships.

Summary

Child welfare services arose in response to a need for substitute care for children whose parents are absent or unable to care for them. As this need has changed with shifting economic and social conditions, the field has expanded to include services to strengthen families through supporting or supplementing the roles of the parents. This has created a trend toward the integration of child welfare services with services to families. Specialization and integration should be regarded as interacting rather than opposing forces. Both are needed if the child welfare field is to fulfill its responsibility for insuring that all children receive the parental care that is necessary to their growth and to their participation in society.

CHAPTER 2

When Families Break Down

Mrs. Ames called a public child welfare agency to request a foster home for eleven-year-old Johnny. Johnny's mother had abandoned him as an infant in the care of Mrs. Ames's sister, who had raised him as her own child without establishing legal custody. After her sister's death, Mrs. Ames had undertaken to care for Johnny, but his acting-out behavior in school and in the neighborhood was creating difficulties for her. She no longer wanted to assume this responsibility.

Mrs. Brown's doctor had recommended emergency surgery, but she refused to accept admission to the hospital because she had no one to care for her five children. The hospital social worker called a neighborhood multiservice center that had had previous contact with Mrs. Brown.

Mrs. Caldwell became extremely depressed after her second husband walked out on her in her seventh month of pregnancy. Her six-year-old son by her first husband became fearful and refused to go to school. Unable to cope with the situation, Mrs. Caldwell sought help from a family service agency.

A family court intake worker called a public child welfare agency to request emergency foster care for a year-old boy. At a hearing to establish paternity, the father refused to accept any responsibility for the child, charging that the mother had abandoned the child in his care. The distraught young mother, Carol Davis, declared that she wanted the baby adopted, but in talking to a social worker after the hearing she admitted that this statement had been made only because was was homeless and without financial resources. She had broken off her relationship with the baby's father after he had abused her, and he had locked her out of the apartment they shared.

A hospital social worker called a public protective services agency to request that foster care be arranged for an infant who had exhibited severe withdrawal symptoms after birth. The mother, Denise Evans, was believed to be addicted to heroin, and the social worker questioned whether she would follow through with treatment plans.

A teacher reported to a protective services agency that ten-year-old Mary had told some of her friends that her stepfather had forced her to have sexual relations with him. Mary's mother and stepfather at first denied but later admitted that the incident had occurred. Mary's mother refused to bring charges against her husband, stating that it was better for children to learn about sex from their parents than "on the street."

Mr. and Mrs. Green, a well-educated couple, were unable to accept the fact that their first child had been born with Down's syndrome. Mrs. Green refused to see the child, and her husband supported her request that the baby be placed in an institution. The hospital social worker referred them to a public child welfare agency.

Joan sought help from a neighborhood service center in arranging for care for one of her six children, a four-year-old twin with cerebral palsy and spinal meningitis. Joan lived in a one-bedroom apartment on the third floor of a deteriorating building. The strain of carrying this child up and down three flights had recently caused her to hemorrhage and made her consider placing the child in foster care since she had been unable to find better housing. (Bush, 1977)

Mrs. Hanson consulted a child guidance clinic at the suggestion of nine-year-old Tommy's teacher. Tommy had become unmanageable in the classroom and frequently provoked fights with the other children. Mrs. Hanson admitted that she was unable to cope with her stepson. He harassed his younger stepbrother and had been accused of several acts of vandalism in the neighborhood. Mrs. Hanson expressed a desire to have Tommy placed in a residential school.

These vignettes illustrate the variety of situations in which child welfare services may be needed, ranging from those in which children have no one to care for them to those in which concerned parents are at a loss as to how to meet special needs of their children. While a child's need is always the focus of service, it may not be necessary to provide services directly to a child if the parents can be helped to meet the child's need themselves. In some cases, both parents and children will need services. Children without caretakers will need some form of substitute care, but they may require other services as well.

Traditionally, the child welfare field has described its population in terms of the children served, rather than their families. This approach reflected the large numbers of children in out-of-home care. The traditional categories of *dependent, neglected, delinquent, handicapped,* and *emotionally disturbed* children had some value for grouping children according to the type of care required. Dependent and neglected children, who had come into care because their parents were absent or unable to care for them properly, could often be placed in foster homes or in child-caring institutions that attempted to create a homelike atmosphere. Delinquent children, who had been removed from their families or communities because of their behavior, were usually placed in residential schools (often referred to as "reform schools" or "training schools"), in which the programs were structured to correct or change the children's behavior. The programs of other institutions were designed to meet the special needs of the handicapped or the emotionally disturbed, providing either treatment or custodial care.

These categories are still used by many child-caring institutions to describe their admission requirements, especially by those that will not accept children who have been adjudicated delinquent by a court. The term "dependent" is used in many states by juvenile or family courts to define any child who has become a public ward through lack of adequate parental care, whether the cause is abuse, neglect, or absence of the parents.

These categories are less useful in describing services being provided to strengthen families so that their children will not become wards of the state. These children are still dependent on their families, but they may be at risk of becoming dependent on society. Services provided by a child welfare agency to prevent neglect or delinquency are usually described as services to children in their own homes, presumably to distinguish them from those involving substitute care. The distinction between these services and those offered generally by the social work and mental health fields to families seeking help cannot always be clearly defined. This is the area in which the boundaries of the field tend to become blurred. The difficulty is in deciding the point of intervention at which child welfare services are required.

Public funding for services to families is tied frequently to the degree of risk that a child will require substitute care. This may be quite clear, as when a child has been abandoned or is being abused by caretakers. For a family under stress, the degree of risk is often less clear. The interaction of forces that may hold a family together or lead it to break down completely is extremely complicated.

The concept of the *social roles of parents and children,* which has been applied by Kadushin (1980) and others to the field of child welfare, offers one way out of this dilemma. This concept provides a framework that focuses on the functions of the family and describes the children in need of services in terms of the deficiencies that may occur in the roles the family is expected to fulfill. Thus, a child may need services because the role of one or both parents is unoccupied, permanently or temporarily; on the other hand, one or both parents may be available but have difficulty implementing their roles for a variety of reasons, such as parental incapacity, parental role rejection, or some type of role conflict (Kadushin, 1980). The most common reasons for the role of the parent to be unoccupied are death, desertion or abandonment, physical or mental illness requiring hospitalization, imprisonment, or a decision by the parent to surrender the child for adoption. Parental incapacity may be caused by chronic illness, physical handicap, ignorance, emotional immaturity, mental retardation, drug addiction, or alcoholism. Role rejection may be expressed in neglect, abuse, or abandonment. Role conflicts may occur between the roles of family members, or they may be experienced by an individual who carries differing roles. An example of the first would be a father who defines his role as limited to that of provider while his wife expects and needs his assistance in nurturing and guiding or disciplining their children. The second can be illustrated by the working mother, forced to occupy or share the role of provider, who feels a conflict between that responsibility and her child-caring role. A similar conflict may be experienced when one's role as a son or daughter responsible for aging parents clashes with the needs of one's children.

Kadushin (1980) noted also the special needs of children who make excessive demands on parents. Thus, parents may be unable to fulfill their roles when emotional disturbance, brain injury, or mental deficiency make a child unable to fill his normal role.

Finally, Kadushin (1980) noted that deficiencies in community resources, such as a lack of housing or jobs, may be an added source of stress to parents, making it difficult for them to fulfill their roles adequately.

These categories can be useful in identifying the point of intervention if it is recognized that they are comprehensive, going beyond the limits of the child welfare field, and that they are not intended to be exclusive. Kadushin (1980) included the supportive services provided to families by other social work and mental health agencies, such as child guidance centers, in his structure. This is a logical way to integrate the family service and child welfare fields, but in practice these services involve interdisciplinary relationships. On the other hand, while any or all of Kadushin's categories may be factors in situations requiring child welfare services, the mere fact that a role is inadequately performed does not necessarily mean that intervention is needed. Extended family members of other resources may be available to fill the gap. Not all families are affected in the same way by deficiencies in community resources:

some manage to stay together in spite of poor housing or unemployment; others break apart under the stress.

Two clues to the point of intervention are the absence of resources to fill a gap in parental care and the lack of access to such resources, either of which may be the product of either inner or outer obstacles. The vignettes that introduced this chapter will be used to illustrate how role theory can be applied to the child welfare field to clarify the population in need of services. In the absence of other resources, intervention will be needed when children have lost their caretakers, either permanently or temporarily, or when their caretakers, though available, are unable to implement their roles adequately. The special needs of children or deficiencies in community resources may be factors in the inability of parents to fulfill their roles.

Permanent Loss of Caretakers

Johnny, the boy in the first vignette, had the misfortune to lose both his mother and his surrogate mother. Even without a legal guardian, he found substitute care through an informal child-care network, which is characteristic of the black community. If Johnny's surrogate aunt, Mrs. Ames, had not found his behavior so difficult to handle, she might never have called for help from a social agency.

Johnny could have lost his caretakers in other ways. His mother might have chosen to surrender him for adoption to a child welfare agency, which would then have assumed the responsibility for substitute care. It is possible that if she had tried to care for him herself, she might have proved incapable of fulfilling her parental role. In that case, Johnny might have come into the custody of a child welfare agency as a neglected or abused child through a court action terminating parental rights.

Temporary Loss of Caretakers

Mrs. Brown's situation, outlined in the second vignette, was fairly simple; she seemed only to require competent substitute care for the children during her expected brief absence and perhaps some supplementary care during her convalescence. Because she could not afford to pay for a caretaker for her children and had no friends or relatives willing or able to step in, she had to call for help from an agency. Homemaker services would be the preferable solution to this problem, representing minimal disruption for the children and offering some support for Mrs. Brown when she returned home.

The need for temporary care is often more complicated. A hospital stay may be prolonged, or it may be of uncertain length when the treatment addresses a psychiatric problem, alcoholism, or drug addiction. Additional support services may be needed when a mother returns home. If Mrs. Brown had been functioning marginally before her illness, a homemaker might have been needed who could assist her in organizing her household tasks more efficiently. Special needs of some of her children would necessitate careful selection of a homemaker and perhaps other supportive services. Moreover, attention might need to be given to Mrs. Brown's own concerns about her illness, especially if these worries were related to chronic health problems.

Children may need emergency care because their mother has been imprisoned, or substitute care may have to be arranged while their mother serves a prison term of several weeks, months, or years. The imprisonment of a father may also affect family stability. The loss of income may make it necessary for the mother to go to work, or the added stress could lead to her breakdown.

When a parent is absent for only part of the day, as when a single parent or both parents are employed, some form of day care is needed. Again, this may be a simple situation, requiring only substitute care, or the case may be more complex, involving other services to parents or children.

Caretakers Available but Unable to Fill Their Roles Adequately

Children in single-parent families are most vulnerable to the loss of caretakers, but when two parents have been sharing this role, the loss of one may tax the capacities of the remaining parent. Whether the loss occurs through death, divorce, separation, or desertion, the parent who is left with the child-caring responsibility usually has to assume additional aspects of the parental role.

Some have the resources to cope with this situation. A woman with job skills and available relatives or friends may be able to fill both the child-caring and the income-producing aspects of the parental role satisfactorily. Mrs. Caldwell and Carol Davis, in the third and fourth vignettes, did not have such resources. It was not the loss of her husband's income that affected Mrs. Caldwell so much as the devastating emotional impact of his desertion during her pregnancy, which made her unable to function as a parent. The most pressing problem for Carol Davis, on the other hand, was to replace the shelter and income she had received from her baby's father before the break in their relationship. Her immaturity probably contributed to her feelings of helplessness and desperation, which had led her to offer to give up the baby; however, she might not have asked for help in the absence of financial need. For both women the loss impaired their ability to perform their parental roles.

In some cases an impairment brought on by a crisis is temporary and is corrected as soon as the crisis has passed. Yet if the functioning was marginal before the crisis, recovery may not come easily. Both Mrs. Caldwell and Carol Davis had suffered early emotional deprivation, which affected their performance as parents. They needed more than temporary support to replace the loss they had suffered. Their ability to function independently had to be strengthened if they were to perform their parental roles without continued support. These illustrations are evidence of the complexity of the problems involved in insuring that a child has adequate care.

The role of parent is a demanding one, and at times any parent may have feelings of inadequacy or of unwillingness to meet all the demands of raising children. Many parents recognize an incipient problem in a child's behavior or in their own discomfort and seek help voluntarily. Others, like Mrs. Hanson, in the ninth vignette, will follow through on the suggestion of a teacher, doctor, or nurse that they get professional help with a problem involving their children. Still others, like Denise Evans, in the fifth vignette, have difficulty facing a problem in caring for their children but may be willing to accept help that is offered when the situation comes to the attention of an agency. Some, like Mary's mother, in the sixth vignette, are unable to admit that a problem exists and reject any offers of help. In such cases, laws providing for protective services have asserted society's right to intervene in order to insure that at least minimal standards of child care are met.

Mary's mother is an example of a parent whose early emotional deprivation was so serious that she may never be able to fill her parental role adequately. If she could be engaged in a program through which some of her own needs might be met, her functioning as a parent might be improved, but some form of supplementary care might still be needed by her children.

The circumstances and stresses that impair the ability of parents to perform their roles may be external or internal, but often they are a combination. Some problems lie within the individual, either parent or child. Some reflect the impact of social conditions on the individual or the family. Most probably result from the interaction of these forces.

Poverty or unemployment, substandard housing, or a deteriorating neighborhood may make it very difficult for parents to give adequate care to their children. On the other hand, the poverty and substandard housing may sometimes be the result of a parent's addiction to drugs and a consequent inability to manage money, or a parent overwhelmed by a multitude of problems may lack the energy to seek solutions. The chronic incapacitating illness of a mother may make her physically unable to care for her home or young children, or she may be unable mentally or emotionally to meet her children's needs.

When the impaired ability of a parent to function makes substitute care necessary and the parent does not have resources for such care, child welfare services have the responsibility to provide such care. However, when earlier intervention is needed to avoid the breakdown that may make such care necessary, services may be provided from many different sources. Some parents may seek help for problems from medical, mental health, or educational agencies. Child welfare agencies may provide similar services to avoid the need for out-of-home care, or services may be provided through the cooperation of several agencies or disciplines.

Children with Special Needs

The inability of a parent to cope with the special needs of a child may stem from a lack of inner or outer resources, or both. In Mrs. Green's case, vignette seven, her emotional state made her unable to accept the fact that her child had been born with Down's syndrome. Joan, in the eighth vignette, had done her best to care for her child with cerebral palsy, but housing problems and her own ill health made it impossible for her to continue.

Child welfare services may be involved in meeting the special needs of children because their parents lack resources or because their parents are unable to take advantage of resources that are available. Many agencies outside the child welfare field serve children with special needs. Organizations in the health field that deal with conditions such as epilepsy, cerebral palsy, sickle cell anemia, and other genetic or birth related handicaps often include support systems for parents in the form of counseling or mutual aid groups. Many parents of developmentally handicapped children have banded together to obtain needed services for their children, especially educational services. Groups held under hospital auspices have been successful in helping parents of children with Down's syndrome to work through their feelings about the condition, thus enabling them to accept and to cope more effectively with the special needs of their children (Murphy, Pueschel, & Schneider, 1973).

Mrs. Green's inability to face her child's handicap was a barrier to utilizing such resources. Even if such a group had been available, she may have been unwilling to participate. Joan needed help because her poor health and her large family left her with little energy to seek out

appropriate resources and especially to negotiate the complicated bureaucratic systems through which services could have been obtained.

Other stressful factors may complicate the situation. Meeting the
needs of an autistic or hyperactive child may exacerbate existing marital
discord. Other children in the family may resent the attention required
by a handicapped child and react by withdrawing or misbehaving.
Many families have been strengthened and drawn together by the effort
to meet the needs of a handicapped member, but some will be torn apart
unless extra support is available.

Within this framework describing the children for whom child welfare services are considered appropriate, we can look at what is known
about the children actually receiving services.

Characteristics of Children Receiving Services

A comprehensive survey commissioned by the Children's Bureau
estimated that in March 1977 approximately 1.8 million children were
receiving social services from public agencies (excluded from this figure
were "children receiving day care primarily to facilitate the employment
or training of their parents") (Shyne, 1980, p. 27). More than two-thirds
of these children lived with their parents (60 percent) or other relatives
(8 percent). Only 28 percent were in some kind of foster care—foster
family homes, group homes, or institutions.

> The largest single category included about 40 percent of the children living
> with mothers only. Fifteen percent lived with both parents, and 5 percent
> with the father only. The second largest category, foster family care, in-
> cluded 22 percent of the children. Group homes and institutions accounted
> for 6 percent, adoptive homes for 2 percent, and a miscellany of other set-
> tings for the remaining 2 percent. (p. 28)

Less than 40 percent of the children being served lived in households
whose major source of support was Aid to Families with Dependent
Children. The fact that fewer than one in ten of the seven million children reported to live in AFDC households was receiving social services
led Shyne to conclude that a wide gap probably existed between the
number of children needing services and those being served and that
services had to be made "more available and acceptable to these economically disadvantaged families" (Shyne, 1980, p. 32).

Child neglect was the most frequently cited reason for providing
services. It was a factor in 30 percent of the cases and the most important
reason for providing services in 15 percent. Child abuse followed as the
most important reason in 7 percent of the cases, although it was a factor
in 12 percent. Financial need, a factor in 22 percent, was the most impor-

tant reason for services in 5 percent of cases. Emotional problems of either parents or children and conflict in parent-child relationships were next in importance, each of these three problems accounting for 4 percent of the cases. The other two significant problems were abandonment of the child or unwillingness to care for the child, each of which was the primary reason for services to 3 percent of the children.

The survey revealed that the public child welfare system was serving a surprisingly low proportion of young people in two categories which have been of wide concern to the community: teenage parents and status offenders. Teenage pregnancy or parenthood was the primary reason for service in slightly more than one percent of the cases. Although three-fourths of the agencies gave service to status offenders, whose behavior had brought them before the courts, this was the most important reason for service in less than two percent of the cases and a factor in only 6 percent.

When the figures on foster care were compared with those from a similar 1961 survey, the number of children in foster homes had almost tripled. The number in child-care institutions or residential treatment centers had increased from forty-five to seventy-three thousand, while the number in group homes had jumped from under a thousand to more than thirty-four thousand (Shyne, 1980, p. 29). The large increase in the number of children in group homes undoubtedly reflects the greater availability of this type of care and its choice as a more appropriate placement for many children who would otherwise have been placed in larger institutions. In spite of the increase in total numbers, less than 15 percent of the children in placement were in institutions. Nearly 80 percent were in foster family care.

Shyne (1980) reported that the median age of children in foster family homes was 9.7 years. Those in group care were generally older, with a median age of thirteen–fourteen. The reasons for entering care and the length of stay in care differed for these two groups. Children in foster family care had been placed most frequently because of child neglect, unwillingness of the parent to care for the child, or abandonment. Their median length of stay in care was twenty-nine months. One in six had been in foster family care less than six months and another one in six had been in such care for at least eight years. Children in group homes and residential treatment centers had been placed most often because of their own emotional problems. Parent-child conflict was the reason for a lesser number of these two types of placement. Some group home placements were neglect cases. Residential treatment centers had some children placed because of mental retardation, but cases in which mental retardation or delinquency was a major factor were found more often in other types of child-caring institutions. The median length of stay in institutions was about ten months; in group homes, six months.

Some ethnic differences were apparent: "Black children were some-what overrepresented and Hispanic children underrepresented among those in foster family homes. . . . Few black children were in group homes or residential treatment centers, but in other institutions the various ethnic groups were fairly evenly distributed" (Shyne, 1980, p. 30). One of the conclusions drawn from this finding was that "such specialized services as residential treatment" appear to be less available to black children. "The principle of equal access to service on the basis of need for service, without regard to race, income, or location, should permeate program planning and funding" (p. 32).

Although only 6 percent of the children receiving services were free for adoption, with an ethnic distribution comparable to that of the total survey group, 40 percent of these children were eleven years of age or older and 15 percent were at least fifteen years old. More than half these children had been surrendered voluntarily, but 34 percent had been freed involuntarily. Only 4 percent were free for adoption because of the death of their parents; 5 percent, because they had been abandoned.

Just as the foster care population had increased greatly, the number of children living in adoptive homes had nearly quadrupled since 1961. Also notable in this comparison was the increasing age of the children. The proportion of those under four years of age had dropped from 66 percent in 1961 to 36 percent in 1977. Adoptive homes had been found for "almost all of those under age 3 and almost none of those 15 or older" (Shyne, 1980, p. 30). Homes had been located for 54 percent of the white children but for only 34 percent of the black children.

These figures provide some information about the population receiving child welfare services, but they should not be construed as an indication of need. The need was estimated at that time by Kadushin (1978a) at between five and six million children.

Where Services May Be Found

Child welfare services are provided by both public and voluntary agencies. The Child Welfare League of America (CWLA) has about three hundred voluntary and fifty public member agencies. All states have either public child welfare agencies or child welfare divisions that function as part of a public assistance or human resources administration. Some of these divisions or agencies are operated directly by the state. Others are administered locally, with the state sharing costs. More than twenty-three hundred public agencies serving children and their families in 1977 were sampled for the data reported by Shyne. Kahn (1977) noted that together, public and voluntary programs formed a network of roughly four thousand sites at which child welfare services were delivered. Some of these agencies had a single function, such as adoption, protective services, or institutional care. In 1961 almost half of the estimated four thousand agencies offering child welfare services were institutions (Turitz & Smith, 1965).

A census of requests for child welfare services conducted in 1975 by the Child Welfare League of America (Haring, 1975) provided some information about the division of responsibility between public and voluntary agencies in the provision of services. While this census has not been repeated, the trends it revealed are still evident today and can be confirmed by the experience of many practitioners. In this census, the trend was for protective services for children (investigation of abuse or neglect) to be provided by public agencies. Employment related day care was also provided more frequently by public agencies, although this service was sometimes purchased with public funds from nonprofit or proprietary agencies. Services to children in their own homes, such as counseling, and group care in residential schools or group homes were more likely to be offered by voluntary agencies. Again, group care is a service frequently purchased with public funds from the voluntary agencies providing it. Foster care and adoption services were almost equally likely to be offered by either public or voluntary agencies.

Some changes have been evident in recent years. Many of the specialized agencies have adapted their programs to meet altered needs and conditions. Those that formerly provided services to unwed mothers, such as operating maternity shelters and finding adoptive homes for surrendered infants, now place more emphasis on supportive programs for young mothers or on finding adoptive homes for older, minority, or handicapped youngsters.

The changing character of the foster care caseload has prompted many agencies that provide foster family homes and residential care for children to expand their programs to include more supportive services to families. The increase in the number of children in foster family homes reflects more selective use of group care, among other influences.

The pressure on both public and voluntary agencies to reduce the length of time children remain in foster care and the number coming into care has stimulated the development of a variety of innovative programs to meet these needs. Among these are community multiservice centers and programs that emphasize permanency planning for children.

The question of where a family will go for services may depend more on the resources available than on the nature of the problem. This fact has been noted often, yet whatever the situation or the agency to which it happens to come, normally the possibility of keeping a family together and providing services to a child at home will be explored first.

The First Line of Defense: Services to Children in Their Own Homes

The traditional agencies providing services to children at home are the child guidance centers and family service agencies, both of which provide a similar range of individual and group counseling services to families experiencing problems with children's behavior or with parent-child relationships. While the orientation and emphases of these agencies differ as a reflection of their evolution, the types of problems they deal with and their treatment modalities overlap to a large degree.

The child guidance centers, which developed out of the movement to prevent juvenile delinquency, receive many referrals from schools and juvenile or family courts when children have difficulty fulfilling their social roles and come into conflict with various social institutions. The centers' funding and structure connect them to the mental health field. Their staffs usually include psychiatrists, psychologists, and psychiatric social workers, functioning as a multidisciplinary team.

The family service agencies, an outgrowth of the charity organization societies, which served the poor, are more likely to provide advocacy, in addition to counseling that may be either psychiatrically or socially oriented. Involvement with children may come as a result of the agency's involvement with a family, while the reverse may occur in a child guidance center. Family agencies often utilize psychiatrists or psychologists as consultants rather than have them on staff. Many family agencies have developed innovative programs to augment their traditional services, reaching out more actively to families who may need supportive services. Programs that combine individual and group counseling, family life education, and advocacy have been found to be more effective than counseling alone (Ambrosino, 1979).

Neighborhood multiservice centers have reached some families who do not or will not seek aid from traditional agencies. By offering a variety of health, educational, vocational, and recreational services, in addition to social services, these centers attract families who may not recognize the existence of a problem in relation to their children. Often, help can be offered, and may be accepted, because the parent does not feel singled out as having a problem.

Public social service and child welfare agencies also provide services to children in their own homes, most often in the context of a protective services program or as an alternative to foster care. If a family requests foster care from a public agency, services may be provided to that family to avoid the need for foster care when that course appears possible. Even without a request by the family, services may be offered if they appear to be necessary to protect children from harm. Most states now have laws that hold a public agency responsible for investigating all reports of abuse or neglect of children. If the investigation indicates that the children are in danger, the agency is authorized to intervene either through the offer of services to the parents or through legal action if necessary. Services may be offered directly by the agency investigating the report, or they may be arranged through referral to a voluntary agency. When services are refused or are ineffective in protecting the children, the children may be removed from the home, but court approval must be obtained for such action. In some areas in which an SPCC has been operating effectively, the responsible public agency has been given the option to contract with the voluntary organization for the provision of protective services.

Substitute care within a child's home may be provided through homemaker services. Both public and voluntary agencies use homemakers to sustain families during the temporary absence or incapacity of a child-caring parent. Some agencies employ their own homemakers, training them to assist disorganized or overwhelmed parents to develop their own skills in home management or child care. If the need is primarily for substitute care, this service is frequently purchased from commercial or proprietary agencies.

The Second Line of Defense: Provision of Care in Substitute Homes

If substitute care is needed, the concern is to provide the child with the most natural setting possible. The principle of the *least detrimental alternative,* proposed by Goldstein, Freud, and Solnit (1973), has been widely accepted as a criterion for determining the appropriate type of care. In regard to placement, this goal is usually expressed as the least restrictive alternative. Settings that approximate family living and allow free access to the community are considered less restrictive than a more structured institutional setting, which may provide schooling, health care, and recreation all within its grounds.

DAY CARE

If substitute care in the home is not feasible but a child has a responsible parent or caretaker available for part of the day, some form of day care would probably be the first alternative explored. This might be provided in a family home, a day-care center, or a program such as Headstart. In-home day care is not usually considered a child welfare service, although public agencies may pay for approved caretakers to enable parents receiving Aid to Families with Dependent Children to work or to enter training programs. The choice of a family home or a group program would depend on the needs of the child, the preferences of the parent, and available resources. For children under the age of three, family homes are usually preferred. If group programs are set up to accommodate infants, higher staff-child ratios are usually required and other standards must be met.

Public social service agencies are frequently responsible for insuring that family day-care homes meet acceptable standards. The state may set the standards, while local agencies find, study, and certify the homes. The day-care mothers may be given special training in educational and socialization activities, and the homes are usually supervised and recertified periodically.

Group day-care programs are more likely to be under the auspices of a voluntary agency, but this service is often purchased by public agencies. Most group day-care programs include an educational or developmental component along with the provision of substitute care. Many of these programs have socialization and educational preparation as their main focus. They may be used as a child welfare service, either to meet developmental needs of a child or to provide respite to a parent, as well as for temporary substitute care. Some group day-care programs include opportunities for parents to assist or observe in order to improve their parenting skills. This is an area shared by the educational and child welfare fields. Unfortunately, the funding support for day-care services has not expanded to meet the growing need, so that families needing such a resource do not always have access to it.

FOSTER HOMES

When temporary substitute care outside the home is needed, a foster family home is usually considered the least restrictive alternative. Foster homes may be provided by either public or voluntary agencies. As in the case of day care, the homes must usually meet standards set by the state, but they are recruited, studied, certified, and supervised by a local agency. Training for foster parents is generally part of the home finding program.

Agencies that specialize in foster home care sometimes provide services to strengthen the child's own family, as well. Aftercare services are frequently provided when a child returns home, and some agencies attempt to sustain families in which placement of children is being considered. A public and a voluntary agency may share these functions, as in the system used in New York City. The intake is completed by the public agency, which retains a monitoring function but purchases the needed foster care service from a voluntary agency.

Some agencies provide different types of foster homes. For example, emergency homes will take children on short notice for brief periods, either until an appropriate placement can be arranged or until the child can return home. Foster homes may be certified to care for one to four children or, occasionally, a larger group of siblings. An agency may employ a couple as foster parents to care for children in a home owned by the agency, an arrangement that gives the agency somewhat more control over the placement of children in the home.

ADOPTIVE HOMES

When permanent substitute care is needed, as when a child has been surrendered voluntarily for adoption, parental rights have been terminated by court action, or an abandoned or orphaned child is without a legal guardian, then an adoptive home is the preferred choice. Many children are adopted by relatives in such situations, but when this arrangement is not possible, a child welfare agency seeks a suitable permanent home for the child.

Adoptive homes are often provided by both public and voluntary agencies. Most of the homes sought today are for older, minority, or handicapped youngsters since the shortage of infants and the waiting lists of couples who wish to adopt them make it unnecessary to recruit adoptive homes for babies. Many agencies formerly screened all applicants and studied all homes that appeared appropriate in order to have an adequate selection available to match the characteristics of infants to be placed. This process is no longer productive in view of the long waiting periods involved. Couples may be discouraged from applying unless they are willing to consider a child with special needs. Adoptive agencies have developed innovative methods of recruiting homes for available children. The home study process differs somewhat for infants and older children, but in either case the agency studies available homes, selects those that meet the needs of children free for adoption, prepares both the child and the family for the placement, and supervises the placement during the period of adjustment until the legal adoption has been completed. Families adopting older and handicapped children often need extra supportive services during this period. Programs providing for subsidized adoption are administered by public agencies in many states. These programs have significantly increased the adoptive homes available for the children most in need of this resource. Federal participation in this important program was finally achieved in the 1980 Adoption Assistance Act.

The former clear distinction between foster and adoptive homes has been relaxed in order to meet the need of children for continuity. Foster parents may be encouraged to adopt children who have become integrated into their families prior to being freed for adoption. For some older children who do not wish to be adopted, long-term foster care arrangements have been developed to provide stability, either through legal guardianship by foster parents or through contracts for care until the child attains majority. These plans usually include preparation of the child for independent living.

The Third Line of Defense: Group Care

Group care, which usually involves a higher degree of structure than is necessary in a family, is considered the least restrictive alternative only when a child's needs cannot be met at home or in an available foster home. Some children respond better to a group living situation, in which peer relationships are an important factor, and others need the structure and services available in a residential program. Group care may range from small group homes for six to twelve young people, through group residences that accommodate twelve to fifteen, to residential schools or treatment centers for larger numbers.

Older children or those with special needs are more likely to require group care. An adolescent who is in rebellion against his own family may find it difficult to fit into another family structure and may feel more comfortable living among a small group of peers. Some group homes are set up in family style with houseparents. Others are staffed by young adults, who can serve as role models for the residents but not necessarily in a parental role. Residential schools can provide therapeutic environments for the emotionally disturbed or for those whose behavior cannot be tolerated by family or community.

Many group care programs have been developed under the auspices of voluntary agencies. Some of these are the religious societies that originally cared for children in large institutions. Most of the former orphan asylums have been converted into residential schools with therapeutically oriented programs. Some agencies provide a variety of types of group care. They may have a short-term diagnostic facility that admits children for a period of observation and testing in order to develop a suitable long-term placement or program. They may sponsor several residential schools with programs for different degrees of disturbance. In addition, foster homes and small group homes may be maintained for less disturbed children or those who have made sufficient progress to leave the residential program.

Some group care programs are maintained under public auspices, but these are more likely to be used for children placed by the courts. Although most state schools are no longer called reform or training schools, and efforts have been made to improve their programs, they still tend to be used for youngsters for whom other resources cannot be found. Courts place some children in residential schools maintained by voluntary agencies, and the cost of these placements may be paid or subsidized by public funds if the parents are unable to pay the full cost. These "private" schools tend to be more selective, with intake policies designed to select the children most likely to benefit from their programs. The publicly administered schools are more likely to have to accept any child sent by the court. As a result, they tend to receive the children who run away from other institutions or who act out in a way that is not tolerated. Publicly administered residential schools sometimes have group homes or foster homes associated with them that can be used as a transition to community life for those considered ready to leave the school.

These "state schools," are usually excluded from the child welfare field, being considered within the field of corrections, although there is considerable overlap in the population served by the two types of group care facilities. Other group care programs for children outside the child welfare field are the facilities providing long-term, or custodial, care to the severely retarded, along with specialized programs for children or adolescents within psychiatric hospitals.

Summary

The population served by the child welfare field consists of children and their families who lack resources to fill a gap in parental care or to compensate for some deficiency in the care that is needed. The absence of parents or caretakers, either temporarily or permanently, or the inability of parents or caretakers to fulfill their roles adequately; the special needs of children, which make extra demands on parents or caretakers; or the unavailability of resources in the community may be factors in the situation that create the need for services.

The services needed are provided through both public and voluntary child welfare agencies. They are drawn also from related fields, such as family service agencies and mental health centers.

In most states, public child welfare agencies have primary responsibility for protective services to children. These agencies are authorized by law to intervene in a family when such action is necessary to protect a child from harm. This intervention usually begins with an investigation to verify a report of abuse or neglect. If a basis for the report is found, the agency is responsible for offering services to correct the situation. Children may be removed from the home and placed in substitute care when the agency determines them to be in serious danger if they remain, but such action must be approved by a court. The services needed by a family may be provided by the public agency or arranged through referral to a voluntary agency.

Both public and voluntary agencies provide substitute care for children through homemaker services, day care, or foster or adoptive homes. Public agencies are often responsible for insuring that such homes meet acceptable standards and for administering programs for subsidized adoption.

Voluntary agencies provide a great deal of the group care needed for children, through day-care centers, group homes, and residential schools. Much of this care is financed by public funds through purchase of services. Voluntary agencies also provide counseling and other services to families to enable children to remain in their own homes.

Whenever possible, in-home services are provided to children in order to strengthen and support the family. Other agencies in related fields may be called on to provide some of the services needed. Family service agencies, child guidance centers, or multiservice centers are utilized for counseling, family life education, advocacy, and other services. Homemaker services may be used to provide substitute care for children within the home when this approach is possible. Homemakers may be employed directly by a public agency, or this service may be provided by a voluntary, nonprofit agency or purchased from a commercial agency.

If care outside the home is needed, the least restrictive alternative is considered. Care needed for only part of the day may be given in either a family day-care home or a day-care center. Employment related day care, needed to enable families to become or remain self-supporting, is frequently provided or financed by public agencies. Foster family homes are the preferred alternative when full-time care is needed temporarily. Adoptive homes are sought when a child is in need of permanent caretakers; for example, in cases of voluntary surrender by parents or termination of parental rights by a court.

Group care is most often used for older children and those with special needs that cannot be met in a family home or through use of community resources. Group homes can approximate family life but provide a structure useful to adolescents. Larger group residences are appropriate when special services are needed. Residential schools are usually the choice when a total therapeutic environment is desirable. Some voluntary agencies provide a continuum of types of substitute care, ranging from foster family homes through residential schools with specialized programs.

Some group care facilities for children are considered to be outside the child welfare field although they may serve the same population. These include specialized treatment programs associated with hospitals, facilities for long-term care of the developmentally disabled, and publicly administered residential schools for children placed by the courts as juvenile delinquents.

CHAPTER 3

Who Can Help?

When Mrs. Ames called a public child welfare agency to request a foster home for eleven-year-old Johnny, the person who responded to her call was Miss Curtis, a caseworker with the agency for three years. In order to qualify for her job, Miss Curtis had passed a civil service examination, which required that she have a bachelor's degree. Miss Curtis had a B.A. in sociology. Her only social work experience before coming to the agency was some volunteer work with children.

Miss Curtis had started out in the home finding unit, screening and studying potential foster homes. After two years, she had been transferred to foster care services. She had received some on-the-job training for her work in the foster care division from her supervisor, Mrs. Rollins, who had an M.S.W. and had been with the agency for eight years. Miss Curtis had also attended some in-service training sessions through the staff development section of the agency. These had reviewed basic interviewing and assessment techniques and some of the principles of permanency planning for children.

After Miss Curtis had obtained enough information from Mrs. Ames over the telephone to determine that this was a situation with which the agency could help, she made an appointment to visit Mrs. Ames at home to continue the exploration of the problem. The meeting was set for early afternoon so that she could talk with Mrs. Ames alone and then see Johnny when he returned from school.

Because Miss Curtis was relatively new in her job, she met with her supervisor to review the various options that she might be able to offer Mrs. Ames. In checking the agency's records, she had discovered that Mrs. Ames had been a certified foster parent for the agency a few years earlier. She had withdrawn from the program when her sister had become seriously ill and had needed her. Mrs. Rollins agreed that the agency could recertify Mrs. Ames as a foster parent for Johnny if she were interested in continuing to care for him with some assistance and support from the agency. Miss

Curtis took with her the necessary forms for this process, as well as an application for services and release forms for Mrs. Ames to sign so that she could obtain Johnny's school and health records.

Somewhat reluctantly, Mrs. Ames accepted this plan as a temporary solution to the problem and only with the understanding that Miss Curtis would continue to explore other alternatives for Johnny in case his behavior did not improve. She agreed that Johnny had gone through a difficult time and that it was better for him to stay in a place that was familiar while Miss Curtis completed her assessment, but Mrs. Ames had obviously reached her limit in trying to cope with Johnny before she called the agency.

Miss Curtis got the impression in talking with Mrs. Ames that her commitment to Johnny was more out of a feeling of obligation to her sister than from an attachment to Johnny himself. When she had a chance to speak with Johnny alone, she had difficulty getting at his real feelings. His affected indifference seemed to cover a deep hurt that he could not express.

Mrs. Ames blamed Johnny's behavior on her sister's indulgence of him, poor peer influences in the city neighborhood in which he had grown up, and the wrong friends in school and the community. Johnny said he did not care whether Mrs. Ames sent him away but that he would stay if she wanted him to. He had no complaints about his "aunt" except that she did not like any of his friends and would not let him bring them home or visit their houses.

Miss Curtis sensed a lot going on under the surface of this dispute, but she felt beyond her depth in trying to mediate. She suggested a referral to a local child guidance center, which might be able to help Johnny stay out of trouble. Mrs. Ames and Johnny both agreed to think about this.

In discussing her impressions with her supervisor after the visit, Miss Curtis felt somewhat pessimistic about the chances of Johnny's remaining with Mrs. Ames. Even if they agreed to accept the referral to the child guidance center and were able to get a therapist without waiting, still the process of resolving Johnny's feelings over the double loss of his natural mother and surrogate mother would take time. She was not sure that Mrs. Ames had the patience or a strong enough commitment to Johnny to go through that process with him.

Mrs. Rollins pointed out that if Johnny did have to be removed eventually from Mrs. Ames's home, his adoptability would have to be considered. Putting him in another temporary home would be likely only to increase his feelings of insecurity and lead him to act out more in order to test his foster parents. Even if an adoptive home could be found, his feelings would have to be worked out before he could accept adoptive parents. But before adoption could even be considered, Miss Curtis would have to undertake to locate Johnny's mother, whose whereabouts were unknown. Only if every reasonable effort were made to find her and this search failed could the agency petition the court to free Johnny for adoption. Mrs. Rollins and Miss Curtis went over the legal steps that would have to be taken, and they discussed the possible approaches to broaching the subject of adoption with both Mrs. Ames and Johnny, the importance of timing the introduction of this option, and the ways in which the search might be used constructively to help Johnny deal with his feelings about his mother's abandonment.

This illustration is given to suggest some aspects of the role played by child welfare workers. Studies of the field (Shyne, 1980) have suggested that most of the direct services in public agencies, and in some voluntary agencies as well, are provided by social workers with a bachelor's degree, which may be in social work or a related field. The typical child welfare worker has been described as a white woman from a middle-class background, working as a caseworker in a public child welfare agency located in an urban, industrialized area. She is likely to have a B.A. in some field other than social work and three years' experience in the field (Kadushin, 1980).

A study of 1.8 million children who were receiving services in March 1977 found that 46 percent of these children were served by workers who had bachelor's degrees in fields other than social work and no graduate training (Shyne, 1980). Only 9 percent were assigned to workers with graduate degrees in social work, and another 16 percent to workers with bachelor's degrees in social work. Nearly a quarter of the children (23 percent) received services from workers with some graduate training but in a field other than social work. The remaining 6 percent had caseworkers with less than four years of college. Data in this study "indicated that, although the direct-line supervisors in the participating agencies usually had many years of social service experience, barely one-third had graduate social work degrees" (p. 27). In this respect, Mrs. Rollins may not have been typical, but in many public agencies a master's degree in social work is a prerequisite for the position of supervisor. Few public agencies utilize their M.S.W. personnel for direct service functions. Generally, they will be found in supervisory or administrative roles, and where M.S.W.'s are very scarce, they may be used primarily for staff development.

Even in the area of in-service training, Miss Curtis's experience was not typical. Another study done for the Children's Bureau found that little of the training given in the public agencies studied related specifically to work with children and their families: "Most training available is related to generic human services or is directed more toward procedures and policy implementation than toward skill and knowledge. . . . Often the first-line supervisor is practically the only source of in-service training" (U.S. Department of Health, Education, and Welfare, 1976, pp. II–72). The sharp cuts in Federal training funds in the 1980s had a limiting effect on efforts to correct this situation. Although recommendations have been made "that a bachelor's degree in social work should be the minimum educational qualification for a caseworker providing services to children and families and that a graduate degree in social work, as well as experience in casework with children and families should be mandatory for supervisory personnel" (Shyne, 1980, p. 31), in reality most direct service functions continue to be performed by staff who are dependent on the quality of the supervision and in-service training they receive for the knowledge and skill that these functions require.

Direct Service Roles

In public agencies, the caseworker's role may include one or more of the following responsibilities: investigation of allegations of child abuse and neglect; in-home preventive and rehabilitative services to families requesting foster care for children or to those found to be abusing or neglecting their children; supervision of children placed in foster care; study and supervision of foster homes; services to pregnant minors and to parents considering surrendering a child for adoption; study of adoptive homes and supervision of adoptive placements; supervision of homemakers placed with families; study and supervision of day-care homes; and evaluation of the need for services and determination of eligibility.

Most of these functions involve visits to the home. When service is involuntary, as in protective services, home visits are a necessity. Clients requesting services, such as institutional care for children or adoption, may be expected to keep office appointments, but in many situations a home visit is an important part of the assessment, especially when the child will remain in or return to the home. For the study and selection of foster, adoptive, or day-care homes, an interview in the home is usually a requirement. Caseworkers supervising foster home placements are often required by law to visit the homes periodically.

A voluntary agency, particularly one that provides counseling to individuals, groups, or families, is more likely than a public agency to utilize M.S.W. staff for direct services. These counseling services are usually provided in the office, and fees may be charged, based on ability to pay. Paraprofessional staff without college degrees may perform advocacy roles and provide concrete services under the supervision of professional staff.

Voluntary agencies providing foster care vary in the standards set for their staff. Many operate like the public agencies in providing direct services through caseworkers with bachelor's degrees and utilizing their M.S.W. personnel in supervisory or administrative roles. When specialized foster homes are included in their programs, more highly trained staff may be assigned to the supervision of these homes.

In residential care, caseworkers with master's degrees in social work often carry major treatment responsibility for individual children. Often they serve as members of a multidisciplinary team, in which the consulting psychiatrists and psychologists, teachers, nurses, and child-care workers cooperate in developing and carrying out individualized treatment plans. The director of social services, for whom an M.S.W. is usually a requirement, is likely to serve as coordinator for the team. The director may also supervise a staff of caseworkers, including some with graduate training. Contributing to in-service training, providing consultation to child-care staff and teachers with regard to individual children, working with parents, and planning for aftercare services are frequently additional responsibilities.

Administrative Roles in Child Welfare

Graduate social workers are found on all levels in the child welfare field, from administrative roles to direct services to families and children. In administration, many are directors or assistant directors of public or voluntary agencies. The programs they run may be on a national, state, or local level. As administrators they perform a variety of functions. These may include any or all of seven basic activities that have been identified as important to the effective management of an organization: planning, controlling, coordinating, directing, representing, staffing, and negotiating (Schneider, 1978).

National organizations, such as the Child Welfare League of America, exert leadership in the field through setting standards, sponsoring research, and applying the findings to policy and program development. The Children's Bureau, which for years promoted the development of public child welfare programs through investigation, research, advocacy, standard setting, service demonstration programs, and coordination, now functions in a more limited role as a part of the Administration of Services for Children, Youth, and Families, primarily in the areas of standard setting and guidance (Kahn, 1977). A number of specialized agencies within ACYF, such as the National Center for Child Advocacy, sponsor research and demonstration programs, disseminating information about the findings for program development, and providing technical assistance and training materials to agencies. As a federation of accredited child welfare agencies, both public and voluntary, the Child Welfare League of America serves as a clearinghouse and performs functions of accreditation, coordination, standard setting, and research (Kahn, 1977; Turitz & Smith, 1965). A number of other national agencies play a leadership role in relation to child welfare. The American Public Welfare Association (APWA) is involved in standard setting. The Children's Division of the American Humane Association sponsors research and takes an advocacy role in the area of protective services for children. The Children's Defense Fund is a major advocate for black children and their families. The Puerto Rican Family Institute is another organization which is active in advocacy for minority children. The Family Service Association of America has furthered innovative programs for families and children. Other specific needs are addressed by the Child Welfare Division of the American Legion, the National Council on Crime and Delinquency, and the National Council of Organizations for Children and Youth. Many national and state groups and coalitions form before and after the White House conferences on children, which have been held usually every ten years since 1909 (Kahn, 1977).

Many of the same functions are performed by administrators of state programs. Some states administer their child welfare programs directly. The service workers are state employees, although they may work out of regional offices. In other states, the service programs are locally administered but supervised and monitored on the state level. In either case, the administrative functions of policy development, planning, setting standards, and maintaining accountability are carried out by the state.

The planning and controlling functions have become increasingly important on all levels as fiscal limitations have increased demands for accountability in the social services. The growing use of computer technology to facilitate planning and monitoring has required more advanced management training for social service administrators. Particularly in the child welfare field, systems have been introduced into the foster care, juvenile justice, and adoptive service programs to improve the tracking of children placed in out-of-home care. These systems are used to monitor service plans, match children with resources, and provide information for planning.

Supervisory Roles in Child Welfare

As supervisors, a major role of graduate social workers is case management and supervision of accountability systems, including court reviews. They also provide on-the-job training to staff without formal social work education who perform most of the direct services to families and children. For these functions a basic knowledge of child development and family dynamics is important. Some knowledge of legal processes is also necessary since the courts are frequently involved when society intervenes in the parent-child relationship. A knowledge of group dynamics is of value, too, because supervisors deal with staff not only as individuals but also as a group. Some supervisors conduct group sessions with parents, foster parents, or young people, both as a support service to participants and as a demonstration to staff of group methods.

Some supervisors perform additional direct service functions in intake. Their controlling and representing functions include managing a caseload and participating as agency representatives in community or interagency planning or coordinating groups. Supervisors need to develop skills in such managerial techniques as the organization of systems for effective work flow, adequate record keeping, accurate reporting, collection of statistics and other information, and maintaining standards of performance. Since computer systems are widely used today supervisors need to have some knowledge of them to utilize them constructively.

A graduate social worker performing direct service functions is most likely to be employed by a voluntary agency for such responsibilities as intake, services to children in their own homes, adoption services, or the supervision of specialized foster homes serving disturbed children. Graduate social workers provide specialized services in many group homes and residential treatment centers.

Roles for Paraprofessionals

Paraprofessional staff have an important role in the child welfare field. As day-care mothers, foster parents, homemakers, child-care workers in residential schools, and paid or unpaid parent aides, lay therapists, or mentors, they have day-to-day direct contact with children and their families. Teamwork between professionals and paraprofessionals is essential to effective service provision. Each has a distinctive role and unique skills to contribute. With professional guidance and support, paraprofessionals or volunteers selected for personal qualities (especially the ability to establish a supportive relationship) can often gain the trust of an inadequate parent or an abused child and meet day-to-day needs or serve as a role model in a way that would not be possible for a professional working alone. A similarity in ethnic background or economic circumstances may make a paraprofessional more sensitive to certain social or cultural influences, thus establishing rapport more rapidly.

One of the findings in Fanshel and Shinn's (1978) foster care research was that the younger, less experienced child-care workers in residential programs had a positive effect on the development of the youngsters under their care. Noting that college students often take jobs as child-care workers to gain social work experience, he speculated that this relationship was stimulating to the children.

Some basic principles of child development and an understanding of the developmental tasks appropriate to each age may be provided as a part of in-service training for paraprofessional staff; such information is useful for all types of workers who have direct contact with children or parents. In addition, child-care workers need knowledge and skill in group dynamics in order to make the daily activities and interactions of a cottage group growth enhancing experiences. The inclusion of child-care workers in meetings of the treatment team helps them to understand the goals of treatment so that the child's daily living activities can contribute to these goals. Consultation with the child's caseworker can assist paraprofessionals in understanding the children they serve and in dealing with their own feelings and reactions to the children's behavior.

Team Models in Child Welfare

Teamwork between professional and paraprofessional staff is an important aspect of the child welfare field that occurs in many different settings. Some agencies have cultivated a partnership between caseworkers and foster parents by bringing them together for joint training that emphasizes their common purpose and the unique contribution each can make. Foster care teams often include the natural families and other service providers, as well, and they may use contracts as "an explicit working agreement among all team members" (Marr, 1981, p. 2).

The concern for efficient utilization of social work manpower has led to the exploration of team models as a means of more effective service delivery. A three-year research and demonstration project published in 1973 recommended one such model.

> One of this project's three objectives was to design a model for achieving improvement in the delivery and management of child welfare services—specifically in a county department of social services, but applicable, with modifications, to voluntary agencies and larger governmental systems as well. . . . In regard to staffing, after an exhaustive review of the literature and a careful study of the implications of employing a variety of manpower utilization patterns as they relate to the entire delivery system, the project's research team concluded that by far the best results are promised by proper use of social service teams. Substituting the team concept for the currently prevalent hierarchical pattern . . . would significantly improve the quality of services and appreciably increase caseload capacity—to say nothing of providing more adequate service to a multiple-problem family. (Madison, 1977, pp. 42–43)

In this model, the team consists of a leader, who is an M.S.W.; social workers (B.A.) with experience in various areas of child welfare, such as foster care, adoption, services to families, day care, and homemaker services; a community worker, who functions as a case aide, providing more concrete services; a consumer member, who is paid on a per diem basis to serve as a consultant; and a secretary. Cases are assigned to the team. Taking into account the particular skills of each team member, the leader designates a coordinator for each case, giving this person primary responsibility for all contacts. Other team members may be called on to share their areas of expertise as needed. Cases are reviewed by the entire team under the guidance of the leader.

Variations on the Team Model

Many protective services programs now utilize multidisciplinary teams to provide services needed for the rehabilitation of families. These teams usually are composed of medical and social services personnel, but many include other professionals, as well as paraprofessionals. Some limit their functions to diagnosis, evaluation, consultation, and monitoring. Others become involved in crisis intervention and coordinating service provision.

An M.S.W. usually serves as team leader and coordinates regular mettings of a team that has been assembled to meet the needs of a particular case. Such a team generally includes a protective services caseworker, who has responsibility as case manager; medical, mental health, and other appropriate service providers; and sometimes a parent aide or homemaker serving the case.

A somewhat different model was developed by the Lower East Side Family Union in New York City. This project demonstrated the use of a team that had a social worker with an M.S.W. as leader. Social work associates, with bachelor's degrees, and homemakers served as team members. The associates were responsible for intake, developing service plans with families, arranging meetings with service provider agencies to reach agreement on service contracts, and monitoring progress and service delivery. The homemakers worked closely with the associates to whose cases they were assigned. The team leader served as consultant, supervisor, and overall coordinator for all cases.

Other Models of Partnership: Parents and Professionals

Another innovative model of social work manpower deployment uses an M.S.W. as director of a program that trains parents as paraprofessional group leaders in family life education programs. Parents who have participated successfully in a group experience and who show an interest and aptitude are trained in group leadership and/or peer counseling or advocacy. The paraprofessional staff receive professional support through supervision and consultation with the director of the program and through professional counseling within the agency. The Parent and Child Training Project (PACT) and the Mothers' Center, both developed by the Family Service Association of Nassau County, are variations of this model (Ambrosino, 1979). PACT was designed

> to reach the most vulnerable groups in the community—families on welfare, those reported for child abuse and neglect, and Hispanic families, isolated and overwhelmed by the demands of their new environment. The vehicles for reaching out were family life education groups that focused on child rearing, helping children in school, and advocacy. (Ambrosino, 1979, p. 584)

The Mothers' Center, developed in a middle-class neighborhood,

> offers groups for pregnant women and mothers. . . . A self-selected group from the approximately 300 women who have used the center have been trained by professional social workers to conduct groups or to be available for individual peer sessions for members who want to examine further personal aspects of issues discussed in the groups. These peer group and one-to-one facilitators, with the assistance of professional staff, identify members who might benefit from counseling, and appropriate referrals are made. [Data collected] about the experiences of the participants . . . [are] used as the basis for advocacy actions with medical and educational resources in the areas of pregnancy, childbirth, and health care. (Ambrosino, 1979, p. 583)

Still another variation can be found in some multiservice centers that use their M.S.W. social workers as clinical supervisors and administrators to develop programs that utilize personnel of many different backgrounds to provide the needed supportive services to families. These may include such programs as a crisis nursery, workshops, self-help or mutual aid groups, and family recreation. Several of these programs are described in Chapter 4.

Job Satisfaction and Stress

Many factors contribute to job satisfaction, but one of the basic elements is the gratification that comes from a sense of accomplishment or of seeing some progress toward goals. People who enter the field of social work usually have a desire to interact with other people and to be of service to them. If the relationships are not satisfying or the problems do not improve, workers may become frustrated and leave the field. One of the key findings in Shapiro's (1975) study of agencies and foster children was that "dissatisfaction with client relationships and problems in satisfying the need to give service were a major factor in motivating social workers to try different jobs in fields other than child welfare or enter graduate work to obtain an MSW" (p. 197). Those who stayed were often dissatisfied with the system, but to some this frustration became a challenge. Shapiro noted that her study "demonstrated that at least one goal—the return of children in foster care to their families—could be achieved given conditions conducive to good casework. It is especially noteworthy that such successes are achieved largely by BA workers with two to three years experience" (p. 198). Another key finding was that "workers' feelings of frustration about the adequacy of the services given and their ability to use informal procedures were associated with early discharge" (p. 197). Since early discharge from foster care was a measure of success, these workers apparently were able to gain some satisfaction from their efforts to overcome conditions that they found frustrating.

> Dissatisfaction with the system was more pronounced in the public sector of the child welfare network than in the voluntary sector. . . . Workers in the voluntary sector had the advantage of working under less pressures. Nevertheless, on a number of performance criteria the public agency's work appeared to be as good, and in some instances better, than that in the voluntary sector. (Shapiro, 1975, p. 197)

Another finding from this study throws light on the question of job satisfaction.

> The longer the children were in care, the more likely they were to be assigned experienced, trained workers with manageable caseloads. These more experienced workers, however, were as likely to feel subjective pressure and dissatisfaction with their work as the younger, less experienced workers who were assigned these children in the earlier phases of placement. What satisfactions they experienced were consistently derived from working directly with children, while satisfaction derived from working with families was limited to the first year of placement. (P. 196)

Lack of gratification from working with families may in part reflect a preference for working with children, but the seriousness of a client family's problems or the lack of responsiveness of parents whose children remain in care for longer than a year could also be factors. Shapiro (1975) observed that "the difficulty encountered by the workers in assessing maternal adequacy is the key reason for continuing placement" (p. 195). Shapiro's study was based on a New York City sample. The national picture, reflected in the 1977 survey analyzed by Shyne (1980), was somewhat different. Shyne noted that "a large majority of the children were assigned to caseworkers without professional education and with limited in-service training, and those in care any length of time were likely to have several different caseworkers. One third of the children had had at least three different caseworkers, and one tenth had had five or more" (p. 31). Recognizing that such changes cannot always be avoided when a placement is of long duration, she suggests that "[a]dministrative practices and in-service training should emphasize ways to minimize the sense of discontinuity and insecurity these changes spell for the child" (p. 31).

In recommending that workers in child welfare have at least under-graduate training in social services, Shyne (1980) cited the "extremely serious decisions [that] caseworkers are called on to make . . . such as whether parental care is sufficiently inadequate to justify removal of the child . . . whether parents can be helped to function adequately as par-ents, and if so, how . . . and whether a mentally ill mother will ever be able to resume her maternal role" (p. 31). In the process of making such decisions, supervisors must not only share their knowledge but also help workers deal objectively with the feelings aroused by the responsi-bility for these decisions.

The awareness of feelings, which is basic to the use of self in social work, is a prominent source of both stress and satisfaction in child welfare work. It is an important factor in the phenomenon of *burnout,* which has become of increasing concern in the area of protective ser-vices for children. This phenomenon has been observed also in child-care workers who have intensive contact with disturbed children (Freudenberger, Maslach, Pines, Reed, & Sutton, 1977). Working with clients who actively reject help by being either hostile or unresponsive deprives the worker of the satisfactions expected from interacting with others and rendering valuable services. The stress associated with the critical decisions that must be made by caseworkers and the pressure of responding to frequent emergencies consume a great deal of energy. If this energy is not renewed by a feeling of some progress toward goals and professional growth, the worker may begin to feel frustrated and exhausted—that is, burned out.

A national evaluation of child abuse and neglect demonstration pro-jects found that almost half of the younger, inexperienced workers were burned out! "Projects with large monthly caseloads and more formal organizational structures had more burned out workers and higher turn-over rates" (Schneiger, 1978, p. 2). Other factors Schneiger associated with burnout were unclear communications, lack of autonomy, and low staff support: "In projects where leadership provided structure and sup-port, only 27 percent of the workers were burned out" (p. 2).

One of the methods that has been found effective in helping workers to manage the feelings that may interfere with good practice and lead to burnout is a support group for staff. The models vary. Some agencies have tried leaderless support groups in which the supervisor sits in as a group member (Bandoli, 1977). These groups may use "techniques of

role-playing, validation exercises and facilitating . . . to raise conscious-
ness and to allow group support for each worker who needs it"
(Davoren, 1975, p. 39). Other groups have used co-leaders to provide
both training and support to community workers from various disciplines who deal with families in the area of child abuse or neglect
(Copans, Krell, Grundy, Rogan, & Field, 1979).

The significant role such groups can play in enabling workers to give
more effective service, thus gaining greater job satisfaction and reducing
stress, has been described by Copans and his colleagues (1979).

> Work with . . . high risk families is difficult, and often it does not help the
> family's problem. In some cases this is because resources are too limited or
> intervention begins too late but in many cases it is the lack of adequate
> training and support for workers that hampers the delivery of care. Work
> with high risk families is particularly difficult because of the highly charged
> feelings aroused by such work. These feelings often prevent workers from
> making proper decisions and mitigate against good management of cases,
> even when the cases are adequately understood. A crucial part of a worker's
> training involves learning to recognize, examine and work with these feel-
> ings. However, the process does not stop with training, and ongoing sup-
> port for such self-examination should accompany any job involving work
> with high risk families. (p. 24)

This study identified "11 major sets of feelings and processes that frequently interfere with effective delivery of care by workers."

- Anxieties about being physically harmed by angry parents and about the
  effects of a decision.
- Denial and inhibition of anger.
- Need for emotional gratification from clients.
- Lack of professional support.
- Feelings of incompetence.
- Denial and projection of responsibility.
- The feeling that one is totally responsible for families assigned to a worker.
- The difficulty in separating personal from professional responsibility.
- Feelings of being victimized.
- Ambivalent feelings toward clients and about one's professional role.
- The need to be in control. (P. 24)

Copans and associates (1979) gave an example of one of these sets of
feelings.

> Anxieties about physical harm are common in work with high risk families.
> In many cases there is a history of violence and it is appropriate and realistic
> to be frightened and to ask for assistance. However, very often the anxiety is
> irrational and unconsciously determined.
>
> For example, one worker visited a mother in a family with a history of
> abuse. She told the mother that it would be necessary to involve Protective
> Services and that she would return the next day to discuss this when both

the father and mother would be at home. The mother predicted that the father, who had beaten her in the past, would surely "beat up" the worker when she returned.

Initially the worker became quite fearful and panicky and felt totally unable to return to the home, although she realized that wives in abusive families often suggest that a worker will be harmed by the man in the house, as a way of telling the worker not to come back. After a discussion with her supervisor, she arranged to have another worker accompany her on her visit with the father and mother. In the group she was able to describe her initial anxiety and inability to proceed with the case as being related to her own childhood experiences and fears of her father. As a result of the group discussion, she was able to return to the family without fear. In fact, once she stopped reacting to the father as if he were her own father, she found him to be in great distress about the family situation and willing to have her help. (P. 24)

In discussing denial and inhibition of anger, group members expressed their awareness that avoiding cases "was one way of expressing anger that they did not consciously recognize. As one worker put it, 'The nice thing about having a large caseload is that when a case gets too difficult or frustrating, you can ignore it for awhile because you always have too much else to do'" (Copans et al., 1979, p. 26).

One of the benefits of the team approach is that shared decisionmaking reduces stress for the individual members while the professional interchange can provide a degree of support. The job satisfaction that comes from increasing skills and professional growth can go a long way toward meeting the challenges of the child welfare field.

Summary

In the field of child welfare M.S.W.'s perform roles at all levels, from administration through direct service provision. In public agencies they are more likely to serve as administrators or supervisors. In voluntary agencies, they may provide direct services as well. A major function of supervisors is case management and the supervision of accountability systems.

Many direct services in public agencies and some in voluntary agencies are provided by social workers with a B.S.W. or a B.A. in some field other than social work. Additional in-service or on-the-job training is usually provided by the agency. Graduate social workers often provide this training in staff development or supervisory positions. Often they are responsible also for the training of paraprofessional staff or volunteers.

A cooperative relationship between professional and paraprofessional staff is of particular importance in the field of child welfare. Child-care workers who serve as surrogate parents in residential schools, foster parents, day-care mothers, and homemakers have most of the direct daily contact with children in care. Similarly, parent aides have frequent direct contact with the families of some of these children. Life experience, personal qualities, and parenting skills are often more important than education or training in these relationships, but teamwork between professionals and paraprofessionals can increase the effectiveness of services.

A team model has been recommended as the best method of delivering child welfare services. Many variations on this model have proved effective in experimental programs. Multidisciplinary teams are widely used in protective services. Graduate social workers often have responsibility for leading such teams or for directing other innovative service programs for children and their families.

A knowledge of child development and family dynamics is important for all workers in the child welfare field. Some understanding of group dynamics is of value, too, since work with groups is common, especially in the area of child care. Knowledge of legal processes also is necessary in many areas of child welfare. Courts are involved not only in questions of the custody of children, but also whenever foster care costs are reimbursed by federal funds through the AFDC program.

Skill in assessment is vital to anyone dealing with intake. In protective services, investigative skills may be needed to complete assessments. A wide range of intervention approaches in both casework and group work can be useful. Because of the stressfulness and the demands of many child welfare jobs, support groups for staff can assist individuals to deal objectively with the highly charged feelings aroused by their work.

CHAPTER 4

Can Breakdown Be Prevented?

In CONSIDERING preventive strategies, it is important for the practitioner to be aware of the various levels at which prevention might be possible. Even though the programs and resources needed may not be available, an awareness of the points at which early intervention might have been effective in reducing stress or strengthening a point of weakness could help to collect the data needed for effective advocacy for such programs.

The earliest level, commonly referred to as primary prevention, has been demonstrated most clearly in the health field, where broad programs of health education and immunization have virtually eliminated certain childhood diseases and reduced others. Efforts to promote this approach in the fields of mental health and social work have met with some success, but inevitably the question arises: where should limited resources be focused in order to bring the greatest benefit? While there is probably consensus that the earliest possible intervention is most effective, do we begin by meeting the needs of a young child, who will then grow into a more capable parent, by providing family life education to high school students, by developing services to prevent teenage pregnancy, or by expanding employment, educational, health, or recreational services for young people?

Some programs developed under health, mental health, and educational auspices aim to strengthen family life on this level, but there has been little governmental support for such programs. Advocacy groups attempting to improve housing conditions or employment opportunities have contributed to primary prevention. Social agencies are sometimes involved in such efforts through community organization programs in relation to specific groups of families or particular neighborhoods.

In reality, the line between primary and secondary prevention cannot always be clearly drawn. Some programs are directed only toward broad educational goals, but others may provide for intervention on several levels, including direct services. Germain has described the possibility of developing such an intervention process in her statement on the importance of the location of services.

> Early or preventive intervention has long been cited as a probably positive consequence of locating services where life-cycle events intersect with institutional or environmental processes; examples include first-time parenthood, initial school entry, departure for college, first job, migration, marriage, retirement, bereavement, and catastrophic illness. Therefore, neighborhood family service centers, autonomous social workers, and ancillary services in Social Security offices, hospital emergency rooms, and housing developments will provide case-finding, case-channeling, case advocacy, consultation, direct services, and educational activities for the public. Such a pattern of service, making help available when and where it is needed in the life-space of people, represents a beginning commitment to the ecological point of view. (Germain, 1973, p. 330)

Despite wide recognition that prevention of breakdown is more effective and less costly than repair, services designed for this purpose have rarely received adequate funding. Legislation intended to expand services, even for secondary prevention, has usually been hampered by so many restrictions that the limited funds appropriated have not been applied either to expanding existing preventive services or to developing new ones. Agency administrators have little discretion in the allocation of resources. The necessity for dealing with crises as they arise, particularly in a public agency which has been given the responsibility of protecting children whose needs cannot be met by other social institutions, leaves little money and manpower for the outreach and early intervention that might have helped to prevent the situation from becoming a crisis.

Although secondary prevention is the area dealt with most frequently by child welfare practitioners, some knowledge of the resources available on other levels is important so that full advantage of them can be taken. For this reason, the major areas in which services to support family life are provided through either public or voluntary auspices will be discussed briefly in this chapter to provide a background for the consideration of preventive strategies. Those unfamiliar with these programs can find more detailed information in the references cited.

Public Programs to Sustain Families: Supplemental Income and Day Care

The social insurance and income maintenance programs represent the major commitment of public funds for primary prevention. Kadushin (1980) classified these programs as supplemental services since they supply a missing aspect of the parental role: income production. By doing so, they enable many parents without a source of income to care for their children. To a lesser extent, public funds are used to supply the child care function, through day care, to enable a single parent or both parents to produce the income needed for the family to survive. Practitioners in the child welfare field need a basic understanding of these public programs on which many of the families they encounter are dependent.

The *social insurance* programs make payments on behalf of dependent children when a wage-earning parent is deceased, disabled, or retires. Children who become totally disabled prior to age twenty-two may be eligible for payments also, under provisions for Supplemental Security Income (SSI) (Kadushin, 1980). The payments to a disabled child formerly continued indefinitely and enabled the families of many severely retarded or mentally disabled children to continue to care for them throughout their lives. As the social insurance programs have come under more economic pressures, new screening procedures have limited eligibility considerably.

Unemployment insurance benefits have assisted many families to survive a period of temporary unemployment of the wage-earning parent. When unemployment is prolonged or the wage earner becomes disabled, families may have to resort to income maintenance programs, such as Aid to Families with Dependent Children. Under certain circumstances, two-parent families who lack a wage earner for reasons of illness, disability, or other problems may be eligible for income maintenance programs. Some states have extended this assistance (without federal participation) to working families whose earnings are less than a minimum level. Supplementary assistance from other programs, such as Medicaid and Food Stamps, has enabled some low income families to survive economically, but the added limitations being placed on these programs through the move toward a new federalism has removed this source of protection from many families.

The AFDC program, which provides support to many families in which the mother has never married or in which desertion, separation, or divorce has left the family without a source of income, has been described as "probably the most successful preventive program for keeping children out of foster care" (Jenkins & Norman, 1972, p. 133). It is necessary, in order to qualify for this program, that a search be made for an absent parent and that legal channels be employed to obtain support payments from this parent. Since such support payments are frequently inadequate, they may be supplemented by an AFDC grant.

Kadushin (1980) reviewed many studies on the effectiveness of the AFDC program and reported that in general it appears to have achieved its objectives of providing children with the economic support they need for health and development and the opportunity to grow up within their own families, sharing in the life of the neighborhood and community and receiving an education that will help them realize their capacities. AFDC has been credited with keeping together the families of a hundred million children in the first forty-five years of its existence. In a 1952 study, Blackwell and Gould stated, "Without this assistance, it is certain that many of these families would have dissolved completely, and the children would have possibly suffered permanent emotional and even physical damage" (quoted in Kadushin, 1980, p. 140).

Contrary to the impression sometimes given that AFDC families are disorganized or deviant, these families "as a whole present a profile of functioning that is quite stable. Relatively few . . . have been charged with child neglect and abuse, and the level of delinquency of AFDC children is similar to that of their peers" (Kadushin, 1980, p. 140).

The AFDC program has sometimes been accused of encouraging family disruption. Kadushin (1980) concluded that the findings in this area are ambiguous. They tend to support the observation that the availability of income support does not precipitate the dissolution of a relationship but provides an alternative for women who wish to separate for the same reasons that separation occurs in nonwelfare groups—often to escape an intolerable situation.

One of the more interesting research results appeared in a group of three negative income tax experiments conducted in New Jersey, Washington, and Colorado in the early 1970s. Families were randomly assigned to experimental and control groups, and the experimental group was guaranteed an income for a three-year period. Although marital dissolution was larger in all three experimental groups, the effects varied with the size of the grant: "At the higher guaranteed income levels, there was little difference in disruption rates between the experimental . . . and control families" (Kadushin, 1980, p. 144).

Some day care is provided through the AFDC program for the purpose of enabling a single parent to work, with the goal of eventual self-support. Although such day care is not considered a child welfare service, it contributes to sustaining single parent families by supplying the function of child care while the parent is concerned with income production. Title XX of the Social Security Act gave states the option of providing this service to self-supporting families with minimal incomes. Both these programs were severely limited by funding cuts which reduced the AFDC Work Incentive program (WIN) and replaced Title XX with block grants to the states. Nevertheless, the day care provided through public funding serves to remove a potential source of stress for some single parent families or those in which both parents must work for the family to survive.

In spite of the success of the AFDC program in enabling many mothers to care for their own children whereas they would not otherwise be able to do so, it is far from offering a complete solution to the problem of keeping families together. Most AFDC grants, even with the addition of other benefit programs such as Medicaid and Food Stamps, still provide a family with an income below the poverty level. Struggling to exist on this limited income, these families are vulnerable to the common human problems faced by single-parent families and to the other problems associated with poverty, such as poor health and inadequate housing.

Public social services are available to these families to assist them in coping with the problems they face. Many of these services were formerly a part of the AFDC program and were offered directly to families by the workers who determined financial eligibility. Since the separation of these functions, families must request these services in order to receive them. This change, which was intended to enhance dignity by giving the individual a choice, has often operated to make services less accessible to those who need them. Several studies reported that a lessened use of services by AFDC recipients came more from a lack of awareness of the availability of services and of the means of obtaining them than from a lack of the need or desire for services. Although eligibility workers and service workers were employed by the same agency, eligibility workers often did not inform applicants of the services available and rarely attempted to motivate them to take advantage of services that appeared to be needed (Citizen's Committee for Children of New York 1978, cited in Kadushin, 1980, p. 138). These findings prompted changes in federal regulations in order to give states the option of reintegrating these services.

Even if accessibility to services could be improved, one problem still remains. As Kadushin (1980) stated, "No amount of social service can substitute for inadequate assistance. Under such conditions it is difficult to implement the rehabilitative aims of the program" (p. 144).

The need for welfare reform has been widely recognized, but the necessity to achieve some compromise among conflicting needs and aims has made this goal very difficult to reach. Efforts to limit spending and to direct scarce resources to those most in need have resulted in eligibility requirements that are a bureaucratic nightmare to negotiate—far beyond the capability of an inadequately functioning family or parents in crisis. While administrators, influencing social policy, attempt to insure that the basic needs of families will be met by these programs, social workers and family advocates working at a secondary prevention level continue to assist individual families to qualify for benefits to which they are entitled and to seek out voluntary resources in the community to supplement inadequate grants.

VOLUNTARY PROGRAMS TO STRENGTHEN FAMILIES. PRIMARY PREVENTION

The major contribution of voluntary agencies to primary prevention in child welfare is probably in the areas of *family life education* and *family advocacy*. While many family life education programs are held under such auspices as adult education, mental health, and religious or community groups, there has been a growing trend for family service and child welfare agencies to sponsor such programs. In 1976, 79 percent of family service agencies were offering some kind of family life education as one of their many programs (Kadushin, 1980). Some of these groups focus on particular developmental stages in the growth of children, such as preschool or adolescence, or particular problem areas, such as helping children in school. Others aim to improve parenting skills in general, through Parent Effectiveness Training or other specific techniques (Turner, 1980).

A noteworthy primary prevention program was developed by the Family Counseling Service of Eugene, Oregon. Birth to Three provides a new parent support network, which reaches out to parents immediately after the birth of a child. A variety of volunteer and professional services are available, from telephone support to educational programs.

Not all these programs are limited to primary prevention. Some attempt to establish mutual aid relationships among some families experiencing difficulty and others that are functioning effectively. An understanding of the potential benefits of such interaction between levels of prevention is useful in planning for intervention.

MULTILEVEL PREVENTION PROGRAMS

One of the most exciting and creative developments in the field of child welfare has been the combining of all social work methods in multifaceted programs that deal simultaneously with all levels of prevention. Many of these were demonstration programs developed by voluntary agencies with financial support from both private and government sources. A brief historical view of their growth and a description of a few of the models will shed light on the type of preventive intervention they can offer.

They originated in the expansion of social services during the 1960s, when funding for antipoverty programs stimulated a rapid expansion of *multiservice neighborhood centers.* Located in low-income neighborhoods, these centers stressed consumer participation and attempted to integrate local services and encourage community action. As a whole, they met with rather limited success, according to a number of studies. Kahn (1976) stated that they tended to provide "centralized intake" rather than "a case integration service" (p. 34). In 1972 O'Donnell and Reid found them to be involved more in counseling than in community action (cited in Kadushin, 1980). In the early seventies the Office of Child Development funded *parent-child development centers.* These also served low-income families and included family counseling and family life education among their services.

During this period traditional social agencies were attempting to adapt their programs to the new trend. The Family Service Association of America (1969) took a stand in support of family advocacy in order to serve the needs of the poor and non-white communities. The Community Service Society of New York, one of the oldest and largest family service agencies in the country, announced in 1971 that after "123 years of family casework and individual counseling" it would abandon this approach to focus on "the community as the client" (*New York Times,* 29 January, 1971, cited in Kadushin, 1980, p. 96). By 1973 the agency had made a partial shift back, including individual counseling as one of its options. Subsequently, it developed an innovative program, the Single-Parent Family Project, which combines primary and secondary prevention in a variety of groups and recreational programs designed to provide needed supports to single parents (Kadushin, 1980).

The expansion of preventive services programs was encouraged by some federal and state funds made available for research and demonstration projects focused on preventing the placement of children. The expectation was that successful projects would receive local support and also would serve as models which other communities could adapt to their needs. The success of some of these programs did lead to expanded services. In New York City, seven demonstration projects funded by the state in 1974, had increased to forty-seven by 1980. A survey and evaluation of these programs revealed many variations on the original models (Interface, 1980). Most were built around a core service of individual counseling, but many offered the entire range of social work methods, including group work and community organization activities. Some were citywide programs developed by traditional child welfare and family service agencies. Others had been developed to serve specific neighborhoods, sometimes by local community groups. Some emphasized mental health services. Others stressed advocacy among other services.

One of the original seven demonstration programs was the Lower

East Side Family Union (LESFU). Initiated by the director of the Henry Street Settlement and assisted financially by the Foundation for Child Development, this program became a joint effort by five settlement houses on the Lower East Side of New York to integrate services for troubled families (Weissman, 1978). These settlement houses, some of the oldest in the country, had long served their neighborhoods in the capacity of multiservice centers, offering a wide range of social services and recreational and cultural activities to the successive waves of immigrants who entered American society through New York.

The project was inspired by an indictment of New York City's child welfare system (Citizens' Committee for Children of New York, Inc., 1971). This report called for more emphasis on "locally based services" with a "family focus" (pp. 27, 32, cited in Beck, 1979). It was logical that the settlement house movement, which had pioneered in offering primary prevention services in the field of social work, should pick up that challenge.

The project operates through four teams, one of which concentrates on primary prevention services in an area of deteriorated housing. Through community organization methods, this team assists the people of the neighborhood in efforts to improve their living conditions. The other three teams are concerned with secondary and tertiary prevention. The social workers, who act as case managers for the families they serve, make extensive use of contracts among LESFU, the clients, and other agencies providing services, as a means of integrating the needed services. The teams include homemakers, who supplement the services provided by the social workers. A public child welfare agency, Special Services for Children, has been drawn into the project and contributes staff for one team (Beck, 1979).

Another multiservice model is represented by the Center for Family Life in Sunset Park, operated in Brooklyn under the sponsorship of St. Christopher's Home. This program deals with all levels of prevention. Individual counseling, recreational and therapeutic groups for all age levels, and active participation in efforts to improve community life are among the components of this program. The center works closely with local schools, providing tutoring services, as well as activities for children while their parents participate in groups and recreational events.

A variation on the multiservice model developed to meet suburban needs was mentioned in Chapter 3. The Parent and Child Training Project (PACT) of the Family Service Association of Nassau County grew out of family life education groups that had focused initially on helping parents to help their children in school. With a minimum of professional staff, who were used to train and supervise paraprofessionals, and with funding obtained first from private foundations and later from public sources, as well, the program expanded to include the full range of preventive services. Educational and supportive groups dealt with the concerns of their members and provided mutual aid. A nursery workshop served the functions of offering respite and training in parenting skills to young mothers. Recreational activities supported family life, and advocacy and individual counseling were available. Mothers who were interested and who showed an aptitude through group participation were trained to run mothers' groups under professional supervision. The program began in a storefront office. Later, branches were set up in other communities through the cooperation of youth centers and churches. A van was used for outreach (Kochman & Gaines, 1977).

A somewhat different suburban model, the Parents' Center of the Central Nassau Action Council, was developed without dependence on government funding through a concerted effort to gain community support. Modeled on a Colorado program to prevent child abuse, the center included a drop-in crisis nursery, discussion groups and workshops for parents, family recreational activities, professional counseling, and a small group of parent aides. Leadership for the workshops and other necessary services were obtained through arrangements with public and voluntary agencies. The project's location in a multiservice community center gave it access to other services at this center, which ranged from a Headstart child development center to a nutrition program for senior citizens (Radowitz, 1979).

In spite of the importance of primary prevention, most child welfare services, whether delivered through a traditional agency or through an innovative program, must concentrate on trying to help families who are threatened, to a greater or lesser degree, with breakdown. The ability to prevent breakdown will depend on many factors. Among the most important are the timeliness of the intervention and the resources available.

The multilevel programs that have been described illustrate a wide range of strategies that can be useful in preventing family breakdown. Sometimes one type of service may be sufficient, but more often a combination of services is needed. Individual counseling may be supplemented by participation in a group, or group participation may lead to a request for individual counseling. Homemaker services may be needed to meet an emergency or to provide support, along with counseling, advocacy, or some type of group service. Day-care services may be utilized in combination with group or individual counseling or advocacy. Whether these services are available through one agency or several, a variety of resources must often be drawn together to meet a family's needs. Accordingly, most of the vignettes used to illustrate the various strategies will be grouped toward the end of the chapter.

Casework Services: Assessment

Whatever the need, the key to the selection of an appropriate strategy is complete and accurate assessment. Although the process may vary depending upon the type of agency, the services it has to offer, and the needs of the family, a good assessment generally involves casework skills.

The initial contact between the family and the agency is exploratory. What need has brought them together? Is it the concern of a parent about a child's behavior, or has the concern of the school or the community forced the parent to seek help? Is there a crisis requiring immediate action?

Both facts and feelings need to be explored. A parent may have certain expectations—that a child's behavior will be changed or that the agency will provide a solution to the problem. As the intake worker gathers the facts that are necessary to understand the situation and attends to the feelings that surround these facts, the process of establishing a relationship begins. Often, applicants to child welfare agencies have very little positive experience on which to base a trusting relationship. They may need concrete evidence that the worker is willing and able to help, and even then it may take some time for real trust to develop, if it does at all. The issue of trust is complicated when an agency must intervene without a request for help, as in protective services.

The initial contact may be brief or extended, formal or informal, concerned with meeting a crisis or with determining whether a problem exists with which the agency can help. Whatever the nature of this contact, the essential element is an effort to reach a mutual understanding as to what is needed, what is possible, and what the next steps will be. The professional social worker brings to this process the ability to empathize with another human being; an understanding of the dynamics of the complex interactions that take place within the individual, the family, and the community; and a knowledge of available resources. To the extent that these elements are present, the initial contact is more likely to result in a clarification of the problem, an accurate assessment of the needs and the resources available to meet them, and a start in the process of solving the problem.

The assessment process is basic to all social work practice; its essential elements are the same whatever the field. What is unique to this process in child welfare is that it may involve a decision as to whether and how a child's family environment can be sustained, or whether a substitute family environment must be developed, temporarily or permanently. This can be a very difficult decision, which may have to be made rather quickly in an emergency situation. A variety of guidelines have been developed to assist child welfare workers in assessing situations more quickly and accurately. These vary in their emphasis, but they have in common a focus on the family and the environment in which the family lives.

GUIDES TO ASSESSMENT

Structured Assessment: A Decision-making Guide for Child Welfare (Dukette, Born, Gagel, & Hendricks, 1978) was designed to facilitate an exploratory study to determine whether a child can remain at home or needs placement. Four criteria are used to evaluate the need for placement.

1. the nature of the problems
2. the parents' parenting capacity
3. the organization of the family and its support systems
4. the developmental status and condition of each child

"The methods used in this guide for gathering data, assessing them, and drawing conclusions for effective case planning are accepted social work methods; interviewing, observation, and the skilled use of a client-worker relationship" (Dukette et al., 1978, p. 2).

The guide suggests questions and sources to be used in gathering data and provides a format both for recording information and for drawing conclusions from the data in relation to each criterion. This guide recognizes also that early intervention may be needed to avoid placement and that such services may go on at the same time that an understanding of the situation is being gained through the exploratory study.

Guidelines for Decision-making in Child Welfare (Janchill, 1980), prepared for the New York State Department of Social Services, presents principles and methods for case assessment, service planning, and service selection. The book includes a set of protocols—diagrams that can be used to insure that all important life space areas and dimensions are included in a problem and needs analysis, an evaluation of assets and resources, and the choice of options in support services. Protocols are included also to suggest the range of services that may be needed for children for whom various types of placement have been selected.

Janchill (1980) identified three minimal criteria for determining whether a child needs to be removed from the family.

1. Whether there is sufficient parental concern or desire to maintain the child at home: a criterion which is often difficult to measure. . . .
2. In the case of an older child, able to express choice, willingness to live at home and work out areas of difficulty. . . .
3. Whether an adequate range of help can be garnered at the community level to sustain the child and family. (Pp. 46, 48)

These guidelines incorporate much of the material presented in Janchill's 1975 publication, *Criteria for Foster Care Placement and Alternatives to Foster Care*, prepared for the New York State Board of Social Welfare for use in connection with the 1975 study of foster care in New York City by Bernstein, Snider, and Meezan.

Guides to assessment that emphasize the principles of permanency planning for children have been developed through a federally funded program in Oregon to find permanent homes for children already in foster care. The strong legal focus of this project is evident in many of its publications. Jones and Biesecker's (1977) *Permanent Planning Guide for Children and Youth Services*, based on the work of this project, takes workers step by step through the process by which a child whose home is in question can be assured of some stability and security. The categories suggested for defining the problem more clearly are those that would be useful if it should become necessary to take protective action through the court system. Parent-child problems are defined within three basic categories: *absence, condition,* or *conduct.* Absence includes both desertion or lack of supervision by a parent and running away by a child. Condition refers to a mental or physical condition afflicting either the parent or the child that prevents the child from receiving adequate nurturing. A condition may involve mental illness or retardation, but it should have a diagnosis and a prognosis. Conduct refers to parental behavior that is detrimental to the child, such as abuse, or behavior by a child that is disruptive to the family, such as destructive or aggressive acts. Resources and alternatives to solve the problem or alleviate the situation are then considered.

ASSESSMENT IN PROTECTIVE SERVICES

A protective services investigation presents special problems in assessment, primarily because of the involuntary nature of the intervention. The initial step in a protective assessment is usually the investigation of a report of suspected abuse or neglect to determine whether it has a basis in fact and whether any danger exists to the child. For this, some knowledge of investigative techniques may be required in addition to the usual social work skills of interviewing, observing, and relating empathetically to a client. If the case must later be taken to court, the evidence presented to justify the need to protect the child must be acceptable to the court.

The parent who is the subject of such an investigation may or may not recognize that a problem exists but will almost certainly resent the intrusion of the agency, at least initially, when no help has been requested. The worker may need to resort to an authoritative approach to make the role of the agency clear, at the same time trying to convey the message that the agency is willing and able to help if the parent will voluntarily engage in a joint problem-solving effort.

An example will be presented to illustrate problems that are often encountered by protective services workers in making an assessment. Although the vignette combines elements from several actual cases, all the features are typical of those found in many protective services case-loads. Italics are used in this illustration to highlight some of the clues that alerted the investigating worker to the possibility of maltreatment. In the face of denial by a parent and lack of any confirming evidence, it is often difficult to establish enough facts in a case to enable an agency to intervene effectively.

A neighbor anonymously reported that an eighteen-month-old child had been left unsupervised and beaten. On an unscheduled visit to the furnished room in which the twenty-one-year-old mother lived, the worker found her about to take the child to the doctor because of a cough. The mother was cooperative, denied beating the child, and allowed the worker to examine him. No bruises were found. The mother stated that either her landlady or a neighbor cared for the baby if she went out. The landlady confirmed the mother's statement that there was no maltreatment of the child.

In exploring the mother's family background, the worker learned that *she did not get along with any members of her own family. She had lived with a relative for much of her childhood. The child's father had deserted her* when he learned of her pregnancy. Her own needs and the needs of the child were discussed. She expressed a wish to finish high school and said she would like a playpen for the baby, who was beginning to walk and was very active. The worker's impression was that the mother was self-centered but conscientious.

The pediatrician confirmed that the child's weight was normal and that he appeared to be getting good care. The worker continued unscheduled visits for a week. No bruises were found on the child during this time. A possible day-care plan to allow the mother to finish school was discussed, but *she did not follow through on this suggestion.* The worker referred her to a resource for the playpen she wanted and closed the case as unfounded.

Three months later a similar report was received. The same worker visited and found the mother in bed with a migraine headache. The baby was quiet in his crib. *A small bruise on his arm* was explained by the mother as having been caused by his bumping into a chair. The landlady brought in food for the child and fed him. *He did not eat very well.* He cried when he was put back in his crib. Otherwise, *he was not expressive.* The worker observed that *the child seemed thin and subdued.* The doctor had some question at this point about the child since *his weight was not at a normal level.* He had not seen any bruises.

Weekly visits were continued for three months. During this time *the mother had a variety of physical complaints.* The possibility of a part-time homemaker was discussed to allow her to get a little rest, but she rejected the offer, saying that she was feeling better. She had gotten the playpen and the child seemed happy in it. No marks were found on him. The other roomers and relatives with whom the worker checked said that the mother raised her voice or slapped the child occasionally but did not beat him. When contacted again, the doctor reported normal growth and no evidence of maltreatment. The case was closed again as unfounded.

A third report six months later charged that the mother had twisted the child's arm. On this visit, the supervisor accompanied the worker. *The mother was belligerent* and complained of being harassed. She denied that anything was wrong with the child's arm. *The little boy was thin and expressionless.* He showed no expression of pain when his arm was moved. *A small cut on his leg had been stitched.* His mother said he had fallen while playing. She refused the worker's offer to take him to the doctor and said she would take him herself. After two follow-up calls she finally did. The doctor reported that the X ray had showed no sign of a fracture or dislocation, but he had noticed scratch marks on the child's back. The mother's explanation that they had been made by another child was credible, and the case was again closed.

A fourth report was received two months later from a public health nurse who had observed, on a visit to another roomer, that the child had two black eyes. His mother said they had been caused by a fall. A worker visited immediately and found the child sleeping in his playpen, alone in the room and unsupervised. She took him to a hospital for examination. The report from the hospital noted healed fractures, lacerations, bruises and welts, poor hygiene, and developmental delay, and the child was placed in foster care. The court ordered evaluations of both mother and child.

The foster mother reported that the child had nightmares, refused to feed himself, would not let anyone come near him, and would go into rages. An evaluation found him functioning on an autistic level and unable to feel pain. Evaluation of the mother found her guarded and suspicious, with no insight and too impaired to nurture her child.

Under pressure from the court, the mother agreed to enter a treatment program and to leave the child in foster care, with supervised visiting permitted. Within a short period of foster care, the child's fears abated and with intensive training he began to make developmental progress.

Some guides have been designed to assist protective services workers in assessing situations involving abuse or neglect and in determining what services are needed. Indicators of abuse and neglect have been developed that can be used to evaluate each individual in the family: "They offer a way of quantifying family problems normally assessed subjectively. Although indicators are not intended to replace professional judgement, they can facilitate that judgement" (Coombes, McCormack, Chipley, & Archer, 1978, p. 43).

A casework handbook published by the American Humane Association breaks the intake and assessment process in child protective services into specific steps.

a. Intake is the first step in the process. It includes:

1. Receiving the referral.
2. Possibly making collateral contacts and checking records.
3. Exploring the appropriateness of the referral.
4. Deciding to commit the agency to the referral as a report of abuse or neglect.

b. Initial assessment (investigation) is the second step. It includes:

1. Making initial contact with the child and family.
2. Making subsequent assessment visits.
3. Assessing the damage to the child.
4. Assessing the potential for continuing risk to the child.
5. Evaluating the family indicators of abuse or neglect.
6. Determining if abuse or neglect exists and continuing the case as open.
7. Determining the need to invoke the authority of the family court.
8. Providing emergency services as needed.
9. Providing feedback to appropriate persons.
10. Documenting the record.

c. The study of the problem and people—the diagnostic assessment—is the third step. It includes:

1. Studying the family problems in more depth from a causal perspective.
2. Individualizing family members.
3. Assessing strengths and areas for improvement.
4. Determining resources available to and needed by the family.
5. Specifying assessment conclusions (diagnostic assessment). (Holder, Mouzakitis, Romero, Sahd, & Salisbury, 1981, p. 7)

A diagram of the full process outlined in this handbook is included in Appendix A of this volume (Holder et al., 1981, p. 7).

ASSESSMENT TOOLS

An ecological approach that can help to capture many of the complexities and interrelationships of the family in its life space is found in Hartman's (1978) *ecomap* (Figure 1) and *genogram* (Figure 2). These "two simple paper-and-pencil simulations have proved to be particularly useful, not only as assessment tools, but in interviewing, planning and intervention" (Hartman, 1978, p. 466). The ecomap developed through a

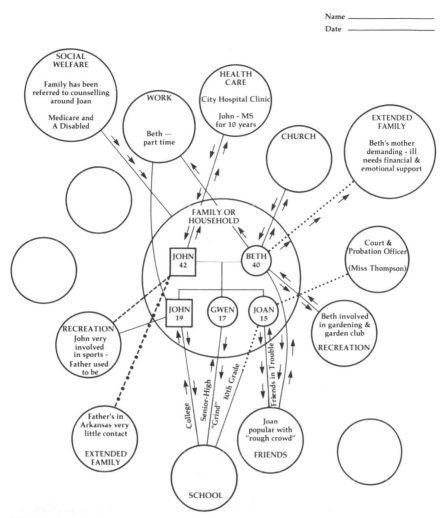

Name _____
Date _____

Fill in connections where they exist.
Indicate nature of connections with a descriptive word or by drawing different kinds of lines;
——————— for strong, —•—•—•—•— for tenuous, •••••• for stressful.
Draw arrows along lines to signify flow of energy, resources, etc.
Identify significant people and fill in empty circles as needed.

Figure 1. Ecomap. From Ann Hartman, "Diagrammatic Assessment of Family Relationships," in *Social Casework,* October 1978, p. 470. Reproduced with permission of the Family Service Association of America, publisher.

federally funded project "as an assessment tool to help workers in public child welfare practice examine the needs of families" (p. 466), is a graphic representation of the individuals (with their ages) who compose the family. Solid or broken lines show relationships among family members and between them and surrounding systems.

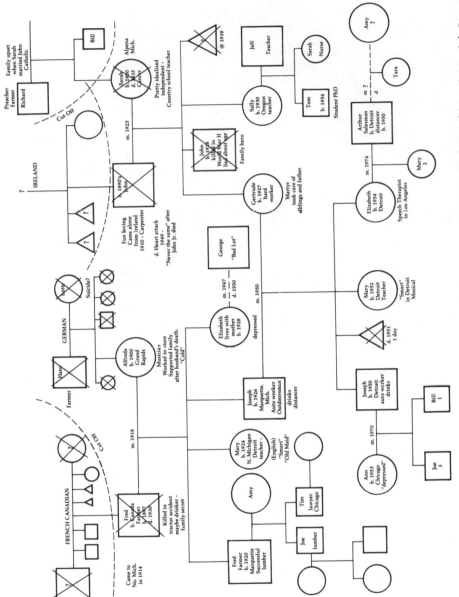

Figure 2. Genogram. From Ann Hartman, "Diagrammatic Assessment of Family Relationships," in *Social Casework*, October 1978, p. 474. Reproduced with permission of the Family Service Association of America, publisher.

Just as the eco-map can begin to portray and objectify the family in space, so can the genogram picture the family system through time, enabling an individual to step out of the system, examine it, and begin to gain a greater understanding of complex family dynamics as they have developed and as they affect the current situation. (Hartman, 1978, p. 472)

Both tools have been tested "in a variety of settings with a wide range of clients" (Hartman, 1978, p. 466). In an extensive test with "natural parents working toward the return of their placed children . . . foster care workers noted that parents who were generally angry and self-protective following placement of their children because of abuse or neglect were almost without exception engaged through the use of the map" (p. 471). A more detailed explanation of the uses of these tools as applied to assessment of adoptive families can be found in Hartman's (1979) *Finding Families.* They can be useful not only in engaging families in the assessment process but also in choosing the strategy or points of intervention that will be most effective.

Sometimes it is obvious that intervention can be successful in preventing family breakdown. If the family has sought help with the problem early enough, and if they are motivated to bring about the necessary changes, traditional casework counseling may be the strategy of choice.

Casework Services: Counseling

The traditional agencies providing this service: Child Guidance centers, family service agencies and mental health centers, generally offer a range of treatment modalities, including both long and short-term therapy, individually and in groups. Problems of children, such as enuresis, stuttering, tics, school phobias, or aggressive, destructive or extremely withdrawn behavior are often referred to Child Guidance Centers. Parents who become aware that marital conflicts threaten to disrupt their family life or are having a negative effect on their children may turn to a family service agency for counseling.

A detailed discussion of the various treatment modalities is beyond the scope of this book. The brief descriptive summaries which will be presented here are intended merely to suggest the range of possibilities which may be available. Fuller descriptions of these methods, the merits and drawbacks of each, and the types of situations to which they are applicable can be found in other literature.

Long-term therapy with a psychoanalytic orientation, which aims at achieving basic personality change through the development of insight into the unconscious sources of behavior and the corrective process of working through a relationship with the therapist to a more mature level of functioning, can be effective when there is a degree of motivation and commitment to the process by the person seeking help. When this is lacking, as it frequently is in families with whom the child welfare practitioner deals, or when adequate resources for longer-term therapy are not available, one of the shorter-term therapies may prove useful. For some situations they may be more appropriate than longer-term therapy. Most of the short-term methods emphasize the establishment of clear but limited goals with a time period set for their accomplishment. The goals are more likely to involve behavioral change or problem solving rather than basic personality change. The conclusion has been drawn from some studies that short-term treatment of parent-child problems has been as effective as more extended services. "Lower expenditures of casework time and effort yielded results as good or better than more extended contact" (Kadushin, 1980, p. 105). On the other hand, some of these studies have been criticized for a "lack of scientific accuracy" (Strean, 1981, p. 163). Treatment methods sometimes become fads and appear to offer easy solutions to difficult problems. It is important to remember that no method is a panacea. Applied appropriately by a skilled practitioner, many different methods can be useful, either singly or in combination. Among the most widely accepted short-term techniques are crisis intervention, task-centered casework, behavior modification and the use of contracts.

Crisis intervention is based on the premise that timely intervention at a point of crisis can be more effective than more lengthy intervention later. Periods of disequilibrium occur both during normal stages of growth (at adolescence, for instance) and following a change in the family's status—the birth of a new family member, a loss through death, a serious illness, the loss of a job—that creates stress. Intervention focuses on the effectiveness of the family's previous coping mechanisms and on strengthening these or substituting new approaches for strategies that have proved ineffective. Restoring equilibrium through these methods often frees energy to achieve a better level of functioning. The effectiveness of crisis intervention is attributed to the lowering of habitual defenses, a by-product of the vulnerability created by the crisis; a greater willingness to accept help; and more motivation for change because of the discomfort of the anxiety that the crisis has produced.

Behavior modification is based on learning theory. Rather than seeking to understand the origins of behavior, this approach utilizes knowledge of the process of conditioning to change behavior in the desired direction. Although it has been criticized in some quarters as being manipulative and mechanistic, comparative studies have shown that in many situations behavior modification has proved at least as effective as, and sometimes more effective than, other therapeutic methods. It appears to be particularly useful in behavior problems of young children and is frequently taught to parents as a means of improving parent-child relationships. By emphasizing methods of observing a child's behavior objectively, defining undesirable behaviors and desired outcomes clearly, and teaching parents how to modify their own behavior so that they reward the desired behavior in their children, behavior modification has enabled many parents to gain more satisfaction from their relationship to their children. This method has the advantage of being clearly structured, which may help a parent feel more secure in applying it.

Task centered casework provides a structured, goal oriented approach that is focused on problem-solving. The caseworker and client together try to define the problem for which help is needed, to analyze the problem, and to agree on steps that will be taken to solve the difficulty. There may be a contract between the parties, which is explicit whether it is written and signed or merely approved verbally. Time limits may be set for completion of the tasks.

Contracts are useful in many situations in which there is a possibility that children may have to be removed from the home. By stating clearly what is expected of the parents and what the agency's responsibilities will be, the contract helps the parents to understand the possible consequences of their actions and creates a more objective view of the situation.

The following example illustrates the use of task centered casework, in combination with other services, to relieve depressive symptoms in a young mother.

A hospital social worker, arranging for the discharge of a twenty-eight-year-old mother of three children, aged eight to ten, after a hospitalization for phlebitis and depression, requested that the public agency that had provided homemaker services for the children during their mother's absence continue this service for part of her convalescence. In addition, the psychiatrist who had treated Mrs. Smith for depression recommended that she receive intensive casework services as a follow-up. Recurring hospitalizations suggested that a relationship might exist between her physical and emotional problems.

In the caseworker's first interview with Mrs. Smith, she observed that Mrs. Smith was devoted to her children. She regarded them as individuals and showed an awareness of their emotional needs and stresses. The fact that none of them had developed serious problems indicated that in spite of Mrs. Smith's depressed feelings and frequent hospitalizations, she was trying to meet their needs. An agreement was reached by the worker and Mrs. Smith that in weekly home visits they would try together to locate the sources of some of her feelings.

Over a period of several months, Mrs. Smith showed an ability to develop insight and to connect her present feelings with past experiences. She recalled that her first feelings of depression had followed a tubal ligation that had been medically recommended after the birth of her third child. Task centered casework was used, with short-term goals set at each interview. Initially, these interviews centered on Mrs.

Smith's feelings of anger toward her husband for having left her and her thoughts of killing him. After a hospitalization for dysmenorrhea, at which time a hysterectomy had been recommended, Mrs. Smith had developed the habit of drinking a few beers, and she found that her violent thoughts were stimulated by this behavior. At the same time, she had developed a food phobia and was often unable to eat because she believed her food had been tampered with, even though she knew this idea was "ridiculous" because she bought and prepared all the food herself.

At one interview, at a time when Mrs. Smith was considering going into the hospital again because of her "bad" feelings, her exploration of the sources of these feelings with the caseworker revealed a gynecological problem, dating from the tubal ligation, that interfered with her desire for physical intimacy. She had never discussed this problem with anyone and was reluctant to do so now, but with encouragement from the caseworker, she agreed to discuss it with both her doctor and her male friend. After making this decision, Mrs. Smith felt better and was able to get some insight into her own anger toward herself and to consider the possibility that her food phobia might be a way of punishing herself.

In the course of planning each week for ways to deal with a threatened eviction, which had the potential to rehospitalize her, Mrs. Smith brought up memories and made associations with her childhood home that revealed additional sources of her depression. She recalled an unhappy childhood in a small, dark, closed-in home; her father had insisted that his wife remain indoors and he had beat her daily. Mrs. Smith had felt happy only when visiting her boyfriend in his grandmother's big, airy house. She had found a house that reminded her of this one and became very depressed when the agency refused to approve the move because the house was substandard. As the caseworker explored with her the positive aspects of her efforts to improve her situation and the reality of the substandard rating of the house she liked, Mrs. Smith rallied out of her depressed, nonfunctioning state to find another house she liked even better. This success boosted her self-esteem and enabled her to modify her view that "welfare" was "out to get her" in denying the first house.

In the course of this process, Mrs. Smith was able to make a connection between her wish to kill her husband, who had views very similar to those of her father, and her earlier desire to kill her father when she had witnessed his beatings of her mother. The alleviation of her depressive symptoms enabled Mrs. Smith to think in terms of getting some training for employment and going for help to Alcoholics Anonymous. The caseworker encouraged these efforts at self-help and utilized them as a preparation for reducing her visits, looking toward eventual termination of her services.

This situation illustrates the frequent intimate relationship between intrapsychic and external stresses. It should be noted, however, that the handling was not typical of most public agencies. In ordinary circumstances, the public agency worker receiving such a referral would not have the time, training, skill, and supervision required to explore the client's problems in depth through weekly home visits. The usual role of a public agency worker would be to encourage the client to accept a referral to a mental health center or counseling agency and then to see that appointments were kept. This process is frequently not successful. For example, Mrs. Smith could not always mobilize herself to keep appointments with her psychiatrist at the hospital for supervision of her medication, which she did not take regularly. Few mental health or family counseling agencies send their therapists into the field. Even if the barriers of getting to the agency and developing a relationship with the therapist had been overcome, counseling that was not concerned with Mrs. Smith's reality problems, such as housing, would probably not have engaged her. In this vignette, the worker's ability to deal with these problems and to relate, at the same time, to the feelings that were aroused by these external stresses contributed to her success in strengthening Mrs. Smith's ability to cope with her own problems.

Casework Services: Advocacy

Often, a more active advocacy role must be taken by a caseworker attempting to prevent family breakdown. This is particularly true when concrete problems, such as housing or health, are an important part of the family stresses and are beyond the coping ability of the family. The case of Joan, which introduced Chapter 2, is a good illustration of this.

Joan came to a multiservice agency, the Family Union, with a request for foster care.

> She and her six children were living in a one-bedroom, rat-infested apartment that was often without heat and hot water. Joan had separated from her alcoholic husband, and was dependent on public assistance. She suffered from asthma and the aftereffects of a gynecological operation. The mother and her children were very close and wanted to stay together. The children were helpful and well adjusted, except for low reading and math scores at school. Joan had tried to get help from several traditional service agencies in the past, but they had failed to improve her situation. A Family Union social-work associate, Miriam Colon, and Joan decided the first step was to get adequate housing. (Bush, 1977, p. 48)

Other services were needed, but if Joan could not get an apartment that did not require her to carry her handicapped child up and down several flights of stairs, the other services would not be enough to keep the family together.

Advocacy was the major method used to solve the housing problem. Over a seven-month period, from July to January, the social work associate encouraged and assisted Joan to use every possible channel to obtain better housing. An effort was made to get the building condemned, which would have given Joan priority for public housing. Violations were reported, but a cutback in housing authority staff delayed the processing of the papers. Meanwhile, Joan and the social worker had found two suitable four- and five-room apartments. They were not successful in getting them approved because regulations required a six-room apartment for a family the size of Joan's.

> Colon wrote letters to five New York City Housing Authority officials and received no response for two months. Joan and Miriam Colon averaged two trips per week to the Housing Authority offices to complain. There the mother was given such a blizzard of forms to fill out that she eventually gave up and refused to go back. Cold weather and no heat in the apartment combined to bring on bouts with pneumonia for the mother and three of her children.
>
> In early January, Colon finally received a written response from the Housing Authoirty's Director of Community Affairs. It said that since Joan had been sent two appointments for housing interveiws but had failed to show up, she was dropped from consideration. Joan had no mailbox, since it had been broken into by drug addicts. She had to wait each morning for the mailman, and said she never received any appointment notice.
>
> Another appointment was made. At the meeting, Joan was again informed that Housing Authority policy made it necessary for her to have a six-room apartment. Joan pointed out that she was currently living in two rooms. The Housing Authority worker said there was nothing she could do but put her name on the waiting list.
>
> Finally, with the help of a journalist, the Family Union reached a sympathetic commissioner in the Housing Authority. Through her efforts, the family was able to move into a six-room apartment in their neighborhood late in January. . . . While the apartment battle was going on, Colon had also arranged for medical care for the family. (p. 50)

Stress was reduced for Joan by providing her with a part-time homemaker to help with household tasks, home management, and budgeting. An evaluation and therapy were arranged for the handicapped child, and educational and recreational programs helped to meet the needs of the other children.

Casework Services: Case Management

For many families threatened with breakdown, a variety of services are needed. In arranging for these, a case manager who has a relationship of trust with the family and the knowledge and experience necessary for effective intervention with available resources is essential. Another of the cases that introduced Chapter 2 illustrates the importance of the right combination of services.

Mrs. Caldwell's request for foster care was made during a period of increased emotional stress. The acute depression she had felt at the time of her second husband's desertion had been alleviated with antidepressant medication, supervised by a psychiatrist, and weekly counseling sessions with a social worker at the family service agency to which she had gone for help.

Her son Billy, who was having difficulty relating to other children, had received therapy as well and had had a college student assigned to him as a Big Brother. For two years, since the birth of her second child, Mrs. Caldwell had been able to manage with occasional help from a part-time homemaker, who not only assisted her with child care and household tasks but also served as a role model and teacher. Whenever Mrs. Caldwell was especially depressed, the homemaker's hours were increased. At times, she came for six hours a day, seven days a week.

Just prior to the request for foster care the family had suffered several mishaps and disappointments. Mrs. Caldwell had slipped on the ice and broken her foot. Growing friction between her and the homemaker had developed into a rift and the homemaker had left. Billy's Big Brother had failed to show up for his anticipated Christmas visit. At Billy's request, Mrs. Caldwell had contacted his father, her first husband, for the first time since their divorce and asked him to visit Billy. He agreed but did not keep the appointment.

After her cast was removed, Mrs. Caldwell was hospitalized for a blood clot. As soon as she was on her feet again, she asked that the homemaker service be discontinued and refused to accept another homemaker even when she felt depressed and ill. The public health nurse who visited to follow up on her medical needs noticed Mrs. Caldwell's irritability with Billy, which sometimes resulted in verbal abuse and threats. About this time, Mrs. Caldwell suggested to her therapist that she felt Billy would be better off in a foster home with two parents.

Two facts emerged when this request was explored with the public foster care agency. Billy was due to have a hernia operation, and his mother, who had almost a phobia about doctors and hospitals, could not face the prospect of caring for both a demanding two year old and a convalescent nine year old. This fear appeared to have triggered the foster care request. Further exploration of Mrs. Caldwell's feelings about foster care revealed that her mother had died when she was nine and that she and her sister had been placed by their father in a child-caring institution. He had rarely visited them, and Mrs. Caldwell had felt abandoned, feelings that had been re-aroused by her husband's desertion and that had contributed to her depression. The loss of the homemaker and the other disappointments also had revived these feelings.

It was evident to the intake worker that weekly therapy sessions and even the previous homemaker service did not provide enough support to Mrs. Caldwell to enable her to cope with the added stress of her son's operation. Arrangements were made with a multiservice center in the neighborhood to assist her with child care for Donald, the two year old, during Billy's hospitalization. Mrs. Caldwell was involved in a mothers' support group at the center, and a volunteer parent aide began visiting her regularly to help in overcoming her isolation. The combination of continued individual counseling, child care, the support group, and a parent aide enabled Mrs. Caldwell to follow through on Billy's medical care. The center assisted Mrs. Caldwell in concrete ways, as well. She was having difficulty managing financially because of irregular support payments. She was helped to obtain Food Stamps to stretch her budget, and a special fund was drawn on to allow her to replace some worn out clothing. The center worker encouraged Mrs. Caldwell to take Billy shopping with her, leaving Donald in the nursery, and to buy some things for both herself and Billy. She was reluctant to impose on the center and felt that she did not deserve anything herself, but she followed this advice and had a good time with her older son.

Both Joan and Mrs. Caldwell had reached a point of desperation before requesting foster care. Although in one case the desperation was brought on by the lack of adequate housing and aggravated health problems and in the other case fears and feelings of inadequacy and lack of self-worth were primary factors, in both cases the workers' activity was designed to reduce the stress for each woman to the point that she was able to cope. In Joan's case it was evident that the strength that had enabled her to keep her family together under difficult conditions could be supported and built on if the concrete problems could be solved. In Mrs. Caldwell's case, emotional supports were needed. The concrete supports of first homemaker service and later child care and financial help reduced the stress somewhat so that Mrs. Caldwell could accept the emotional support offered by the mothers' group and the parent aide and begin to think in terms of getting day care for Donald and preparing herself for employment.

GROUP SERVICE METHODS

Group methods include various types of joint or family therapy, peer groups, groups formed around a particular problem the participants share, and mutual aid and self-help groups. Group methods have been used effectively to prevent family breakdown in many different settings. They may be used alone or to supplement individual therapy. Since the problems of a child almost inevitably involve other family members, the counseling or therapy often involves more than one family member. The parents may be seen together, with or without a child or children. A parent and child may have joint sessions to resolve a conflict or improve communication. *Family therapy,* as introduced by Ackerman (1958), was based on the belief that "the existence of problems in a child always implied that there was a disturbance in the entire family network" (Strean, 1981, p. 165). With the application of system theory and role theory to social work, the family was viewed "as a dynamic system with interacting partners, all of whom contribute to the system's functioning and dysfunctioning" (Strean, 1978, p. 169). The concept of "family homeostasis" examines the subsystems within the family in their interaction: the marital subsystem, the parent–child subsystem, and the sibling subsystem. Changes in one system, such as the birth of a baby, may upset the balance of forces which previously maintained equilibrium in the family (Strean, 1978). In the following example, a family therapy approach was used in the assessment process:

> Leon is a 14 year old boy . . . who was brought to the Center because of his refusal to attend school. Many attempts had been made to help him, but to no avail. The Center's therapist immediately called in the entire family for a brainstorming session. As they reviewed the development of Leon's truancy, they realized that he had always been fearful, and had managed to go to school when accompanied by an older sibling attending that school. When his brothers and sisters graduated, Leon stopped going.
>
> Further exploration revealed that Leon's father had died when the child was five years old, and that Leon had been at school when it happened. In his child's mind, he felt that he was responsible for his father's death. As he matured, this fantasy was repressed, while his guilt and fears were expressed through his behavior. When the repressed material was brought to the surface and discussed, the child was able to re-integrate the experience more realistically. Today Leon is back at school and doing well. An understanding of his behavior saved Leon from placement in a residential center and kept a family together. (North Shore Child Guidance Association, 1978–1979)

Family therapy is frequently the choice when one family member has become a scapegoat for the family's problem.

Mrs. Miller was referred to a multiservice center by a legal aid society to which she had gone for help when her twelve-year-old son, Richard, had become involved in several delinquencies. His disruptive behavior in school had resulted in his being referred to a committee on the handicapped for a school transfer.

During the assessment at the multiservice center, it became apparent that there were many sources of severe stress in the family. Mrs. Miller was confronted with the possible need for major surgery. She had been unable to free herself from dependence on her husband, who became abusive fairly regularly when he had had too much to drink. Ten-year-old Sally was overcontrolled and had developed an ulcer, and seventeen-year-old Anne was depressed and struggling with many problems of individuation.

A family treatment process enabled all the family members to break out of their rigid role ascriptions. Once Richard realized he was not "the" family problem, he became less defensive, more open to intervention, and more mature in his participation in the family. He was able to graduate from school without further behavioral problems. Sally became secure enough to shed her angelic posture and begin to test limits in an age-appropriate manner. Anne was able to avoid psychiatric hospitalization, which was threatened when an overdose of pills required emergency medical attention. The incorporation of mother-daughter issues into the treatment plan helped her to become stabilized and successful in school.

Mrs. Miller tended to make after-hours calls to the center's director in times of severe anxiety, but these decreased as she became involved in treatment and in planning for the reality needs of her three children. Mrs. Miller's background had included a series of unhappy foster home placements in childhood, but concern for her children led her to work on her own problems, with the result that she began to develop a better sense of her potential and new life interests. (The Center for Family Life in Sunset Park, Brooklyn, New York)

Individual therapy with one or more family members may be combined with some sessions in which part or all of the family participate.

The O'Connell family was referred to child guidance center by a church worker because the whole family was suffering from Mrs. O'Connell's depressed state. She was unable even to get out of bed in the morning. Mr. O'Connell was struggling valiantly to keep the family together, but financial and emotional strains made him even more short-tempered than usual. The family was heavily in debt, and much energy had to be spent in staving off bill collectors.

The center brought the family's problems to a case coordination conference attended by representatives of both the public child welfare agency and a local community center, a public health nurse, and a school social worker. It was agreed that the social worker from the center and the public health nurse would make a joint visit to the home for purposes of assessment. Although serious consideration was given to hospitalizing Mrs. O'Connell, the decision in a follow-up conference was to try to keep the family intact with a combination of services. The public health nurse, who had psychiatric training, and the social worker from the center undertook family therapy in weekly visits to the home. A part-time homemaker was placed by the public agency to assist the family with shopping and household tasks. The school and recreational needs of the children were worked out with the school social worker and the community center representative.

Gradually, Mrs. O'Connell began to respond to this program, first getting out of bed and finally going outdoors. The relationship between the parents and between parents and children was dealt with in the family therapy sessions. Attendance of family members varied with the needs of the moment. As the stress on Mr. O'Connell was reduced, he was able to admit his concern about his own irritability and lack of patience and to look for better ways to deal with his family. (North Shore Child Guidance Center, Nassau County, New York)

Peer groups may be formed around a particular type of problem or developmental stage. They may be based on age or sex. Adolescents are frequently more comfortable and responsive in groups than in individual therapy.

A mother asked for help because her youngster had gotten into trouble with the law. When he came in it was soon clear the boy was not a delinquent. He was shy and self-conscious. But he was involved with a group of "acting out" types. He went along with what they did to try to fit in. It was like buying friendship. The under-lying problem was depression. He felt alone and apart and needed the group identification to escape these feelings. Once he could acknowledge this, he was able to give up these friends. He got involved with a group of peers who were also getting therapy at the center. He was able to turn himself around, be graduated from high school and go on to college. (Zinman, 1977)

The creative use of group methods with adolescents is illustrated by two projects developed by the North Shore Child Guidance Center of Nassau County, New York. This center sends an outreach worker into the public schools to work jointly with the school social worker in leading groups for students having difficulties. In another project, court-referred adolescents helped to remodel an old house for use as a community center. The project was both an adjunct to therapy and a means to increase employment and socialization skills. Such activity centered groups may be used with therapeutic effect for latency-aged children. Planning a trip or a social event brings about interaction with others and develops problem-solving skills under professional guidance.

Mothers' or fathers' groups may be based on stages of child development or on behavior problems of children. Groups may deal with the problems of new mothers, single parents, mothers of preschoolers, fathers whose sons have become involved with the courts, or stepparents. Couples with handicapped children, remarried couples, or those experiencing marital conflict may find groups a better source of support and insight than individual therapy. Such groups may combine some didactic material—information about stages of development—with an expression of feelings, which leads to the development of insight and serves as encouragement to experiment with new ways of handling situations.

Mutual aid and self-help groups often begin to function somewhat as extended families, providing the type of support that is often lacking in our mobile society.

> Ann was banished by her family when she insisted on keeping her interracial child. She lived in an area of deteriorated housing where she was frequently robbed and afraid to sleep at night. During the day she was too tired to cope with her active three year old. She yelled and hit, and he reacted with tantrums and destructive acts. A friend told her about a mutual aid group, and she began attending. The group connected her with another mother, a mature woman with a large family and a warm heart, who "adopted" Ann and her son. This gave Ann some respite and the freedom to begin to seek a way out of the conditions under which she was living. (Kochman & Gaines, 1977, pp. 12, 13)

Parents Anonymous has become well known as a self-help group for parents concerned over a tendency to abuse their children. While these groups are run by nonprofessionals—parents who have benefited from the program—they usually have a professional sponsor, who is available to serve as a consultant and to provide or arrange for professional counseling when it is needed. Groups offer an exchange of experiences, alternatives to abuse, and the support of other parents, who may be called on by a member in distress. For those who are able to take part in them, such groups can be effective in reducing the isolation that is often a factor in abuse.

HOMEMAKER SERVICES AS A PREVENTIVE STRATEGY

Homemaker services may be used appropriately when the child-caring parent is temporarily absent from the home and there is no one available to care for the children. Absences caused by a mother's illness are the most frequent reason for the use of such services (Kadushin, 1980). When a mother is expected to return in a few days or weeks, it is usually less disruptive for the children to stay together in their own home than to have to adjust to emergency foster home placements. Moreover, the larger the family, the more economical homemaker service is in comparison to foster care, especially if the father or another relative is available to give the children part-time care. Even if twenty-four-hour homemaker services are needed, this alternative may still be preferable.

For school-aged children, homemaker services make it unnecessary for them to adjust temporarily to a new school or neighborhood. For preschool children this consideration is less important, but when they have suffered the loss of their mother, familiar surroundings can help to give them a degree of security.

When a mother's absence is permanent, as in the case of death or desertion, or when it is of uncertain or indefinite length, as is often the case in mental illness, a homemaker may be used appropriately to allow time for a complete assessment of the situation to be made. If it should become necessary to place the children, a homemaker can be of value in assessing their individual needs and in allowing time for a permanent plan to be developed and for the children to be prepared for the change.

Homemaker services are also appropriate when the child-caring parent is available but temporarily incapacitated. If the primary reason for homemaking service is to allow a mother to convalesce at home, the supplementary care given to the children by the homemaker may be the only service needed. More frequently in situations of this type, a homemaker is needed who can not only perform the tasks the mother is unable to fulfill but also serve as an instructor or role model for the mother to help her manage her home more effectively.

Two of the cases already cited illustrate this use of homemaker services. Joan needed help because her large family and her physical condition made it difficult for her to perform household tasks and give adequate care to her handicapped child. The homemaker not only assisted with the household tasks but also showed Joan ways of managing her work so that she could conserve her strength and get more done. Mrs. Caldwell had only two children, but her depressed emotional state left her unable to meet the needs of an active two year old and a disturbed nine year old. Her own lack of mothering in childhood made the homemaker of value to her as a role model.

When homemaker service is used as an adjunct to therapy in this way, it is important that the homemaker receive the kind of supervision that will enable her to participate as a member of a treatment team. This may be difficult when the therapy and the homemaker services are being provided by different agencies. If friction occurs, as it did in Mrs. Caldwell's case, it is important that this development be related to the goals of therapy. A better understanding of this problem could help the homemaker deal with it more objectively and perhaps avoid an abrupt termination of service. For this reason, the Lower East Side Family Union includes homemakers on its service teams. The homemakers participate in setting goals with the families they serve and evaluating progress toward these goals, as in the following example.

Family A was referred to the Union by a municipal hospital. The family consisted of a married couple with three children, ages six months, one and one-half years, and two and one-half years, respectively. The hospital had diagnosed the two older children as retarded, and the six-month-old baby was also showing signs of retardation. The parents were not cooperating with the hospital staff, and, in fact, had refused to recognize the hospital's diagnosis as valid. The parents claimed that they had been told that if they did not show a willingness to meet the special needs of their children, the case would be referred to Special Services for Children for a decision as to placement of the children in foster care. To assist the family, the hospital enlisted the support of the Family Union.

In addition to a social-work associate, the Family Union supplied Family A with a homemaker to help the mother schedule her time and organize her household. It soon became apparent to both the social-work associate and the homemaker that the parents had been giving the children no stimulation. For most of the day, the children just lay around, virtually ignored by their parents. The homemaker spent considerable time convincing the mother of the importance of talking with the children, playing with them, and stimulating them to play by themselves. Almost immediately, there was a visible improvement in the children's development. Meanwhile, the social-work associate was able to persuade the parents to enroll the two older children in Step One, a program that works with youngsters who are slow to develop. The parents subsequently became active in the Parents' Association of Step One and began to attend the organization's meetings on a regular basis. At first, a worker from the Union accompanied them; later, they went entirely on their own.

In conjunction with staff workers from the hospital's psychiatric division, the parents, and with representatives of Step One, the Family Union drew up a contract to plan for the needs of the children. At one of the planning meetings, both the Step One and the Union workers made the observation that the oldest child did not seem to be retarded. Furthermore, the Union worker felt that the six-month-old baby showed no signs of retardation. The hospital agreed to reexamine both children, confirming the workers' impression that neither was retarded. In fact, the baby was unusually bright.

It became clear, however, that the middle child's retardation was genuine. A therapist was sent once a week from the hospital to work with the child. The Family Union homemaker worked with the therapist to teach the mother how to provide daily therapy. Later, the therapist was withdrawn, and the mother continued to work on her own with her child.

Over the course of a year, the Union was gradually able to reduce the amount of time the homemaker spent with the family, from five days a week at the initial stages of the Union's intervention, to three days a week, to two, and, finally, to only one. (Beck, 1979, p. 11)

A homemaker is usually not expected to cope with adolescents or with children who have severe behavioral or emotional disturbances. Whenever a child in the family has special needs, it is important that the homemaker be carefully selected and prepared for the assignment.

When Mrs. Tate was hospitalized temporarily for alcoholism, sixteen-year-old Cindy undertook to care for her three younger siblings, aged seven to twelve. She had frequently carried the maternal role in the family when her mother was drinking, and she objected to sharing it with anyone. Contact with the children's schools revealed that they had been coming to school dirty and inadequately clothed and that Cindy had been doing poorly because of her inability to concentrate on her school work. The caseworker, in discussing this situation with Cindy, was able to persuade her that she need not carry the whole burden of the family but was entitled to some life of her own. A mature homemaker was chosen who could share some responsibility with Cindy and also serve as a role model for her. The caseworker kept in close touch with the situation until she was sure the plan was working.

DAY CARE SERVICES AS A PREVENTIVE STRATEGY

Day care is frequently used, in combination with other services, to provide respite to an overburdened parent under stress.

Mrs. Perry, twenty-five years old and the mother of year-old twins, came to a multiservice center at the suggestion of a friend. Deserted by the children's father during her pregnancy, she was overwhelmed by reality problems, as well as ambivalent about being a mother. Holding herself responsible for being with the children constantly, she nevertheless regretted that she had not learned to read well and could not prepare herself for employment. Finally, Mrs. Perry came to an emotional crisis in which she felt she might "kill the babies or myself." The center worker planned with her for family day care, which was a great help. As she tended to worry considerably about the children's health, a student nurse visited Mrs. Perry regularly to talk with her about health matters, child development, and discipline. Mrs. Perry obtained considerable support from a women's group at the center, and her isolation lessened considerably. She began to take some decisive steps toward self-improvement. (Center for Family Life in Sunset Park)

Family day care is usually the choice for very young children. In addition to providing respite for an overburdened mother, a family day-care home can be the source of more effective parenting skills. A day-care mother who is supportive and tactful may become a role model for a young, inexperienced mother. When a day-care home is to be used therapeutically, for either a child or a mother, the day-care mother will need careful preparation. Closer supervision or more intensive support may be needed from the caseworker until a relationship begins to develop between the mothers who are sharing the care of the child. A child who comes from a disturbed home may present special problems in a day-care home that the day-care mother will need help in handling.

For older children, the choice between a day-care home and a day-care center may depend largely upon accessibility and availability of resources. A disturbed or immature child may benefit from the individualized attention of a family home if enough support can be given. On the other hand, some children may need the understanding and attention of a professional staff, available in day-care centers.

Headstart or child development centers are frequently used to stimulate the development of children who have been deprived in some way and to prepare them for school entrance. These programs sometimes involve the parents, as well, teaching mothers ways of interacting with their children that will stimulate the child's general development.

Two relatively new developments in the child welfare field are *crisis* and *drop-in nurseries*, now part of many protective services programs. A crisis nursery may be open twenty-four hours a day, seven days a week, to provide emergency care for children. A drop-in nursery is usually available only during daytime hours. Such a facility gives a mother under stress the chance to be away from her children for a few hours. Drop-in nurseries also may provide child care while parents attend a therapeutic or a mutual aid group; if the parent is dropping off children and leaving the premises, the time limit is usually two or three hours. Sometimes a drop-in nursery may include a nursery workshop at which parents are asked to share in the child-care responsibility under the direction of a professional teacher, thus learning more about child development and child-care skills.

PREVENTIVE ASPECTS OF PROTECTIVE SERVICES

Protective services represent society's effort to reach those families who need child welfare services but do not seek them voluntarily. The requirement in many state laws that professionals report all cases of suspected child abuse or neglect may sometimes permit intervention before a crisis develops; in a sense, this is a form of outreach as it permits services to be offered to a family who did not request them. At the other end of the protective spectrum, the public agency is authorized to intervene to insure that a child's minimal needs are being met. In either case the difficulty lies in persuading an apathetic or actively hostile family to accept services. There has been government supported emphasis in the child welfare field on the development of innovative methods for facilitating parental acceptance.

Methods of assessment have been briefly described. The first step is the investigation of a report to determine whether it is true. A time limit, usually ninety days, is set for making this determination. When a report has no basis in fact, it can usually be dismissed within a few days. In many cases, though, the question is one of degree. Is the abuse or neglect serious enough to warrant intervention by society? In such cases, the assessment period involves not only a diagnosis of the causes and the seriousness of the problem but also an active effort to engage the family in recognition of the problem.

Mrs. Dalton told her doctor that she had never wanted to be a mother and that she sometimes felt like killing her children, Jimmy, who was four, and Patty, age six. The protective worker who visited after the doctor reported his concern learned from Mrs. Dalton that she often used extreme methods of discipline. She had locked Jimmy in the trunk of her car and had held Patty out a window by her feet, threatening to let go if she would not behave. At times, she overprotected both children and would not let them out of her sight. Mrs. Dalton was unahppy in her marriage, depressed to the point of considering suicide at times, but unwilling to see a psychiatrist.

The protective worker was gravely concerned about the children's safety. Mr. Dalton, who had grown up with emotional deprivation, was too dependent emotionally on his wife to oppose her methods of discipline. Supports had to be found outside the family if it was to be preserved. Fortunately, a multiservice center was accessible that had a drop-in nursery associated with a supportive program for parents. The worker persuaded Mrs. Dalton to accompany her there to learn what the program had to offer. Mrs. Dalton did so reluctantly and was very distrustful initially. When she refused to sign intake forms, she was not pressured to do so, but the worker offered her a contract. If Mrs. Dalton would agree to attend the center for a full day each day for a week, leaving her children in the child-care program, the worker would agree not to initiate any action to remove the children from the home during that period. At the end of the week, the situation would be reassessed.

Reluctantly, Mrs. Dalton signed the contract. She attended activities for mothers at the center while her children were in the nursery. Within two days she was sufficiently reassured to sign the intake forms. By the end of the week, she had agreed to the doctor's recommendation that she enter the hospital for a week of observation and rest. Arrangements were made for the center to continue to care for the children during their father's working hours that week.

Mrs. Dalton was unable at this point to relate to, or benefit from, a traditional mental health program, but she did respond to some degree to the support that was available from a program that offered a combination of child-care and informal group counseling sessions and other activities. In one session she recounted how she had first lost her father, to whom she had been very attached, and then her grandfather, "who had taken his place in my heart." "They both died on me," she added. When another mother commented that those experiences must have made her feel fearful of losing her children and angry at them when they left her, she remarked, "You know, I never thought of it that way. The psychiatrist told me that, but I didn't know what he was talking about."

After taking a workshop led by a psychologist, Mrs. Dalton voluntarily entered therapy, which involved the whole family for a period of time. Later, after her family had participated in a recreational camping trip with other families, she exclaimed ecstatically in the group, "I can't believe my family is still together. I never really thought my children could be taken away from me."

As in Mrs. Dalton's case, a variety of services are frequently needed by a family in which serious abuse or neglect exists.

The Snyders were a young couple with a five-year-old daughter, Sally, who had been less than a year old at the time the Snyders met and married. Sally, Mrs. Snyder's daughter by a previous relationship, had never been adopted by her stepfather, although she regarded him as her father. The referral to protective services came from the hospital at which Sally had been treated after a beating by her mother. Mrs. Snyder had expressed a fear that she might lose control and kill Sally.

The protective service worker referred this family to a special project that had been set up to give intensive services to families with problems of abuse and neglect. The assessment of the project was that there was "a seriously disturbed mother-daughter relationship and an unhealthy marriage. Mrs. Snyder had been physically and sexually abused by her father and neglected by her mother while growing up. Mr. Snyder was an angry, passive, inadequate male who had been reared in a neglectful home situation by an alcoholic mother.

Because of the neediness of both parents and their conflict-ridden relationship, they were assigned to individual counselors and in addition had weekly marital counseling sessions. Sally was involved in play therapy. As the dynamics of the relationship emerged, it became clear that both parents were replicating their original families. Their child was placed in the role of parent by being the object of rage or having to supply emotional gratification through perfect behavior. The expectations, especially of the mother, were unrealistic and had little to do with the child's level of development.

The initial focus in individual sessions was supportive, with establishing a strong therapeutic relationship as a primary goal. Both parents were immature, growth-arrested individuals who required re-parenting themselves. Included in the service plan were short and long term goals of individuation for both, with the awareness that individual growth might result in the termination of the marriage. As treatment progressed over a period of six months, there was positive movement with all three clients. The parents did effect a marital separation while continuing to maintain a social relationship. As the therapeutic relationship strengthened, some prescriptive and behavioral techniques were introduced. Marital sessions were terminated at the time of the separation.

Mrs. Snyder became actively engaged in a training program and in obtaining her high school equivalency diploma. She joined a Parent Education group at the project and showed a great deal of motivation for change. Mr. Snyder continued to struggle with his mixed feelings about the marriage.

While Sally continued in play therapy, there was a great deal of ongoing advocacy on her behalf with day care mothers and school personnel, sensitizing them to her unique problems. Mrs. Snyder gained some insight into her harshness toward Sally as her own needs were met by her involvement with the project. (Sunley, 1978)

Long-term supports are often needed in a case like this: Mrs. Snyder's ability to nurture Sally was still very limited after six months of therapy, and Sally continued to have many difficulties in relating to others.

Among the innovative techniques that have proved successful in protective services are two that promise to bring a relatively large return for a relatively small investment. One of these, the use of multidisciplinary teams, will be discussed more fully in chapter 7. The other, the use of volunteers or paid paraprofessionals to supplement the services of professional caseworkers, has been rather common in efforts to help meet the needs of parents like Mrs. Snyder.

Alternately called *parent aides, lay therapists,* or *mentors* (Withey, Anderson, & Lauderdale, 1980), these paraprofessionals, either paid or volunteer, provide regular, ongoing support to an inadequate parent. This may include acting in the role of a friendly neighbor, that is, someone who listens and responds in a nonjudgmental way. As a relationship of trust develops, the mentor may become a role model for the parent, offering guidance in parenting when it is requested. Concrete services may sometimes be offered, such as help with shopping or transportation, but in most cases the volunteer or aide serves to reduce isolation by being a concerned listener, a safety valve for verbal ventilation, and a source of information on child rearing. Training and professional supervision are important in enabling paraprofessionals or volunteers to fulfill this type of responsibility.

Summary

The effort to prevent family breakdown will be most successful if it begins early. On a primary level, both public and voluntary agencies contribute to the strengthening of family life through reducing some stresses that could cause breakdown. Public agencies sustain many single-parent families by supplying missing aspects of the parental role—either economic support or child care. Economic support is provided through social insurance and income maintenance programs, such as Supplemental Security Income (SSI) for the disabled and Aid to Families with Dependent Children. Child care, provided through day-care programs, enables many single parents to support their own families.

Under voluntary auspices, many types of family life education help to strengthen both intact and single-parent families, and advocacy programs seek to improve conditions for neighborhoods or groups of families. Some programs include both primary and secondary levels of prevention. There has been a recent growth in community based and family focused programs that utilize all social work methods to provide a range of resources to strengthen and sustain families.

On the secondary level of prevention, individual families under stress often need a combination of carefully coordinated services. The choice of services will depend on an accurate assessment of the needs and desires of the family and the availability of appropriate resources. Several guides have been developed that can be helpful to child welfare workers in making such assessments, especially when they involve a decision as to whether to remove a child from the family.

Casework methods are basic to the assessment process and individual counseling is frequently one of the services needed. In addition to traditional psychotherapy, many forms of short-term therapy have proved effective, including crisis intervention techniques, task centered casework, behavior modification, and the use of contracts.

Group methods may increase the effectiveness of services by involving the entire family. Joint counseling sessions with the parents or with parents and children may be combined with individual sessions, or the entire family may be included in sessions that are focused on identifying and modifying patterns of family interaction or on improving communication among family members. Peer groups may be structured by age or based on types of problems or developmental stages. Adolescents, struggling with peer relationships, often benefit from group counseling. Some groups include elements of mutual aid and provide the type of extended family support that many families lack. Self-help groups, such as Parents Anonymous, functioning with a minimum of professional consultation, are successful in engaging many families who might not otherwise seek help. Participation in a group leads some members eventually to seek help through individual counseling.

More concrete services are often needed to make it possible for a parent to take advantage of counseling help. Homemaker service may be used appropriately to keep a family together during the temporary absence of a child-caring parent or to supplement the parental role when a parent is temporarily incapacitated physically or mentally. An inadequate parent who is severely depressed or a mother overwhelmed by responsibility for a large family and afflicted by health problems may need a homemaker both for help with household tasks and for assistance in improving home management and parenting skills.

Child care is another concrete service that may be used to enable a mother to attend group or individual counseling sessions. Day care, in either a family home or a day-care center, may be used both to provide respite to a parent under stress and to promote child development. Crisis or drop-in nurseries have proved a valuable adjunct to other services in many situations in which children need protection from abuse or neglect. Day care may also be used as a means of improving parenting skills.

Protective services for children can serve a preventive function by reaching out to parents who do not recognize or accept their need for child welfare services. Special skills and techniques are needed if hostile, resistant, or apathetic parents are to become engaged in the process of developing a more adequate family environment for their children. The basis for agency intervention must be clearly defined and the worker must be able to present this role objectively, with a degree of empathy that can keep the way open for the parent to participate voluntarily.

Innovative programs are beginning to develop some of the special resources needed to support families with serious problems. Existing services may be coordinated by a case manager or through the establishment of a multidisciplinary team that meets regularly to review the progress of the treatment plan. The multiservice center, which provides a range of services in one location, is another model that has proved effective.

Volunteers and paraprofessionals, trained and supervised by professional staff, are being widely used today to supplement professional services. As parent aides or mentors, they give day-to-day support to inadequate parents, reducing their isolation and serving as extended family or as role models.

Basic to the decision to attempt to maintain a child at home is the desire of the parent to care for the child, the desire of the child to remain at home, and the availability of resources that are appropriate, accessible, and adequate to meet the needs of the family. When problems are multiple and a number of services are needed, a case manager who can coordinate and monitor the provision of services and whom the family will trust is essential to the success of the plan.

CHAPTER 5

Can Damage Be Repaired?

PREVENTIVE SERVICES are not always successful, or a case may come to the attention of an agency during a crisis, when it is too late to keep a family intact. Substitute care outside the home may have to be provided if the children's needs cannot be met through placement of a substitute caretaker in the home or some combination of supportive and supplementary services.

This chapter deals with the methods used to restore a family once a decision has been made that placement of a child is necessary or such placement has already taken place. Ideally, such a decision will have been made only after "a thorough assessment of problems and needs at the personal, interactional and environmental levels and a search for the resources to meet such needs in an integrated service plan in the community" (Janchill, 1975, p. 25).

The criteria for determining whether placement is necessary were discussed in Chapter 4. Primary considerations are the degree of risk to the child's health or safety, the willingness of the parent to care for the child, and the resources available to assist the family. The willingness of a child old enough to express the choice to stay at home and work out problems may also be a factor in the decision.

The Placement Process

NECESSARY STEPS AND GUIDING PRINCIPLES

The steps in the placement process do not always take place in neat order. When emergencies arise, the process may be completed in reverse order or all at once, but the necessity for each step should never be overlooked.

When assessment indicates a need to remove a child from the family, usually the child is placed temporarily in the custody of a social agency. This may be done voluntarily by an agreement with the parents which must be reviewed by a court, or through an order of removal approved by a court if a need for protection can be demonstrated. Court approval of a voluntary agreement is required in order to secure federal reimbursement for a percentage of placement costs. Such temporary custody gives the agency both the right to determine where the child shall be placed and the responsibility for meeting the child's needs. The parents retain guardianship and the right to make important decisions affecting the child's life, such as permission for surgery or for a minor to marry or to enlist in the armed forces (Kadushin, 1980).

To the extent possible, the parents should be involved in the entire placement process, including the determination of the goals of placement, selection of a placement setting from among the resources available, and preparation of the child and family for placement. Decisions should be based on a full assessment of the needs of both the child and the family and on certain guiding principles of placement planning. An understanding of how these principles have evolved may help to emphasize their importance. The *principles of permanency planning for children*, as they have come to be known, now govern the entire placement process in child welfare.

CONCERNS IN PLACEMENT PLANNING

A major concern in selecting a setting is to maintain as natural an environment for the child as is possible. The principle of the least detrimental alternative, enunciated by Goldstein, Freud, and Solnit (1973), recognizes that separation of a child from the family, even though necessary sometimes for survival, always has potentially detrimental effects. Breaks in the continuity of relationships with caring adults can have serious effects on a child's growth and development. The consequences differ with the age and developmental stage of the child. Especially for very young children, their ability to form emotional attachments and to establish a sense of trust can be affected, thus limiting the achievements that are based on identification with the parents.

The effects of separation on children were eloquently summed up by Germain (1980).

> The child who must be placed in substitute care at any age, and regardless of the reason, is torn from the biological and symbolic context of his identity. No matter how nurturing the substitute care, the child's ongoing task will always be to reweave the jagged tear in the fabric of his identity, to make himself whole again. (Pp. 175–176)

For the child whose family has been disrupted, placement in foster care has some of the hazards of surgery. These hazards affect the family, too, as the Iowa Child and Family Services recognized by adopting the slogan "Healing a Hurting Family without 'Amputation' " to describe its program of family services to prevent the need for placement.

The healing process may be facilitated if some continuity of relationships can be maintained through either keeping a child with relatives or in a familiar neighborhood or keeping siblings together. For this reason it has always been good practice to explore resources available through relatives, friends, and neighbors before placing a child in foster care. In reality, although placement with relatives might help to maintain kinship ties or an informal neighborhood child-care network might be available, a variety of obstacles (bureaucratic, legal, or attitudinal) often interfere with the use of these resources (Jenkins and Norman, 1972; Laird, 1980).

A resourceful worker or agency can occasionally overcome some of these obstacles. Some agencies, for example, have established group homes specifically for large sibling groups who did not wish to be separated. Frequently, the only alternatives for a large sibling group are to be divided among several foster homes, often with different caseworkers, or to stay together in a less natural institutional setting.

Although the effects on children of separation from their families have long been a major concern of child welfare workers, interest in, and systematic study of, the effects on parents of separation from their children is a recent phenomenon. The first report of a major study of filial deprivation found that the "varied and complex" feelings with which parents respond to separation from their children often "fall into definable clusters . . . related to reasons for placement as well as demographic and socio-economic characteristics and attitudinal patterns" (Jenkins & Norman, 1972, p. 266). Six major factors were identified among these feelings: "interpersonal hostility, separation anxiety with sadness, self-denigration, agency hostility, concerned gratitude, and self-involvement" (p. 266). In applying the findings of this study to practice, Jenkins and Norman recommended that "a study of parental feelings may provide a kind of mapping to help workers develop an individualized approach to different situations. . . . An approach to parents which focuses only on child needs and ignores parental concerns is not likely to be effective" (p. 267). The study noted that parents tend more frequently to be angry at each other, or perhaps their own parents, than at the agencies.

Most parents regarded agencies as facilitators of child care and helpful to families in times of crisis. A vocal minority, however, saw agencies as usurpers of their parental rights. Others perceived agencies as parent surrogates. . . . Knowing how parents perceive agencies can help workers in their efforts to facilitate discharge. (P. 268)

Jenkins and Norman suggested that further analysis of the data should compare " 'socially acceptable' reasons for placement, e.g., mental or physical illness of the mother or emotional problems of the child [with] 'socially disapproved' reasons for placement, e.g., abuse, neglect, abandonment, and severe family dysfunction" (p. 266).

This increased concern with the effects of separation on both children and parents has been expressed in the emphasis on permanency planning for children. There are three major aspects of such planning. The first is an exploration of all possible resources for keeping the family together and for strengthening it without removing the child. The second aspect is an effort to minimize the effects of separation by maintaining a relationship between parents and children while the children are in temporary foster care and by involving the parents in a plan to return the children to the home. If such a plan is not feasible or does not work out, the third aspect is planning for a stable family environment for each child, one that will provide the child with the basic elements necessary for healthy growth. Crucial to this goal is the continuity that will allow the child to develop an emotional attachment to substitute parents that will enable them to become psychological parents. When there is some doubt that a plan for repairing the family will succeed, planning for repair and replacement must often proceed simultaneously. The selection of a placement setting may have to take into account a child's need for permanency, even while efforts to repair the family continue.

Although adoptive planning will be discussed in Chapter 6, stages in planning are not always clearly separated. They may overlap, as they do in some of the examples presented in this chapter. These case histories, drawn from a wide variety of sources, were selected not necessarily to represent ideal practice but to illustrate some of the better aspects of child welfare at this time. Some cases from earlier periods reflect changes in practice that have occurred over the years.

Placement Strategies

EMERGENCY PLACEMENT

Emergency placement is often necessary when a family crisis arises or a child is in serious danger of abuse or neglect. Temporary shelters were widely used for such placements in the past, but recognition of the damaging effects of congregate care on young children and the tendency for such emergency placements to become prolonged has resulted in a preference for family homes willing on short notice to provide emergency care.

For most children, and especially very young ones, family homes are preferable because they can provide more individualized care. If the crisis cannot be resolved quickly and a need for longer term care becomes apparent, an emergency home can allow for an assessment of the needs of the child and the family and preparation of the child for the move to a longer term home.

Careful selection of a new home is important in order to preserve as much continuity in relationships for the child as is possible. The process of matching a child with an appropriate foster home usually starts with a discussion of the child's characteristics and needs with the prospective foster family. If the foster parents feel able and willing to accept the child into their family, the characteristics of the foster home are then discussed with the child and family and a preplacement visit is arranged at which the child and the foster family can get to know each other a little. Except in cases in which the child's safety or the success of the placement might be jeopardized by the involvement of the child's parents, it is desirable to include them in a preplacement visit. Adjustment is usually easier for a child when parents accept the placement.

Families providing emergency care need adequate backup services from the placing agency. Agencies have found that when consultation is readily available during the initial phase of placement and twenty-four hours a day for emergencies, families can often cope with the behavior of disturbed and upset children. Without such support, they may experience failure and drop out of the program.

Ideally, the range of resources available for emergency placements should include group homes, which may be more appropriate for many adolescents, and residential diagnostic facilities, which can be useful for older children when problems are more complex. The opportunity for intensive professional study and observation within a controlled therapeutic milieu may "make it possible to sort out the various personality, familial and environmental conflicts which may not have been recognized when the crisis erupted . . . to clarify complex personality problems . . . or to clarify the choice among types of placement" (Janchill, 1975, p. 28). If it appears that a child can return home with adequate supports, such facilities may arrange for the services needed by the family and provide aftercare supervision. When longer term placement is needed, the necessary "degree of structure, therapy and social systems involvement" can be determined (Janchill, 1975, p. 28).The following example will illustrate some of the problems involved in emergency placement.

Emergency placement was the first strategy used when Mary, the child reported to have been sexually abused, was found to be in need of protection. In the judgment of the caseworker assigned to assess the situation, Mary's mother would be unable to protect her daughter from further abuse. A strong defense pattern of denial, which had been useful in helping her to survive her own extremely deprived childhood, now prevented her from responding appropriately to her children's needs. Even after she finally admitted that she knew about one occurrence, which had been witnessed by Mary's brother, who had reported it to her, she was unable to perceive her husband's actions as harmful to Mary. She justified his behavior by saying that most children learn about sex on the street. Her dependence on him, both emotionally and economically, made her fearful of taking any action that might drive him away. She saw no need for therapy or any other supportive service that could be offered.

Although there appeared to be little hope that Mary's home would ever be able to meet her needs, a full assessment would take time. An emergency foster home could give Mary immediate protection and allow time for the careful selection of a longer term home. Foster parents were needed who were willing to make a long-term commitment to care for Mary, even to the point of considering adoption if that became the goal. When such a home was found, careful planning was necessary to prepare Mary for her new placement.

During the week Mary spent in the emergency home, she adjusted well, seeking adult approval through her behavior. The preplacement visit also went well, and arrangements were worked out for her transfer. Testing had put her in a borderline retarded range and revealed a low self-image. After careful consultation with school personnel regarding Mary's needs, it was decided to place her in a regular class but to give her individual attention and remedial tutoring. A special class might have reinforced a feeling of being different, and allowance was made for the possibility that Mary's actual potential was higher (as later testing confirmed). Precautions were taken within the school to insure that confidentiality would be maintained when Mary's needs were shared with her teachers.

Although Mary's behavior was not a problem, arrangements were made for her to receive therapy at a local mental health clinic to assist her in working through her emotional reactions to the experiences that had led to her placement. Her new foster parents planned to attend some sessions with her in order to gain a better understanding of their role in contributing to Mary's growth.

Visits between Mary and her mother were particularly difficult. Her mother's inability to accept the need for placement made it advisable to hold the visits in a neutral setting, where there would be less risk of her disrupting the placement. The court had approved the agency's recommendation that the visits be supervised. Mary's caseworker observed that her mother often counseled her not to accept help but to "do for herself" and not to listen to her foster parents or her caseworker. Having found her caretakers in her own childhood undependable, she tended to pass on her lack of trust to her children.

Rather than have the foster parents bring Mary to these visits, the caseworker drove her back and forth, using this time to help Mary explore her feelings toward her mother. Although Mary's mother was often critical of her during the visits and sometimes provoked feelings of guilt, Mary looked forward to seeing her mother. She conversed actively and tended to imitate her mother's sometimes childish mannerisms. On the way home, she often fantasized that the visit had not ended. Although a good foster home had been found for Mary in which she had adjusted well, she still needed help in dealing with the reality of her relationship to her mother if she was to complete the task of mending her identity and making herself whole again.

Three months after Mary's placement, there was a final, or dispositional, hearing on her case. The agency's recommendation that both Mary and her brother, John, be placed in its custody was approved by the court. A full evaluation of the family had revealed that its inadequacies were having a serious effect on both children. John had not been abused, but he was a victim of role reversal. His mother, who had not herself achieved a level of maturity that would enable her to perceive her children's needs as separate from her own, depended on them, as well as on her husband, to gratify her needs. Many of the homemaking tasks fell to John. He often had to prepare meals for himself or for the family, and his mother relied on him for much of the house cleaning. Because neither she nor the stepfather had ever learned internal controls, they were unable to teach them to the children. Methods of discipline were often harsh.

The evaluations required by the court showed that John's intelligence was above average but that his emotional development had not gone beyond the earliest levels. He was isolated from his peers and found an outlet for his abilities in a solitary preoccupation with insects. He read about them avidly and collected them, keeping some as pets and killing others.

Residential treatment had been considered for John because the agency recognized that adjustment to a foster home might be difficult for him. It finally decided to try a less restrictive setting first, the emergency home which had been used for Mary. This did not work out as well for John as it had for his sister. The foster parents were unable to tolerate his restlessness and his subtly provocative behavior. He sometimes wandered through the house in the middle of the night or hid the foster parents' possessions to see whether they would notice the loss.

A temporary group residence offered a setting in which John could receive intensive professional help with the problems he faced in separating from his mother, learning to trust others, and developing social skills. At the same time, it gave the agency an opportunity to gain a better understanding of his needs in order to select a home that could meet them. The residence offered intensive casework therapy, milieu therapy (which included a rap group and a behavior modification program), and an individualized school program.

In two months John made considerable progress. Although he had tended at first to be a scapegoat for the group, provoking his peers with his superior vocabulary, he responded well to both the behavior modification program and the rap group. A tic, which often appeared when he was upset, was controlled at first with medication and later by behavior management techniques (casually removing John from the group had a calming effect, and the medication could be discontinued).

It took longer for John to develop trust in his caseworker. Storytelling and drawing were used to help him express feelings that he found difficult to reveal. Eventually, as his ability to trust grew, human beings began to enter his stories of animals, which had previously been concerned with themes of violence and isolation. His caseworker was concerned not only with helping him adjust to the setting of the group residence but also with providing nurturance and support for the transition from the relationship to his mother and lessening the need for his intellectual defenses.

The multidisciplinary conference at which John's progress was reviewed concluded that a carefully selected foster home would be preferable to a group setting for John. His tendency to become a scapegoat was more likely to be reinforced in a group. A home was found with a professional couple in an area near his sister's home. Joint supervised visits were arranged for the children and their mother. John was engaged in therapy at the same clinic his sister attended.

Both John and his foster parents needed considerable support from the agency during his initial adjustment to this home. For a while his tic and his tendency toward isolation returned. These symptoms lessened as he began to feel more comfortable. The foster parents needed help with John's tendency to provoke them. The foster father was encouraged to share some interests and activities with John, and they started a stamp collection. John's participation in neighborhood sports was supported by his foster parents, and through this activity he began to gain some satisfaction from peer relationships.

TIME-LIMITED FOSTER CARE

Temporary foster care is probably one of the most frequently used strategies when placement of children in a family home is possible. Since temporary care often extended indefinitely in the past, "time-limited foster care" is the term more frequently used today to describe this strategy. Time-limited foster care is a way to involve parents in the planning for their children, whether the outcome is return home, adoption, or long-term foster care or guardianship. The goals of foster care and a definite time period for accomplishing them are established at the onset of care.

In the past, John and Mary might have remained in so-called temporary care for years, until they reached the age of eighteen. Their mother showed interest by visiting regularly and would not voluntarily surrender them for adoption, but her ability to fulfill her parental role did not improve. This case illustrates one of the most difficult dilemmas faced by child welfare workers and agencies. What is in the child's best interest when a parent who lacks the capacity for parenting clings to a child who helps to meet the parent's needs? For a mother who has depended on her children to meet many of her own needs, both practical and emotional, the void left by their removal is evident. Too often in the past, such parents in effect were abandoned by the agencies concerned with the welfare of their children.

The concept of time-limited care is not new, but a brief look at its evolution will help clarify the strategy's current use. At the turn of the century, Charles Birtwell and the Boston Children's Aid Society began to envision foster care as a temporary means of providing for a child's needs until restoration to the family was possible, in contrast to Brace's view of foster care as permanent substitute care. Rather than relying on free homes, as Brace had done, Birtwell attempted to professionalize practice through systematically studying and supervising homes, and compensating families for the costs of caring for children (Kadushin, 1980).

The family foster home, as we know it today, evolved largely from Birtwell's work in establishing standards for foster families and matching the home to the needs of the child. Homes are recruited, studied, and certified as meeting acceptable standards by an agency, which then provides supervision of children placed in the home. In addition to a board rate, adjusted to the age of the child, medical expenses and a clothing allowance are provided. Special rates may be paid for children who require extra care because of physical or mental handicaps.

The emphasis on improving the quality of foster care to meet children's needs tended, over time, to obscure the aim of returning the child to the family. Providing the child with a suitable substitute environment was often easier than attempting to restore the child's home to an adequate level of functioning. Factors contributing to this tendency were lack of services needed to rehabilitate families, lack of time for active or intensive intervention, lack of needed skills or direction, lack of structure for accountability, attitudes, and legal obstacles. When placement could not be prevented, it was often an indication that the needed supportive services were not available. Overburdened workers generally found it more gratifying to work with relatively cooperative foster parents, whose middle-class values they shared, than with resistant or actively hostile parents who might perceive their efforts as unwanted intrusion. Even when the parent was cooperative, the problems were apt to be frustrating. The average foster care worker would not have been able to undertake the kind of housing advocacy provided to Joan by the Family Union as described in Chapter 4.

Foster care workers sometimes observed that parents who were satisfied with the care their children were receiving lacked motivation to make the changes needed in their own lives to enable them to regain custody (Fein, Davis, & Knight, 1979). Some parents were content to remain part-time parents, with regular or occasional contact with their children. Others lost interest and drifted away. Laws requiring periodic court reviews of placements had some effect in holding both parents and agencies accountable for planning for children, but agencies were sometimes discouraged from pressing for termination of parental rights by court decisions favoring biological parents who had shown minimal interest. In an era in which more infants were available for adoption, older or handicapped children were often perceived as unadoptable. An agency might be reluctant to seek voluntary surrender or initiate court action when no prospective adoptive home was available.

Foster care workers experienced in dealing with these obstacles were not surprised when studies revealed that an alarming number of children stayed in temporary foster care indefinitely, often until they became of age. "Nationwide reviews of the performance of the system, by two different child advocacy groups, indicted the system for its failure in meeting children's needs for permanence" (Children's Defense Fund, 1978; National Commission for Children in Need of Parents, 1979) (Kadushin, 1980, p. 383). The observation of experienced workers, confirmed by earlier research (Maas & Engler, 1959), that if a child could not be returned home within a year to eighteen months, the chances of returning home were greatly reduced was disputed by Fanshel and Shinn (1978): roughly 25 percent of the children in their sample had been discharged by the end of one year and another 25 percent after two years in care. They concluded from these figures that caseworkers should not give up hope, but they also recommended that government funding be increased to improve services to parents of children in foster care.

In the seventies the concept of time-limited foster care was refined through a number of federally funded demonstration projects designed to counteract the tendency to prolonged temporary care. The intent was to provide each child with maximum stability through arriving as early as possible at a decision as to whether the home could be restored. In cases in which this goal was not possible, the emphasis would be on developing an alternate permanent home for the child, preferably an adoptive home. Standards proposed by the American Public Welfare Association in 1975 set one year as the maximum length of temporary foster care when the goal was return to the family. A maximum of two years was allowed when adoption was the goal. The projects approached the problem from several points of view and developed many techniques and tools applicable in various situations. Many that proved effective were disseminated through regional training centers for child welfare workers. Several are reviewed here.

Contracts as a Method in Time-limited Foster Care

One of the most widely used and effective techniques demonstrated in these projects was some form of agreement or contract between the parents and the placement agency as a means of clarifying goals and keeping track of progress toward them. Some of the variations of this technique, as applied in time-limited foster care with differing goals, are illustrated in the cases that follow.

Time-limited foster care was the strategy used to assist Carol Davis, the young woman described in the fourth vignette in the introduction to Chapter 2. The public child welfare worker who responded to the request from the court for emergency foster care for fourteen-month-old Roy learned from his mother, Carol, that she had just broken off her often stormy relationship with Roy's father, with whom she had been living. In retaliation, he had locked her out of the apartment, refusing even to give her her clothes. Although Carol had applied for AFDC, her eligibility could not be established until she had a place to live. The one friend with whom she could stay had no room for the baby, and her mother's landlord did not allow children. In desperation, she had taken the baby to his paternal relatives, who had agreed to care for him temporarily. When the judge at the paternity hearing ordered the adjudicated father to contribute $25 weekly toward Roy's support, he angrily refused to accept any further responsibility and charged that Carol was an unfit mother who had abandoned her child.

Carol impressed the worker as caring for her child but being immature and emotionally needy herself. A mutual agreement was reached that the agency would place Roy in temporary foster care for three months to give Carol a chance to find housing and employment and to get her life "straightened out," as she expressed it. Carol agreed to go for counseling and to visit Roy regularly in the foster home.

Carol followed through on the plans that she and the worker had developed together. She applied for public assistance for herself and accepted a public works job that the agency arranged for her. She contacted a community mental health clinic for counseling. Because she was nervous about her first visit to Roy in his foster home, the worker accompanied her. She had some difficulty communicating with the foster mother, which the worker helped her to clear up.

By the end of two months Carol had succeeded in finding a suitable apartment, which she began to paint and fix up. The worker discussed with her the required thirty-day notice for return of her child, and she gave this in writing the next day. Carol followed through on providing the documentation needed to obtain her AFDC grant and arranged with her therapist to transfer her records to a clinic nearer her new apartment.

The worker made weekly visits during the first month after Roy's return to his mother. Things appeared to be going well. Carol had taken Roy to a pediatrician for a checkup, and she was waiting for the mental health clinic to give her an appointment as soon as they received her records. The worker began discussing plans to terminate the case.

The day before the case was due to be closed, Carol's mother called the agency to notify them that her daughter had been arrested, along with her new boyfriend; stolen goods had been found in her apartment. Emergency arrangements were made for the maternal grandmother and the boyfriend's parents to care for Roy until Carol could be contacted in jail. She requested that neighbors who had previously cared for Roy be asked to do so now. They agreed, and the worker confirmed that the arrangement was satisfactory. When Carol was released, after a two-week delay caused by difficulties in arranging bail, an outreach worker who had contacted her in jail agreed to continue seeing her. The program of the outreach agency appeared to be more suitable than the mental health clinic for this young mother. This service seemed to meet Carol's needs, and the child welfare agency closed its case. Carol's responsiveness to joint planning with the agency for return of her child and her ability to follow through on a mutually agreed upon plan reassured the worker that she could make use of supportive resources in the community to strengthen her performance as a mother.

This case illustrates the traditional use of time-limited foster care: to sustain a family through a crisis period or to provide time for a parent to work out plans for strengthening the family (through treatment, training, employment, etc). The agreement in this case was informal rather than written.

Many of the demonstration projects made more specific use of contracts. They often proved to be an effective means of involving parents in planning for their children; when such planning was not successful, written contracts helped to document failure of the plan and to facilitate development of an alternate permanent plan for the child.

A project in Alameda County, California, experimented with a service delivery model in which case management services were provided to the family by a voluntary agency while workers in the public agency supervised the children placed in foster homes. Contracts written in behavioral terms were the major method of involving the parents in planning for their children. As Wiltse (1979) noted in describing this program:

> A particularly effective tool in providing a framework within which case planning and implementation was carried out was the written contract. Parental objectives (e.g., to have their child returned to their care), visiting and progress assessment schedules were put in writing. Plans were developed and steps to accomplish these plans were outlined and attached to the contracts. Alternative actions, such as referring a case for adoption should parents not follow through with plans mutually agreed upon with the caseworker, were also spelled out, together with time limits within which each part of the plan was to be accomplished.
>
> Each agreement was somewhat like a sector of a decision tree, specifying the alternatives to be confronted as each step was or was not accomplished. . . . The willingness to sign a written agreement proved a useful indicator of parents' continuing participation in planning. (P. 14)

One example from this project illustrates the use of the behavioral approach.

John Woodall, 9½ years old, was said, in allegations to the juvenile court, to have been abused by his father. He was placed in emergency foster care, and the case was immediately given to the project. There were two other nondependent children at the home at this time.

The project worker first visited the parents two days after John was placed in foster care. During the visit the parents said they wanted their son to be returned to them. Together with the project worker, they identified the problems that would have to be solved before John could come home: (1) the children did not comply with the parents' requests to help with household chores, (2) Mr. Woodall drank what he and his wife described as an excessive amount of alcohol each day, and (3) Mrs. Woodall had no time for herself.

The plan of intervention did not focus on Mr. Woodall's abusive behavior. The worker believed, after he assessed the situation, that the abusive behavior, stimulated by what the father described as his "frustration" with the children's failure to follow through on household responsibilities, was aggravated by the father's drinking. The parents and the project and county workers formulated a contract that identified the following general goals:

Goal 1: To engage the parents in a program to increase the frequency with which the children completed assigned household chores.

Goal 2: To decrease Mr. Woodall's drinking from 6 6/7ths drinks to 2 drinks per day. The worker and Mrs. Woodall had observed that Mr. Woodall did not show any behavioral effects of alcohol until he had a third drink. Thus they determined that he could "safely" consume two drinks a day.

Goal 3: To increase Mrs. Woodall's free time from no hours to two hours per week. The amount of free time was determined solely by Mrs. Woodall. She defined free time has having no at-home responsibilities. Since one of the children at home was a preschooler, she had no time during the day when she was completely free.

Intervention Plans—the intervention plan for each of these goals follows:

Goal 1: The children were expected to do these household chores each day: pick up their clothes, make their beds, get dressed, feed the dog, and set the table. The goal was to increase the number of times the children completed the tasks with a minimum of direction by the parents.

The children earned a specified number of points for each chore they completed. They received 5¢ for every ten points they earned and could either spend the money immediately or designate some item or privilege they wished to save for. One point was subtracted for each chore they did not finish. No other punishment (e.g., spanking) was used.

The parents kept a weekly chart for each child of the number of points earned for each chore. On the chart one column listed the chores, and there were columns for each day of the week in which the points were marked.

The workers checked the chart every week to see how many points each child had earned and discussed any problems that might require alteration in the plan.

Goal 2: The goal was to reduce the number of alcoholic beverages Mr. Woodall drank each day from 6 6/7 to 2.

Mr. Woodall said that alcohol quenched his thirst and helped him relax. To achieve his goal, he agreed to do the following: Before he could drink alcohol, he first had to (1) quench his thirst by drinking a nonalcoholic beverage and (2) try to relax through such activities as watching television, reading, and taking a bath.

If he met these two conditions, he could have an alcoholic beverage, but could not exceed the designated maximum of two. In addition, he received these two reinforcers: (1) his wife would allow him to discuss his job with her (which previously she had been unwilling to do) and (2) for each day he had two drinks or fewer, he would earn one hour of time to be by himself.

To help her husband achieve his goal, Mrs. Woodall agreed to do the following: (1) to keep a sufficient amount of nonalcoholic beverages in the refrigerator, (2) to refrain from discussing her husband's job with him until he met the two previously stated conditions, and (3) to maintain records of the free time he had earned and to negotiate with him when he could use that time. The social worker monitored the plan at his weekly interviews with the parents, discussed any problems found in implementing it, and made alterations when necessary. He also agreed to refrain from discussing the father's job with him unless Mr. Woodall met the two conditions on the day of the interview.

Goal 3: The goal was to provide Mrs. Woodall with some free time as a respite from child care and as an opportunity to pursue her own interests. Mrs. Woodall's free time was contingent on her fulfilling the three steps involved in monitoring her husband's drinking program, as mentioned in Goal 2. If she complied with that program, she would earn two hours of free time per week.

In turn Mr. Woodall agreed to negotiate with his wife as to when she could use her free time and to care for the children and do the household chores during her free time. As with the other two goals, the worker monitored the plan at the weekly interviews, discussed the problems in implementing the plan, and made whatever alterations were necessary.

Outcome—within 2½ months, Mr. Woodall reduced the number of alcoholic beverages he drank from 6 6/7 drinks per day before intervention, to an average of 2½ drinks per day; at the time of writing he had stopped drinking alcoholic beverages. Mrs. Woodall's free time increased from no hours to two hours per week and is now eight hours per week. The parents reported that the children's compliance with household responsibilities increased, but they did not maintain records in this area.

After 3½ months of intervention, the project worker recommended that John be returned to his parents for a trial visit, since they had completed the intervention program. John was returned to his parents a month later, and at the time of writing, has been at home for eight months. The worker visited the family once a week and telephoned them once a week for six months after John returned home. (Stein & Gambrill, 1976, pp. 35–36)

While behavioral techniques have been used very effectively in some cases, they are not always applicable or appropriate. The project found that sometimes it lacked "access to incentives (such as financial remuneration for remaining in a drug program or homemaker services to give the parents some free time) equal to those that would be lost by altering their current life-styles" (Stein & Gambrill, 1976, p. 38).

Not all child welfare workers have behavioral techniques in their repertoire of skills, but some of the advantages of this method have been utilized in other programs. The process of breaking down the activity needed to accomplish a goal into clearly defined, small steps can assist both the worker and the parent in understanding what changes are required and what responsibilities each will assume.

The Oregon project—Freeing Children for Permanent Placement— used contracts, not necessarily expressed in behavioral terms, to involve parents in planning when their children were placed in foster care. A model contract, reproduced in Appendix C, spells out the objectives of the parents, the steps by which they are to be achieved, and the responsibilities of both the agency and the parents (for visiting, receiving counseling, etc.) (Pike, Downs, Emlen, Downs, & Case, 1977).

Since this project focused on children who had been in foster care for a year and who had been assessed as unlikely to return home, its handbook (Pike et al., 1977) emphasizes the use of legal methods to achieve a permanent status for the child. Before termination of parental rights should be considered, however, "an exhaustive effort" should be made to accomplish the goal of returning the child to the family. Surprisingly, the project reported that 26 percent of the children were eventually returned to their parents (Pike, 1976).

One example from this handbook of a case in which restoration was accomplished illustrates the importance of clearly spelling out at the beginning of care the objectives and the steps to be taken.

> Mr. Wilson, an American serviceman in Japan, married a Japanese woman. They had one child, Donald, and returned to the U.S. When the boy was two, his father sexually molested him. Mr. Wilson was criminally convicted and sent to prison. Donald was placed in foster care, and remained in the same foster home for the next seven years. His mother visited about three times a year, at her (rather than the agency's) initiation. In the meantime, the mother remarried, had two more children, and she and her husband had a good stable home. After seven years, it was decided that a permanent plan was needed for Donald. When asked, the mother said she had always wanted her boy back, but, perhaps because she was a foreigner with language difficulties, she hadn't known it was possible to have her child return. Donald also said he wanted to go home. Even though he had spent seven years in a good foster home, he had apparently never given up strong ties to his real mother. Some preparatory visits were arranged, and Donald was permanently returned to his mother. His former foster parents have become a foster aunt and uncle to him. (Pike et al., 1977, pp. 18–19)

Preserving the continuity of relationships for a child like Donald is an important part of planning. Today, Donald's original placement might have been avoided altogether. It could certainly have been shortened if his mother's desire to have him returned had been clarified at the time of his original placement. Separating a child from a long-term foster home to which there has been good adjustment poses the same psychological hazards as does separation from the child's own family. In Donald's case, the hazards were minimized by enabling him to continue to have contact with his foster parents. This made it easier for them to accept the separation, which in turn contributed to Donald's well-being.

In making the often difficult decision as to whether a child should return home after a long stay in foster care, the question should be asked: "Where does the child feel that he belongs?" (Pike et al., 1977, p. 15). When the goal of foster care is return to the family, it is important that the plan provide some means of preserving the continuity of relationship for both parents and children. The accessibility of the foster home for visiting, the attitude of the foster parents toward the biological parents, and other supports that will enable parents to gain satisfaction from their relationship to their children are all important aspects of this process.

Planning for the Child's Return to the Home

A case of time-limited foster care that used the contracting model favored by the Lower East Side Family Union illustrates the type of planning that may be needed. Family Union contracts often involve a group of service providers and specify coordination of services.

Mr. and Mrs. Wu were referred by a hospital psychiatric department because Mrs. Wu, who was six months pregnant, had just been discharged after a month's hospitalization. Her emergency admission followed an incident in which she had screamed uncontrollably, broken her third-floor window, and thrown glass onto the street. It was her third hospitalization in a ten-year period, two earlier ones having been in Hong Kong prior to the couple's arrival in the United States.

The couple, who spoke only Chinese, were in financial need since Mr. Wu had had to leave his job to care for his wife after her discharge. The Family Union assigned a Chinese social work associate, who arranged immediately for the couple to obtain emergency financial assistance.

The first contract had the goal of enabling the family to care for their baby with the aid of a homemaker. The Family Union agreed to help the family qualify for financial and medical assistance and to obtain a homemaker after their child was born. A psychiatric nurse from the hospital aftercare department agreed to provide family therapy to the couple, in addition to following up on Mrs. Wu's treatment.

By the time of the baby's birth, the couple felt they could manage on their own. They decided not to accept the homemaker service. After six weeks Mr. Wu went back to work. Almost immediately his wife became delusional. He quit his job, and the Family Union arranged another conference on the case. A new contract was drawn up in which the parents agreed to place their two-month-old daughter in temporary foster care. The Family Union arranged this placement through the Bureau of Child Welfare and a well-known child-care agency.

After three months, at a conference to review the placement, it became evident that longer term care would be needed. Mr. Wu had been willing at first to consider adoption because of his wife's mental illness, but it was agreed at the conference that Mrs. Wu should be given an opportunity to stabilize her mental condition before any decision as to permanent placement was made.

The child remained in care for eighteen months. During this time the contracts between the parents and the agencies were reviewed and renewed periodically. The child-care agency agreed to seek an Oriental home for the child and to arrange for an interpreter for the parents' biweekly visits. The psychiatric nurse continued to provide therapy for Mrs. Wu and agreed to arrange for an evaluation as to her ability to care for her child. The Family Union worker continued to coordinate and monitor the plan and to counsel the family and assist them with keeping appointments and solving other problems. Mrs. Wu was counseled on how to interact with her child prior to the scheduled visits, and she was assisted in getting and keeping a job in a garment factory. Mr. Wu was encouraged to find a job in the neighborhood so that he could spend more time with his wife. The parents' feelings about their child were discussed with them—the father's disappointment that he did not have a son and his fears that his daughter would become mentally ill like his wife, the mother's fears that her daughter would interfere with her relationship with her husband. Eventually, the couple was stabilized enough so that plans could be made to return the child to them. Mrs. Wu had cooperated fully with her therapy program, had been able to keep a full-time job, and had participated in a mothers' group. Mr. Wu had agreed to look for a job that would allow him to come home every night.

When the child was returned, the Family Union assigned a five-day-a-week homemaker for a period of three months to teach Mrs. Wu child-care skills. This service was reduced gradually as mother and daughter became more comfortable with each other. After six months the staff began working to reduce the family's dependence on Family Union. After the case was closed, the family returned once for assistance in making an application for day care for their daughter. Mr. Wu was working steadily, his wife was continuing to attend her therapy program regularly, and their daughter seemed well cared for and happy.

In this situation, preventive services had been effective for a while in keeping the family intact. When a crisis required substitute care for the child, careful planning, made concrete through the use of contracts, enabled a relation to be maintained between the parents and the child, leading to the child's eventual return. Supplementary services were necessary for a while after her return, but eventually the family was able to function effectively on its own.

Another example of the use of this type of contract illustrates its value both as a motivating and as a coordinating mechanism.

The mother of a 5 year old boy who was admitted to a municipal hospital for a sickle cell anemia crisis was referred to the Family Union by the hospital's social worker. Staff at the hospital had observed that, on a number of occasions, the mother appeared to have been drinking. The hospital's social worker had learned that the mother and her son lived in a fourth-floor walk-up apartment in a semiabandoned building that was without heat, hot water, or electricity. In addition, since the mother's welfare benefits had terminated and her attempts to have them reinstated were unsuccessful, she had begun to beg for food from friends and acquaintances. Under the circumstances, returning the child to his mother was impossible. Referral to the Family Union was an alternative to foster placement.

The Family Union worker, who saw the mother while the child was hospitalized, learned that the mother had a history of alcoholism and, as a result, eight of her nine children had been placed in foster care. Although the mother had been involved with three foster care agencies, the worker noted that none had offered her any assistance. Convinced that the mother had the ability and the desire to care for her son, the worker involved the mother in designing a plan that would make this possible.

The mother signed a work agreement that required her to enroll in and attend an alcoholism program; see a legal services attorney to help her get back on welfare; contact the New York City Housing Authority and the Department of Buildings to find suitable housing; find a special school for her son whose illness precluded his attending a public school; plan a permanent arrangement for her five children still in foster care (three had been freed for adoption); and arrange for custodial care of her son upon his release from the hospital until she was ready to care for him.

The worker called a meeting of a number of the service providers at which a Family Service Contract was signed and the following agreements were made:

The mother would keep all appointments and adhere to the plan;
Special Services for Children would accept a time-limited placement;
The municipal hospital, where the child would have regular, routine treatment, would schedule appointments in different clinics on the same day;
The child care agency would find a temporary foster home for the child and would return him to the mother when she found a new apartment.
The Family Union worker would help the mother with her tasks and coordinate the activities of the service providers.

The plan was followed, as agreed. Within three days of the mother's move to a new apartment, her son was returned. (Dunu & Clay, 1978, p. 23)

In most of the cases described thus far, the parents agreed voluntarily to the foster care plan. Court ordered, or involuntary foster care may be used to protect children when the parents are unwilling or unable to take the actions necessary to meet their children's needs or to plan with the agency toward this goal.

The Use of Court Ordered Foster Care

Mr. and Mrs. Warren, both of whom were alcoholics, had been found by a protective services agency to have neglected their children's medical needs. The family, which had 6 children, was referred to a special project for intensive services. For 6 months, the project staff worked with this family. The initial assessment found the home in a state of gross neglect. Neither parent accepted responsibility for providing the basic needs of the family—food, laundry, utilities, etc. Despite the efforts of the oldest daughter, the children were inadequately cared for. The mother had apparently been a greater nurturing figure in the past because there were evidences of ego strength in all the children. The father's sociopathic pattern had been evident before the marriage, but the deterioration of the family's functioning had occurred over a three year period in which both parents had become involved in a restaurant business and bar.

The staff focused on engaging the mother supportively and applying pressure on the father to provide basic necessities. The mother was seen weekly at her home by the social work associate in supportive counseling sessions, and was offered other services, such as homemaker, cleaning service, debt counseling and advocacy for medical care for herself. All these services were refused at first as both parents were resentful and mistrusting.

The father was seen by the case manager, who counseled him directly concerning the status of the house and the care of the children. He was verbally cooperative, but actually resentful of agency "interference." He "often broke appointments and neglected vital family responsibilities."

The two oldest girls were involved both in individual counseling and in a weekly adolescent group. Very meaningful relationships were established with these girls "who had assumed most of the parenting in the family." As they learned to trust their counselors, they were able to ventilate the fear and rage they had felt due to their parents' emotional neglect. Their involvement meant so much to them that they kept appointments, even against their parents' wishes.

Mrs. Warren's health continued to deteriorate due to lack of food and too much alcohol. In midwinter she had to be hospitalized, and the entire family had to be evacuated because utilities were shut off in subzero weather due to unpaid bills. The protective services agency, with the cooperation of the project, moved to place the children in temporary foster care through a court petition.

As soon as Mrs. Warren was released from the hospital, she engaged an attorney. The temporary foster placement of her children became "a powerful motivating force" which had a positive effect on this mother. The father had continued in his behavior patterns, removed himself from his family, and made no effort to see his children. The mother "started divorce proceedings, removing herself from a pathological relationship of long standing." She put the restaurant up for sale and got a job. She resumed seeing her counselor at the project, gave up drinking, and became re-involved with her children, showing more care and responsibility than she had at any time previously. Her efforts became focused on regaining custody of her children (Sunley, 1978).

In this case, court ordered foster care was used to meet an emergency situation after several months of preventive services failed to bring about significant change. The reality that her children could be removed helped this mother to mobilize her strengths and to modify her behavior. For John and Mary's mother, court ordered foster care did not have the same motivating effect. Her deprived background had not given her the strengths to mobilize to meet the situation. Before an agency gives up on an inadequate parent, court ordered services may be tried to see whether the authority of the court will persuade an apparently unmotivated or resistant parent to accept the need for services. Parents may be ordered to attend therapy, or an agency may be ordered to place a homemaker in the home for a temporary period. If such measures are ineffective, a petition to terminate parental rights on the basis of permanent neglect may be considered by the court to allow the agency to develop permanent plans for the children.

Group Services as a Method in Time-limited Foster Care

Group methods have been used effectively with many parents who are motivated to get their children back. Group counseling may take various forms. A group may be composed exclusively of parents whose children are in foster care, or it may include parents who are at risk and those whose children have already returned. The peer support available through such groups is often very helpful to an inadequate parent in need of more support than an individual therapist can provide or to one who finds a relationship with an individual therapist somewhat threatening. The sharing of common problems and feelings in a group can encourage a more objective approach to problem-solving.

Mutual aid groups provide additional support, similar to that which might come from an extended family, in helping to gratify the parents' own unmet needs.

Anna Ray had lost her two young sons to foster care when she was 22 and they were 3 months and two years old. Her unemployed husband had deserted her while she was pregnant with their third child. Cut off from her family, she was in despair and living on the streets. Her court-appointed lawyer involved her with a social worker in a legal services project who sent her to an outreach program developed by a family service agency. Anna began to attend weekly meetings of a mother's group. In the beginning she hardly spoke. She seemed beaten and defeated and perceived herself as a victim. Gradually, she began to open up in the group, and to take advantage of counseling and other services available. She became friendly with another mother in the group who had been depressed and unable to meet the needs of her two small children. Anna spent time with this mother, helping her with her household tasks and her children, and through this relationship, she began to feel more at ease with her own children when she visited them in their foster home.

Anna received much support from the other mothers in the group in her determination to regain custody of her children. She completed her High School Equivalency course and received her diploma. She learned how to be her own advocate, as she struggled to improve her housing situation, and utilized the Fair Hearing process to establish her rights. She developed a positive relationship with her Protective Services worker and began to take advantage of all available support systems. During this process Anna matured. When her children were finally returned after almost two years in foster care, Anna continued in the program. She became a trainee so that she could pass on her experience to other mothers, who like herself lacked the vital supports that enable adequate parenting. (Kochman & Gaines, 1978)

Anna's case is a good example of Shapiro's (1975) finding that the determination of the parents to have the child returned is one of the best predictors of the return of children in the third year of care. This vignette also illustrates many of the obstacles, both inner and outer, that such parents must overcome in their determination, as well as the kinds of support services that are needed to assist them.

Using Foster Parents as Teachers as a Method in Time-limited Foster Care

Foster parents may be called on to play an active role in the treatment plan. Besides providing the child with care that will correct environmental deficiencies and allow for optimum development, their involvement with the child's parents can often be a key to restoration to the home. When this is the plan, the attitude of the foster parents and the accessibility of the home for visiting are important considerations in placement.

Jane's twins were placed in foster care when they were two years old. They had been hospitalized with anemia, and their developmental level was evaluated by the hospital at about eighteen months. A protective services agency had been involved with Jane for several months prior to the hospitalization. A concerned neighbor had reported that the babies were kept indoors all day and were never taken outside. The worker investigating this report found the apartment, which Jane shared with her boyfriend, cramped and dirty. There were no cribs for the babies. Jane seemed concerned, but immature and ineffectual in caring for her children. She had barely turned sixteen when they were born. After living with her mother for a year, she had moved out because she felt the twins were too much of a burden on her mother, who was in poor health.

Jane's boyfriend resented the worker's visits and refused to let Jane accept any of the services the worker offered—a homemaker, day care, or referral to a mutual aid group. Jane was very dependent on him and evasive with the worker. The worker had considered initiating a neglect petition and had discussed this possibility with Jane. When the babies were hospitalized, the agency had the evidence it needed to intervene. The twins were discharged into foster care.

Because the goal was to return the children to their mother, a home was selected in which the mother would have the interest and patience to work with Jane, teaching her child care. Weekly visits were arranged at which the foster mother allowed Jane to bathe and dress the twins and encouraged her to play with them. Both Jane's mother and the worker had accompanied her on the first visit. When the worker observed that Jane's mother tended to direct her daughter's actions, she arranged for Jane to visit thereafter on her own.

Jane's mother offered to find a larger apartment and to make a home for the twins, but Jane began to take action on her own. She found a three-room apartment for herself and applied for public assistance, sacrificing her own needs in order to pay the rent so that she could be ready to take her children back. Her boyfriend moved back with his own family. Jane became involved with a mutual aid group. She enjoyed the weekly meetings with other mothers and found there some of the emotional support she needed. She attended court ordered therapy at a mental health clinic and worked at a public works job, which was a requirement for financial assistance. With the help of various community resources, Jane began to acquire cribs and toys in anticipation of her children's return. She explored the possibility of registering them in a Headstart program.

After ten months, the worker observed that the interaction between the twins and their mother was positive. They went readily to her and seemed to enjoy her visits. A conference of all the agencies involved was called to assess Jane's progress and consider her request to have the children returned. Jane was there with her attorney. It was agreed that the children could begin weekend visits with Jane in preparation for their return. Jane picked up the children and returned them on time and in good condition. She made the necessary arrangements for an extra food allowance for the children's weekend visits.

A month later, another conference set down conditions under which the agency would agree to recommend to the court that the children be returned. The home was to be kept clean, the children were not to be left alone, and they were to receive routine medical care. Because Jane had some difficulty in travelling to the clinic, the therapist agreed to visit two or three times a week initially. The mutual aid group offered weekly sessions, with child-care provided. Jane's mother was doubtful about her daughter's readiness to resume care, but she agreed to offer support.

Jane, who had been overprotected in childhood because of health problems, demonstrated a growing independence during the year her children spent in care. With the active encouragement of the foster mother and the support of a mothers' group, she developed some of the parenting skills she lacked and took steps toward maturity. Supportive services were still needed for a period.

Foster Parents as Members of a Treatment Team

As the use of homemakers and other supportive services to keep children in their own homes has increased, the majority of children coming into foster care are those from families with the most severe problems. Many of these children have suffered from various forms of abuse or neglect. In addition to the usual reactions of separation anxiety and identity problems, disturbed emotional reactions or behaviors are common; these patterns generally are difficult for foster parents to understand or handle without special training. Some agencies have experimented rather successfully with intensive training of selected foster parents and the provision of support services that will enable a specialized foster home to be used as a treatment site for a disturbed child. Foster parents may function as members of a multidisciplinary team serving these children (Harling & Haines, 1980).

A program of intensive treatment homes, developed by the Sacramento, California, County Welfare Department, indicates what can be accomplished through such methods.

> Henry, who was 5, had violent nightmares. Sometimes he was out of touch with reality—for example, he talked about his arms and legs being cut off by a man chasing him with a knife. Swearing, hitting and kicking were his methods of relating to others. Four previous foster home placements had been disrupted by his behavior. His sister, who suffered visual and auditory hallucinations, was confined to a residential treatment center. . . .
>
> When Henry was evaluated after being in an Intensive Treatment Home for six months, his I.Q. had increased 10 points. His language and concentra-

tion had improved markedly and he was better able to control impulsive behavior. His nightmares have ceased. Weekly therapy sessions and a volunteer who worked with Henry have helped considerably.

Prior to Henry's entry into the program, his mother decided to relinquish custody of him. During termination of parental rights proceedings, Henry's father—with whom he had had no contact for several years—was located. After meeting with the therapist, teacher, social worker and foster parents, the father agreed to cooperate in a reunification program. Three weeks later, Henry was reunited with his father, who has continued to follow through with school therapy programs. Now a year later, Henry and his new family are doing well. (Harling & Haines, 1980, pp. 17–18)

Other programs have provided special training to foster parents to enable them to work with retarded children or those with serious developmental delays (Drydyk, Mendeville, & Bender, 1980; Stone, 1980).

Residential Placement

Selection of an appropriate setting for an adolescent is often difficult. A foster home may be tried first, but adolescents may adjust more successfully in a group home, whose structure can incorporate peer influences, which are important to the adolescent's maturational tasks.

Sandra's mother filed a Persons in Need of Supervision (PINS) petition in family court when Sandra was fourteen. Sandra had rebelled against any restrictions placed on her and had rejected all her stepfather's efforts to win her over. She compared him unfavorably to her real father, who existed primarily in Sandra's fantasy since he had not visited in several years. She also had fond memories of the foster home in which she had spent three years of her childhood and wished to return there.

Sandra's earlier stay in foster care had been occasioned by a family crisis: her mother had deserted the family abruptly, in fear of her life, after a violent altercation with her husband. Sandra's father placed his three young daughters in foster care. Sandra was seven at the time. As the oldest, she had borne the brunt of her parents' often stormy marriage. She was placed in one foster home; her two younger sisters, in another.

Three years later, Sandra's mother reclaimed her children; she had gotten a divorce and remarried in the interim. The two younger girls responded favorably to their stepfather and adjusted well, but Sandra felt and acted like an outsider. As she entered adolescence, the strains in the family became unbearable. Frustrated by the failure of all her efforts to improve the situation, Sandra's mother finally resorted to court action.

The judge placed Sandra in the custody of a public child welfare agency for foster home placement. Sandra was disappointed that it was not possible to return to the foster home she remembered, which was in another county. Shortly after her placement in an emergency foster home, she was brought to court on a charge of shoplifting. The court placed her in a detention home until this case was settled. Then the agency found a new home for her.

Sandra continued to have difficulties in adjusting. Behavior problems and conflicts with the foster family's own children led to her removal from this home. She was unhappy in the next home because it had too much structure and asked to be removed. Finally a home was found in which Sandra made a somewhat better adjustment. Nevertheless, during the four months she remained there some problems developed with school, smoking, and late hours. Once she stayed out all night and was brought home by the police.

Rather reluctantly, Sandra agreed to try therapy at a local mental health clinic. Her mother, who visited regularly, had entered therapy herself. Having gained some insight into her daughter's feelings and having had some respite from the problems for a while, she began to consider taking her daughter home. Both she and Sandra had become aware that foster care was not providing a solution. The same problems existed, more or less, no matter where Sandra was living. After two weekend visits at home, Sandra did not wish to return to foster care, and her placement was terminated.

Both Sandra and her mother continued in therapy. For a while the situation improved, but there were ups and downs. Sandra's therapist was changed upon the closing of the clinic, and her acting out began again. After several runaway episodes, arrangements were made for her to enter a group home for girls. A foster home could no longer meet her needs, and she could not tolerate the closeness of her own family.

In some cases the choice between a foster home and a group care facility depends on available resources rather than on the needs of a particular child. Group care may be selected because an appropriate foster home is not available, or a foster home may be tried because there is no opening in an appropriate group care program. A group care program is the appropriate choice when a combination of professional services are needed that cannot be obtained in the community. The reluctance of either the parents or the child to accept a foster family arrangement is another factor that must be considered. The appropriate use of a residential placement is illustrated in the following case.

Fourteen-year-old Kevin Harris and his mother were referred to a public child welfare agency by a child guidance center at which they had been involved in therapy for two years. The center had asked that a residential placement be found for Kevin on the ground that his mother was not capable of providing adequate structure and emotional support for Kevin at home. He continued to do poorly in school and to get into trouble in the community, and the therapist saw little improvement possible unless Kevin could be placed in an environment that would provide him with consistent structure and an individualized school program.

Mrs. Harris had been referred to the child guidance center by the school for a diagnosis of Kevin's learning problems. He had been rebellious at school from an early age, but his mother's frequent moves had prevented his getting help earlier. His parents had divorced before Kevin's birth. Neither of them had come from a stable background and they had not been able to provide one for him. His mother, the oldest of four children, had married at nineteen to get out of the house. Kevin's father, one of eight children, was a gambler who had never worked steadily. Although Mr. Harris visited frequently, he was undependable in providing financial support, and Mrs. Harris had to rely on public assistance.

Both Kevin and his older sister, Marion, had difficulty with peer relationships. Marion, who had been diagnosed as having minimal brain dysfunction, was frequently a scapegoat among her peers, and Kevin found himself in the position of having to defend her. Mrs. Harris tended to overprotect both children but was too involved in her own needs to be able to meet theirs or to guide them toward maturity.

The agency arranged a preplacement visit for Kevin to an appropriate residential school that was willing to accept him. Kevin responded positively to this visit, and his mother accepted the placement. The school encouraged Mrs. Harris to visit regularly and to become involved in a program for parents. Unfortunately, the distance at which the school was located made it difficult for Mrs. Harris to follow through on this plan. Kevin did go home for holiday visits, but he reported to his worker that he was bored at home.

After some initial difficulties with scapegoating at the school, Kevin adjusted well to the program. He was placed in a small cottage group, and a school program was planned to meet his needs. He was involved both in individual therapy and in group interaction sessions. In the individual therapy he was able to develop a trusting relationship with his therapist in which he became freer to express his true feelings. The group interaction sessions gave him experience in relating successfully to peers.

When the agency caseworker visited Kevin at the residential school to see how he was doing and to attend a multidisciplinary conference at which his progress would be assessed, Kevin told her that he would like to stay until he graduated from high school. His school work had improved, he had begun to make friends and to gain satisfaction from the recreational activities, and he was looking forward to attending the high school in the community during his senior year.

The agency caseworker discussed future plans for Kevin with both the school staff and Kevin's mother. Since it was doubtful that the gains he had made at the school could be preserved if he returned to his home environment, a group home placement was considered as a transitional plan. At the eighteen-month court review of Kevin's placement, both his parents appeared. This gave Kevin a chance to renew his relationship with his father, whom he had not seen for some time. His father visited him at the school after the hearing, and they both enjoyed the visit. The possibility of living with his father was explored briefly, but his father had remarried and his young wife was not willing to accept responsibility for a teenage boy.

Eventually, the agency worker was successful in finding an appropriate foster home for Kevin, near enough to his home community for him to keep in touch with his mother but away from direct contact with his previous peer group. It took considerable discussion with Mrs. Harris before she was willing to accept this plan for Kevin. Her feelings of inadequacy as a mother were expressed indirectly as fears that Kevin would again get into trouble in the community. She was reassured that the agency would continue to supervise the placement and that her acceptance would make Kevin's adjustment easier.

Careful planning was necessary to help Kevin make the transition from residential school to foster home. The first preplacement visit was only for a day. Then an overnight visit was planned, with the option of extending the stay to a second night if Kevin wished. Kevin enjoyed the weekend and took the option of extending his visit. Before the actual placement was made, a meeting was held among Kevin, his mother, and the foster parents at which the expectations for Kevin in the foster home were clearly laid out; Mrs. Harris let Kevin know that she could not take him home and that she approved of the plan.

There were some initial difficulties in adjustment that the agency worker helped Kevin to work out. He had to deal with his feelings of resentment toward the natural son in the home, who was a few years younger than he. Once this hurdle was overcome, the placement was successful.

Eventually, Kevin's older sister, Marion, was referred for placement, too. While a special educational program had been arranged for Marion in her community school, she continued to have difficulty with peer relationships. Her mother's over-protective attitude, which was hampering Marion's growth toward maturity, did not appear amenable to modification. The agency was successful in arranging a placement for her in a girls' school, which provided her with services similar to those Kevin had received. In addition to receiving individual and group counseling and participating in a special school program, Marion, who was than sixteen, was able to hold a part-time job as a nurse's aide in a nearby community hospital. She, too, had initial difficulties with scapegoating in her peer group, but as these were overcome, she made considerable progress in developing social skills. She gained confidence through her employment experience, and after a few months at the school, she began to date, showing good judgment in her choice of boyfriends.

The agency worker encouraged Mrs. Harris to keep in touch with both Marion and Kevin, although the distance to Marion's school made visiting difficult. Nevertheless, Mrs. Harris had enrolled in nurse's training for herself, and the worker was able to utilize this common interest to strengthen the bond between mother and daughter.

Residential placement helped both Kevin and Marion compensate for the deficiencies of their family life through a combination of educational, social, and psychological services within a flexibly structured environment. Multidisciplinary teams in both schools met periodically to evaluate the children's progress and to adjust the program for each young person to meet his or her changing needs. The role of the worker in the agency that had arranged the placement was to assist in maintaining contact between the parents and their children in placement, to keep abreast of the progress of both children, and to assist in developing plans for the living arrangements and services that would be needed when they were ready to leave school.

The treatment plan for a child in residential placement frequently involves services to the parent or the family as an integral part of the plan. Sometimes, as in the case of Mrs. Harris, the inaccessibility of the school limits the parents' participation. This is an important consideration when the plan involves returning the child to the home. Even though it was unlikely that Kevin and Marion would again live at home, their relationship to their mother was an important factor in the success of the treatment plan. Mrs. Harris had to be helped to see placement not as evidence of her failure as a parent but as an opportunity through which she could contribute to a fuller development of her children's potential and her own, as well.

Residential placement can also be helpful when a child's ability to form trusting relationships with adults has been so damaged that a relationship to a foster family is not possible. The more neutral environment of a residential school, with enough structure to provide security and a variety of services readily available, may be effective in repairing the damage and enabling trust to be reestablished.

Lennie had been placed at birth with a foster family. His mother completed the surrender papers by mail when Lennie was a month old. Although the foster parents had indicated interest in adopting and the agency encouraged them to do so, they kept postponing the decision for one reason or another. The agency explored other adoptive homes for Lennie. Each time a potential adoption failed to materialize, the Rays expressed relief that Lennie could remain with them. Nevertheless, they still procrastinated.

When Lennie was eight, his foster parents divorced. Each received custody of one of their own children; they requested that the agency find another home for Lennie. He was placed in another home in which there were other foster children. Lennie had done well in school until his foster parents' divorce. His school work had begun to suffer during the period of stress that preceded their breakup. In the new home, he made a good adjustment initially. He showed talent for music and began to play the guitar. Then he suffered another blow. The foster family decided to adopt one of the boys in their home, but not Lennie. He began to fail in school. The agency found another adoptive placement for him. Although Lennie was eager for adoption, he found it necessary to test the concern of these parents for him. After several episodes of stealing and running away, the family asked for his removal.

Realizing that another foster placement would only contribute to Lennie's sense of failure and need to test, the agency arranged for placement in the more neutral setting of a residential school that had a cottage program simulating family life. After a year there, Lennie was able to establish a trusting relationship with his counselor. He was doing well in school and seemed ready to return to the community.

He had kept in contact with his original foster parents, who remained his psychological parents. Even though they felt unable to make a home for him, they visited him at the school and brought him gifts. Lennie, who was now thirteen, was cautious about another foster home. Two placements were arranged for him, but in both he precipitated incidents that led to his rejection. A group home was finally selected as a more acceptable alternative.

Lennie's initial adjustment at the group home was good. He was doing well in school and liked his counselor. However, when this counselor left a few months later, Lennie could not cope with the loss and disliked the new counselor. A third counselor tried hard to reach Lennie but without success. He began to fail in school and to test limits in the home. A psychiatric evaluation recommended a therapeutic milieu, since it was too difficult for Lennie at this point to form a therapeutic relationship with an individual.

Another residential placement was found for Lennie in a setting that provided him with a peer oriented structure for developing social skills. The program included opportunities for educational achievement, work experience, recreational activities, and the development of skills in communication and social competence. Although Lennie complained about the structure when the agency worker visited him at the school, he had become involved in the program and was doing better in school. Since adoption appeared to be unlikely in view of Lennie's age and his continuing ties to his original foster parents, the agency's planning focused on preparing him for eventual self-support and assisting him in maintaining whatever meaningful family ties remained to him.

Residential placement was appropriate for Kevin and Marion because it provided the needed structure and services and because both parents and children found it easier to accept this solution than a foster home placement. For Lennie, the residential placement provided a more neutral setting in which he could begin to repair his damaged relationships with others. In both instances, the preservation of ties to the family was important, even though the young people would not be returning home.

Family Centered Group Care: A New Strategy

One of the problems a residential program must face is the need to reintegrate a child into the family and community after a period of residential treatment. A child who goes back to an unchanged family situation risks losing much of the progress that has been made in the residential setting. Unless an environment that will support the gains can be arranged, regression in behavior may occur.

Some residential programs are attempting to meet this problem by developing innovative family centered programs. The Parsons Child and Family Center in Albany, New York, works with a family prior to placement, providing services designed to bring about the needed changes in the family system without removing the child. If this approach is not effective, the same worker continues to work with the family during the child's placement and after the child returns home. This continuity of service, when it is possible, is a great advantage for families who have difficulty developing trust in an agency. Flexible use of residential placement may involve weekend visits of family members to the institution, as well as the usual visits home by the child.

> The primary goal of placement is to help the child and family live and cope together. The child's adaptation to the institution is secondary. The residential milieu can provide safety, predictability and behavioral expectations for the child. Through involvement in the residential center at least twice a week, over time, the parents can learn from and with the child care workers how to communicate more productively. Parents learn how to be in charge of their youngster and how to evaluate intervention options. (Finkelstein, 1980, p. 35)

A program in Philadelphia employs paraprofessional home management specialists to work as a team with the social worker, providing services to prevent placement or to prepare parents for the return of their children (Spinelli & Barton, 1980). These teams work in conjunction with both a day treatment program and a residential treatment program.

Another innovative model provides a residential program for mothers and their young children together. Mothers who have abused or neglected their young children may enter this program, sponsored by the New York Foundling Hospital, for several months. They receive therapy, learn child-care and parenting skills through a close relationship with a lay worker who "mothers" the mother, and participate in planning for the support services needed when they leave. If necessary, the program helps the women find housing, as this is a serious problem for many of the mothers. Other aftercare services are provided. This program has proved most effective with depressed, dependent, and inadequate mothers; less effective, with those diagnosed sociopathic or schizophrenic (Fontana and Robison, 1976).

Many residential programs are continuing to experiment with ways of utilizing their facilities to strengthen families. Some are developing a range of levels of care, from foster homes to treatment centers, which can provide a continuum of services to meet individual needs.

Summary

If it is not possible to provide a child with adequate care at home, through either supportive services for the parents or some form of supplemental or substitute care, such as homemaker services, then out-of-home care may be necessary. A foster home is usually the first choice if the child is able to relate to another family and to make use of community resources. Foster homes are generally studied and certified by a social agency, which supervises the children placed in them. Different types of foster homes exist. Some accommodate children for emergency placements. Others take from one to six children for short-term or temporary placements or for longer term care. Emphasis has been placed recently on establishing clear goals for foster care at its inception and developing a permanent plan for the child as soon as possible. The first aim is to return the child to the family once changes have occurred in the family system that will enable the child's needs to be met at home. If the family cannot be restored, a permanent family is sought for the child, preferably through adoption. When that cannot be arranged, the alternative may be some form of guardianship that will provide the child with stability.

Various forms of contracting with the parents of children placed in substitute care are being widely used today to involve parents in planning for their children and to monitor the progress of these plans. Most states also have laws requiring court review of foster care placements to insure that foster care is being used appropriately.

Foster care may be voluntary or involuntary. If parents request the assistance of a social agency in providing care for their children, they may choose to place their children temporarily in the agency's custody. The parents retain legal custody, but the agency takes physical custody and becomes responsible for meeting the needs of the child. When children are found to be in need of protection but the parents will not agree to place them in the custody of a social agency, the agency may petition the court for such custody. If the court approves, the placement will be reviewed periodically; return of the children to their parents also will depend on court approval.

Group methods have been used effectively with the parents of children in foster care to improve communication among parents, agencies, and foster parents and to improve parenting skills through parent education. Mutual aid groups can often provide needed support for inadequate parents.

In addition to caring for children, foster parents may sometimes be involved in a teaching role with immature or inadequate parents. Many agencies are placing emphasis on special training for foster parents to enable them to cope more effectively with disturbed children, who represent a larger proportion of the children in care today than in the past. In some programs foster parents have provided care and individual training for developmentally disabled children. In others they have served as members of a multidisciplinary team and provided intensive treatment homes for disturbed children.

Various types of congregate care may be used with children for whom placement with a foster family is not suitable. Some forms of group care approximate family life. Adolescents who would have difficulty accepting a foster family but who can adjust to a group and use community resources may be placed appropriately in a group home or residence. Group residences generally offer more professional services and have less familylike staffing patterns than do group homes.

For children whose behavior cannot be tolerated by a family or community or who are too disturbed to make use of community resources, residential programs can provide intensive professional services in a therapeutic milieu. In a structured environment, with a variety of services readily available, disturbed or acting-out children can be provided with both a stable routine that gives them the security of knowing what to expect and a program adapted to their individual needs. Multidisciplinary conferences assess progress so that treatment plans can be modified as needed. When a child is ready to leave such a program and return to the family or community, planning to assist in this transition is required. Some residential programs have developed innovative methods to involve the families of children in their care in the treatment program. These efforts frequently involve the sharing of child-care methods and responsibility between the child-care staff and the parents. Such programs have been found effective in facilitating progress in treatment and a more lasting adjustment when the child leaves.

Whenever a child is removed from a family, the effects on both the child and the family must be weighed. If the feelings that the separation engenders in both child and parents are not dealt with, the child's growth and development can be impaired. Recognition of these feelings can help a worker plan appropriately to enable a child to retain psychological ties to a parent or to develop substitute ties when necessary.

CHAPTER 6

Is Replacement Needed?

WHEN FAMILIES CANNOT be repaired, the parents may have to be replaced. Permanent substitute families may be needed when the parents are dead, when children have been abandoned, or when parents cannot fulfill their roles effectively. Adoption is usually preferred when parents must be replaced permanently. Not all adoptions involve child welfare services. When parents have made adequate guardianship arrangements for their children's care, there is usually no need for society to intervene. Orphaned children are frequently adopted by relatives without the services of an agency. Many relative adoptions involve stepparents, grandparents, or aunts and uncles. A child welfare agency might become involved in arranging for a relative adoption for children already in its custody. When children have been abandoned by their parents, or when it appears that parental rights will have to be terminated because the parents are afflicted by chronic mental illness, alcoholism, or some other condition with a poor prognosis, the resources available among relatives are usually explored first. If a relative is willing to adopt, this course may be more acceptable to both parents and child. Relative adoption also has the advantage, especially with an older child, of maintaining ties with the extended family.

Nonrelative Adoptions: Historical Perspective

Although adoptions have been recorded throughout history, nonrelative adoptions have had wide legal sanction in this country only in this century. In the past, even after the establishment of orphan asylums, indenture and binding out continued to be accepted methods of providing substitute care for children old enough to work. Laws were sometimes passed approving adoptions in individual cases. In 1851 Massachusetts passed one of the first general adoption laws, which became a model for other state statutes. The Massachusetts statute required written consent from the biological parents, a joint petition by the adoptive parents, court approval, and legal severance of the relationship with the biological parents. By 1929 all states had some kind of adoption legislation. Some of these laws required the judge to conduct an investigation of the adoptive parents to insure that a child would not be exploited by unscrupulous people. Many later laws incorporated a requirement that a social agency conduct a detailed investigation of the adoptive parents and make a written recommendation to the judge as to whether the adoption should be approved (Kadushin, 1980). This is the method most commonly used today.

In the early 1900s impetus was given to adoption by the establishment of a number of agencies that specialized in finding adoptive families for children. Many of these agencies provided services to unwed mothers who were considering giving up their babies for adoption. Shelter care was often provided for those who could not remain at home during their pregnancies. Women who decided to keep their children were assisted in making plans to care for them. Those who chose to surrender their babies for adoption were assisted, if they wished, in planning for their own lives afterward. Adoptive families were selected for the babies, and placements were supervised until they had been legally approved.

Kadushin (1980) reported that today most adoptions by nonrelatives involve children born out of wedlock: in 1971 these accounted for 87 percent of the total. Children abandoned or neglected by their parents formed the next largest group available for adoption, and true orphans comprised a rather small percentage of the total. Reports from the National Center for Social Statistics showed an increase in adoptions from 57,000 in 1957 to 175,000 in 1970. About half of the 1970 adoptions were by nonrelatives. Since then there has been a slow steady decline in nonrelative adoptions (Kadushin, 1980).

Changing social attitudes, which now allow pregnant women more options, have had a significant effect on adoption services. The number of infants available for adoption has been sharply reduced as more women choose to keep their babies or to take advantage of the greater accessibility of abortion or birth control methods. By 1975 most adoption agencies had stopped taking applications for white, unhandicapped infants and informed applicants that there was likely to be a wait of three to five years for such a child. Many shelters for pregnant women closed because they no longer had a client population to serve. Some that remained open shifted their emphasis to assisting young mothers in developing parenting skills.

In an era in which infants were readily available for adoption, many older, minority, and handicapped youngsters were considered unadoptable and remained in foster care until they reached maturity. As a shortage of infants developed, prospective adoptive parents became increasingly willing to consider older or handicapped children.

Standards for the selection of adoptive parents were recommended by the CWLA in 1973. Through setting certain requirements as to age, health, financial stability, marital status, and emotional health, agencies attempted to insure that a child would not suffer another loss through breakdown of the adoptive home. These requirements were sometimes used also to limit the number of applicants when there were more parents desiring children than there were children to be adopted. For example, couples might be required to prove infertility in order to qualify.

In an effort to find permanent homes for all the children who remained in long-term foster care, some of the requirements were relaxed for those interested in children who were less in demand. Middle-aged parents who might not be considered suitable for an infant were quite acceptable for an older child. Financial subsidies were arranged to help a family meet the medical needs of a handicapped child. Parents who already had children were able to adopt more, and even single-parent adoptions were considered. Matching of religion and ethnic origin received less emphasis. The main criteria were the stability of the home and the family's ability to meet the needs of a particular child.

The failure of the traditional adoption process to place many minority children who were legally free but remained in foster care led to special efforts to find homes for these children. For a time transracial adoptions were advocated as one solution to this problem, but controversy over the possible effects of such adoptions on the identity of the children spurred efforts to develop new approaches to recruiting adoptive parents among ethnic minorities. Demonstration programs utilizing social workers and other adoptive parents from the same ethnic groups as the children were successful in finding families for many minority children. Homes were recruited for particular children and supportive services were provided.

Today the view is that no child is unadoptable. Many adoption agencies now specialize in finding homes for children formerly considered hard to place.

Changes in Adoption Practices

The concepts of the *child's sense of time* and *psychological parents*, as presented by Goldstein, Freud, and Solnit (1973), have contributed to a number of changes in adoption practices. These concepts stress the differing consequences of disruptions in continuity at different ages.

In infancy, from birth to approximately 18 months, any change in routine leads to food refusals, digestive upsets, sleeping difficulties, and crying. Such moves from the familiar to the unfamiliar cause discomfort, distress, and delays in the infant's orientation and adaptation within his surroundings.

Change of the caretaking person for infants and toddlers further affects the course of their emotional development. . . . When infants and young children find themselves abandoned by the parent, they not only suffer separation distress and anxiety but also setbacks in the quality of their next attachments, which will be less trustful.

For young children under the age of 5 years, every disruption of continuity also affects those achievements which are rooted and develop in the intimate interchange with a stable parent figure, who is in the process of becoming the psychological parent. The more recently the achievement has been acquired, the easier it is for the child to lose it.

For school-age children, the breaks in their relationships with their psychological parents affect above all those achievements which are based on identification with the parents' demands, prohibitions, and social ideals. Such identifications develop only where attachments are stable and tend to be abandoned by the child if he feels abandoned by the adults in question. . . .

Resentment toward the adults who have disappointed them in the past makes them adopt the attitude of not caring for anybody. . . . multiple placement at these ages puts many children beyond the reach of educational influences and becomes the direct cause of behavior which the schools experience as disrupting and the courts label dissocial, delinquent, or even criminal. (Pp. 32–34)

Even for the adolescent who is revolting against parental authority in order to establish

his own independent adult identity . . . for a successful outcome it is important that the breaks and disruptions of attachments should come exclusively from his side and not be imposed on him by any form of abandonment or rejection on the psychological parents' part. . . .

The significance of parental absences depends . . . upon their duration, frequency, and the developmental period during which they occur. The younger the child, the shorter is the interval before a leavetaking will be experienced as a permanent loss accompanied by feelings of helplessness and profound deprivation. (Goldstein, Freud, & Solnit, 1973, pp. 34, 42)

This time is a few days for an infant or toddler, possibly two months for an older child under five, and six months for a younger school-aged child. Within this period, the child can be expected to replace parents with whom there is no significant contact with psychological parents who provide care.

In traditional adoption practice, a baby is usually placed in foster care until the surrender is completed. This placement is used primarily to protect the interests of the parents, both biological and adoptive. Even if a pregnant woman is determined to give up her child, the legal surrender is not made until after the birth to allow the mother to change her mind if her feelings change when confronted with the baby. The adoptive parents are thus saved from disappointment if the mother changes her mind. It is not unusual, even when everything goes smoothly, for the process of surrender and adoptive placement to take as long as six weeks—long enough for firm bonding to occur between infant and foster mother. More than one foster mother has requested that an infant be removed from her care because her feeling of attachment was growing too strong.

Foster homes are used also to observe babies. Traditionally this was done

> to make sure they were developing properly and had no "defects." . . . [This effort] to guarantee that the child was adoptable [took] precedence over the possible harm to the child resulting from having to move. . . .
>
> The most important shift in adoption practice in recent years has been the slow and halting change from viewing adoption primarily as a service to childless couples to redefining adoption as dedicated to finding families for children who need them. (Hartman, 1979, pp. 14, 13)

As one result of this change, some agencies now attempt to provide more continuity by direct but conditional placement into the adoptive home. The adoptive parents must be prepared, in such a case, to accept the mother's decision if she should change her mind. When a mother is ambivalent before the birth, the adoptive parents may prefer not to take the risk.

Continuity as a Principle in Permanency Planning

Permanency planning places the emphasis in adoption squarely on the needs of the child. Concern for preserving whatever meaningful family ties remain to the child and providing for as much continuity in relationships as possible means that permanency planning begins whenever disruption of a family is threatened. In the absence of parents, adoptive planning begins immediately, and when there is question about the parents' ability to continue or to resume care, an effort is made to reach a decision within a definite period.

When parents are ambivalent about their desire or ability to fulfill their parental role, the agency has the responsibility to help both the biological parents and the foster or adoptive parents focus on the needs of the child and how they can be met. With this focus, surrogate parents can be sought who are willing to make a commitment to care for a child either temporarily or permanently, depending on the child's needs, even when this involves arrangements for the mother to visit while a final decision is being reached. Sometimes such visiting is more easily carried out at the agency.

An Example of Planning for Continuity

Denise Evans, the young mother described in the fifth vignette that introduced Chapter 2, illustrates the problems involved in planning for continuity of relationships for a child. When the hospital social worker called the protective services agency to request placement for the infant, who had been born with withdrawal symptoms, a decision among resources had to be made. The worker had to decide whether a temporary foster home or a home with adoptive prospects was needed. The choice would depend on the mother's feelings and on the prognosis for her rehabilitation. Without an emphasis on permanency planning, the worker would have tended to place the child in temporary foster care. An adoptive home might not have been considered until the child had been surrendered. If the mother proved unwilling to surrender but did not follow through with a rehabilitation program, the temporary care could have been extended for a year or more while the agency went through the process of petitioning the court for termination of parental rights. During this period a strong attachment could have formed between the foster parents and the child they had nurtured from birth. Breaking this bond could be traumatic for both.

Permanency planning attempts to provide as much continuity as possible for the child. If the assessment of the mother raises strong doubt as to her motivation to carry through on a plan that will enable her to assume the care of her child, then a home may be sought in which the parents are willing to give foster care to the child, with the understanding that they will have the opportunity to adopt if the child becomes legally free. Planning with the mother involves a clear delineation of the steps she will need to take to reach her goal of getting the child back. These may include participation in a drug rehabilitation program, a plan for financial support of the child, and a visitation plan that will enable the mother to develop a relationship with her child. The progress that can realistically be expected within three to six months will be spelled out. The alternatives that will be considered if there is no evidence of progress will be clearly stated at the start. These might include an agreement by the mother to surrender the child if she finds herself unable to follow through on the plan or an understanding that the agency will initiate court action to free the child if the mother can neither carry through the plan nor reach a decision herself. The plan can be reviewed and modified if the mother demonstrates a serious intent to work toward return of her child but needs more time or other services. Even if the child has to be placed in temporary foster care, such a plan would insure against indefinite temporary status.

Aspects of the Adoption Process

The adoption process has two major aspects: a child must be separated from one family and joined to another. The first part of the process involves termination of the child's legal relationship to the biological family. Termination may be based on a voluntary decision by a parent, made with or without the assistance of an agency, to surrender the child for adoption, or it may come as a result of an agency decision to seek termination of parental rights through a court. In either case, the decision may be difficult. Some voluntary decisions are made under the pressure of confronting these alternatives.

A young single mother frequently is ambivalent about surrendering her child for adoption. Even if she wishes to keep the child, her plans to care for the baby may be unrealistic. It was not uncommon in the past for children to remain in temporary foster care for several years while the mother deliberated.

Laws that require court reviews of placements after eighteen months and every two years thereafter have been used to help some parents arrive at a decision. A parent who expresses a desire to care for a child but fails to carry through on a realistic plan may be told by the judge at the eighteen-month review that the child will be freed for adoption if specific arrangements for care have not been made by the next court hearing. The three examples that follow illustrate some of the variations that may occur in making the decision to surrender a child.

AN UNCOMPLICATED DECISION

Beatrice was referred to an adoption agency by a hospital social worker, to whom she had confided her decision to give up her baby for adoption. She was a competent twenty-two year old, and her life plans did not include this unwanted pregnancy. Beatrice had chosen to complete her pregnancy and to surrender the baby at birth. All she wanted from the adoption agency was the selection of a good family for her child and help in completing the legal procedures. The adoption agency had a waiting list of parents who had already met general qualifications as suitable adoptive parents. This list was screened to select those parents whose characteristics and desires appeared to be most closely related to the information given by Beatrice about herself and the baby's father. Beatrice had expressly requested that the baby's father not be contacted. If possible, an effort generally is made to involve the father in the decision to surrender, and some state laws now protect the rights of the father. In this case, though, Beatrice's decision was respected. While the surrender was being arranged and the adoptive family selected, the baby was placed in foster care. Within six weeks the arrangements had been completed and the adoptive placement made.

RESOLVING AMBIVALENCE

Janice was twenty and in her third pregnancy when she was referred by a family service agency to an adoption agency. Her first child, born four years earlier, had been reluctantly surrendered for adoption because of pressure from Janice's mother. Public assistance and a supportive program for young mothers had enabled Janice to keep her second child, born two years later. However, she was barely managing to survive on her own and realized that she was not prepared to take responsibility for another child. Janice's unresolved feelings about the first surrender made the decision about the third pregnancy a difficult one. This child remained in foster care for eighteen months while Janice worked out her feelings. She finally decided that it would be best for both children to allow this one to be adopted.

It is difficult sometimes for an adoption worker to be objective in a situation like Janice's. Knowing that couples who are likely to prove excellent parents are eagerly waiting for a child and confronted with a young mother who is struggling to survive both emotionally and economically, the caseworker may be hard put to decide where the child's best interests lie. The investment of time, money, and emotional energy needed to strengthen the mother in her role may seem high compared to that required to place the child in a good adoptive home. In truth, it is difficult to foresee the outcome of many situations and often the decisions that adoption workers must participate in would tax King Solomon.

USE OF THE COURTS TO RESOLVE AMBIVALENCE

Louise, age twenty-three, was referred to an adoption agency by a hospital social worker because she had expressed interest in adoption for her expected child. After the baby was born, however, she changed her mind. The child was placed in foster care to give Louise a chance to establish a home. She was given information about public assistance, housing, and other supportive services. At the eighteen-month review of the foster care placement, Louise had still not been able to make a home for her child, although she had visited and continued to express a desire to have the baby with her. The worker offered to set up monthly sessions with Louise to discuss her plans for the baby and review progress. The judge scheduled a hearing to review her progress over the next two months. This hearing was postponed twice at Louise's request to give her more time; at the third date, she agreed to sign a voluntary surrender rather than have her parental rights terminated by the court.

A conviction as to the value of permanency planning can be useful in helping an ambivalent parent arrive at a decision about a child's future. Three aspects of the situation that need to be discussed as early in the process as possible, preferably before the baby's birth, are the child's need for continuity of relationships, the parent's own needs and desires, and the supportive resources available to assist the parent in fulfilling a plan. Spelling out a plan, with steps that need to be accomplished to reach the goal, provides a means for measuring progress objectively and moving toward a realistic decision.

The use of this process with the families of older children who have been taken into care because of abuse or neglect was discussed in Chapter 5. Practitioners involved in a decision to free children for adoption without the consent of the parent(s) need some knowledge of legal procedures. In order to justify a decision that the child's best interests would be served through adoption, they must be able to document to the court's satisfaction the efforts that have been made to locate parents if they are missing or to assist parents in providing an adequate home for the child.

Another aspect which the assessment must take into account is the availability of an adoptive home. With an infant, this is rarely a problem, unless the child has special needs, but with older children it can be an important consideration. An agency may hesitate to move to terminate parental rights unless an adoptive home is available for a child. Subsidized adoption has been an important factor in helping to meet this need, especially in enabling many foster parents to adopt children who were placed in their care before being freed for adoption.

When a two-parent family chooses to surrender a child, the reason is often their inability to cope with the child's special needs. Many agencies will not accept such a surrender unless they have a prospective adoptive home. If the agency's assessment of the situation confirms the parents' inability to meet the child's needs, temporary custody might be provided while an adoptive home is sought. The parents will continue to have legal and financial responsibility and will be encouraged to maintain some relationship with the child if they are capable of doing so.

A decision by an agency to move to terminate parental rights also must take into consideration the availability of a permanent home for the child. This sometimes involves helping foster parents resolve their ambivalence about adopting a child who has been placed in their care.

Facilitating the Finding of Adoptive Families

Families interested in adopting older children and those with special needs are different in many ways from those who want to adopt infants without handicaps. Agencies have been forced to look beyond their traditional recruiting methods to find families for these children. The availability of supportive services has been as important as recruiting in enabling many of these children to find permanent homes. *Adoption exchanges, demonstration projects,* and *subsidized adoption* are among the factors that have contributed to success in this area.

Adoption exchanges have widened the pool of potential adoptive applicants and available children. The success of some early statewide exchanges led the Child Welfare League of America in 1967 to establish a national adoption resource exchange, which included Canadian agencies. Between 1967 and 1976 the Adoption Resource Exchange of North America (ARENA) placed a total of 1,760 children. In 1978 about a thousand children were registered with ARENA: nearly half of these were described as slow or retarded; slightly over half were school-aged black children (Kadushin, 1980).

Since that time, homes have been found for many of these older minority and handicapped youngsters through innovative methods developed by government funded demonstration projects. A project in New York State that attracted nationwide attention was Operation Placement, developed by the Nassau County Department of Social Services. The methods used built on the experience of the adoption exchanges in recruiting homes for individual children through a presentation of photographs and pertinent facts that might strike a response in a family interested in adopting a child. An audiovisual presentation of children available for adoption was taken to community audiences by professional staff who were ethnically similar to the children in need of families. The adoption process was facilitated by scheduling interviews during evening hours for the convenience of the families and streamlining the home study procedure. Members of an adoptive parents' group known as ABC (Adopt Black Children) were utilized to assist in both recruiting and supporting new adoptive parents. Foster parents were encouraged, through the use of subsidized adoption, to adopt children placed with them.

Subsidized adoption has permitted many low-income parents to adopt. Legislation providing for a financial subsidy to adoptive parents under certain circumstances has made it possible for many foster parents to adopt children who have been in their families for years. Medical expenses for handicapped children may be covered by such programs. Subsidies have been used also to permit sibling groups to be adopted into one family.

In Massachusetts, Project IMPACT, a special needs adoption net-

work, identified certain characteristics of families who had been successful in adopting children with special needs. Many of these families

- were on a low to middle income level,
- were unsophisticated, with simple lifestyles,
- had parents who themselves had been foster or adopted children,
- had mothers who were fulltime homemakers and fathers who were
  hardworking and proud to be good providers,
- had parents who were handicapped or who had had experience with
  retardation or handicaps in their families,
- had parents with religious motivation who relied on the church as a
  community support group (Adoption Resource Center, 1980, p. 9).

Adoption subsidies and support groups enabled these families to adopt
children who would not have appealed to the "typical" childless couple
looking for an infant.

Considerations in the Adoption of Children with Special Needs

The availability of adequate support services is often the key to successful adoption of children with special needs. Wider understanding of
the various types of developmental delay, greater accessibility of
therapeutic and educational programs for these children, and the possibility of financial subsidies to help with the cost of needed services
have encouraged many more parents interested in adoption to be open
to children who need special help.

The process of permanency planning for these children begins at
birth. With adequate support from medical personnel and hospital social
work departments, many parents can find the strength to cope with the
special needs of their children. The value of early intervention and the
success of support groups in building a positive relationship between
these parents and their children were discussed in Chapter 4. When
these methods are not successful, the planning process is the same as for
a normal child. A home is sought that can meet the child's needs, and an
effort is made where possible to place the child directly into a prospective adoptive home. Some of the problems that may be encountered in
this process are illustrated in the following vignettes.

Carl's mother and father were only nineteen and twenty-one, respectively, when he
was born with severe cerebral palsy. The couple lived with the mother's parents,
who were helping to support a rather shaky marriage. Carl's mother was immature
and very dependent on her husband. Carl's father had grown up in foster care.
Although he had remained with one family, his relationship with them had not been
positive. Carl's father was especially resistant to accepting the baby's handicap. The

parents rejected all efforts by the agency worker to discuss the positive aspects of cerebral palsy or to accept a referral to a support group or other helping programs.

Carl was placed in foster care directly from the hospital. A widow with a ten-year-old daughter, who enjoyed helping with the baby, was willing to care for Carl as long as necessary. However, she did not think that she could adopt Carl because of the possibility he would become a burden on her daughter at some future time. Carl participated in a developmental program and made good progress. His mother visited occasionally and showed some concern but felt she could not accept responsibility for him. The year following Carl's birth, the couple had a normal child.

At the two-year review, the agency reported to the court that the child was considered adoptable. Both parents saw Carl in court and agreed to surrender. Shortly thereafter, Carl was placed in an adoptive home.

Lisa had Downs' syndrome; her twin sister was normal. The family also had a teenage son and daughter. They were willing to keep the normal twin but felt unable to cope with Lisa's handicap. At the time of Lisa's birth, developmental programs were not as accessible as they are today. Placement in an institution was often considered for these children. There was no difficulty in finding a foster home for Lisa, but the foster parents were ambivalent about adopting. Lisa's mother continued to visit her from time to time, although the father opposed visiting. She was pleased with the care Lisa was getting and with her development and hoped that the foster family would be willing to adopt. Eventually, they did. The fact that the agency had a potential adoptive home for Lisa enabled the foster parents to resolve their conflicting feelings and to decide that they really did not want to lose her.

Considerations in the Adoption of Older Children

The main concerns in arranging for the adoption of an infant are assessment of the needs of the child and the capability of the adoptive family and resolution of the feelings of the biological parents. When older children are to be adopted, the situation is more complex. A baby can generally be counted on to develop bonds with any adult who provides consistent warm care. An older child who has been abandoned, neglected, or abused must transfer already established attachments, whether these be positive or negative or a mixture of the two. A child's ability to adopt new psychological parents will depend on working through these feelings about previous attachments.

The process of assessing a child's needs and determining how they can best be met requires the utmost skill of the child welfare worker. Each step along the way entails sensitivity to nuances of feeling, clear judgment, and knowledge of and experience with underlying dynamics. Many of the guides to permanency planning cited in Chapter 4 offer child welfare workers some help in this process.

A SUCCESSFUL ADOPTION OF AN OLDER CHILD

When Dorothy was six, her mother requested foster care placement because she felt she could no longer cope with her daughter. Dorothy had a scar on the back of one hand from having had it held under a hot water tap as punishment. Often she had been locked in her room. Sometimes she had been locked in a closet. She had lived with relatives for awhile, because her mother could not stand the sight of her, but they were not in a position to keep her.

Dorothy had been born only ten months after her brother, Donald. Her mother freely admitted that she had been upset to learn that she was pregnant again so soon. When Dorothy came home after a few extra days in the hospital because of her low birth weight, the two babies were more than she could manage. She did not receive much support from her husband, who was eking out a living for the family through marginal jobs.

In spite of her request, Dorothy's mother was ambivalent about the placement. She seemed to feel some guilt, but when she almost changed her mind, Dorothy's father encouraged her to follow through with her decision.

Dorothy adjusted well to placement at first. In the foster home, there was a girl her own age, with whom she got along well. She became upset, though, after visits from her mother. Dorothy's mother was always critical during her visits and regarded foster care as a punishment for Dorothy. She brought Donald with her and sometimes provoked fights between the two children. After her mother left, Dorothy often expressed the feeling that she had been placed because she had been bad. She wished she were a boy so that her mother would love her.

Her worker tried to help Dorothy with these feelings and to get the mother involved in therapy. Dorothy's mother expressed some interest in Parents Anonymous but did not follow through. Eventually, arrangements were made to have both mother and daughter seen separately by the same psychiatrist. He recommended at one point that the mother's visits be discontinued since they were so upsetting to Dorothy.

Dorothy stayed in the foster home for four years. During this time, the possibility of surrendering Dorothy for adoption was discussed with her parents, but her mother remained ambivalent and her father relatively uninvolved. In the meantime another foster child, a young boy, had been placed in the home with Dorothy. The foster parents became interested in adopting him, but when the agency suggested that Dorothy might also be freed for adoption they were not interested.

At the next court review of foster care, the agency recommended that Dorothy be freed for adoption. Although she was already eleven years old, they felt sure they could find an adoptive home for her. She was bright, doing well in school, and enjoyed sports. Except for a tendency to stutter during and after her mother's visits, Dorothy had no serious problems.

Within two weeks of the court approval, the agency found a family who seemed right for Dorothy. After hearing about her and seeing a picture of her, they felt they would like to have her as a part of their family. They already had two adopted children, a girl and a boy, one older and one younger than Dorothy. They shared her interest in sports and were very involved in church activities. They prepared a small album to introduce themselves to Dorothy. Since the school year was almost over, the worker waited a little while to show the album to Dorothy so that if she were interested, the interval between her introduction and the move would not be too long. After looking at the album, Dorothy decided to meet the family. The visit went well, and Dorothy joined her new family as soon as the school year ended. She adjusted well: her stuttering stopped and she no longer needed to see a psychiatrist.

The fact that the other two children in the family were adopted helped Dorothy feel accepted, not different, as she had before. Moreover, the opportunity to adopt an older child enabled this couple to have the larger family they had wanted. Finding the right adoptive family for Dorothy had to be preceded by the decision that the negative relationship with her mother could not be improved and that Dorothy would have a better chance for growth in a new family who valued her. The agency's conviction that such a home could be found was an important part of the process.

ADOPTION OF AN OLDER CHILD WITH SPECIAL NEEDS

One of the greatest challenges in adoption is finding a home for an older child who has physical or developmental handicaps in addition to the inevitable emotional problems. To illustrate the type of supportive services that are often needed, the evaluation of Operation Placement (1978), cited the case of a child who was placed successfully after two disruptions.

Christine had a number of difficulties immediately after her birth, including a low birth weight and the need for oxygen. Perhaps because of her troubled beginning, she had learning disabilities, including perceptual problems and a hearing impediment. She was placed directly into a foster home where she received good care and adjusted well. Unfortunately, although the foster mother would have liked to adopt Christine, her health and marital problems interfered. She had a sister who was interested, however, and this seemed like an ideal family for Christine. The Gordons had three children who had been born to them, an adequate joint income (Mrs. Gordon was a teacher), and they had known Christine all her life.

The reality of having Christine as a member of the family proved somewhat different than the Gordons had expected. She did not live up to their expectations, especially in her school performance. They felt that her presence was retarding the growth of their biological children. They found her stealing money from the family, and felt she needed constant supervision. They asked that she be removed.

Although her foster mother was willing to take her back, another adoptive home was found for Christine. Nine months after her first placement, she was placed in the

Jackson home, another family with three biological children. Christine remained in this home for seven months, but she did not adjust and appeared to be mourning the loss of her previous family. The Jacksons reported that Christine was polite but covertly hostile and rejecting. She was also observed stealing small items from children at school. The behavior presented by Christine is not unusual among children who have lost their families, whether they are in foster or adoptive homes. They may act out feelings of rejection, express hostility indirectly, test the commitment of their new parents, or mourn the loss of previous attachments in this way (Many examples of such behavior are cited in Jewett, 1978).

Christine was attractive, polite, had a good natured personality, and appeared of normal intelligence. Her efforts to cover up the fact that she could not hear or understand many things made her behavior seem stubborn and disobedient to adults who were not aware of its meaning.

Again a choice had to be made. The deteriorating health of Christine's foster mother made it unlikely that she would be able to care for Christine as long as necessary. The caseworker looked for another adoptive home. A family with eight children, four of whom were adopted, expressed an interest. They had recently adopted a handicapped child through Operation Placement. Arrangements were made for them to provide foster care for Christine with a view to adopting if it worked out. This placement was successful. Christine found a place in this family, and with special help from the caseworker in obtaining an appropriate school placement and the services of a reading tutor and a hearing specialist, she began to adjust better in school. (Nassau County Department of Social Services)

The openness of this couple, their tolerance of differences, and their commitment to the children they had taken into their home all contributed to their success as adoptive parents. Their biological children, who were older and had begun to move out of the home, also were supportive.

Finding Adoptive Families: Selection and Preparation

The large number of minority children in need of adoptive homes is still a challenge to the child welfare field. The search for adoptive families for children with special needs has forced agencies to modify their view of the ideal family. Supportive extended families often enable single parents to fulfill their parental roles effectively, whether as biological or as adoptive parents. Even a single male can adopt successfully in such circumstances. Single parents are often interested in older children, who require less care because of their greater degree of independence.

The selection of an unconventional home for a child depends on both the ability of the home to meet the child's needs and the supportive resources available to the family. In the following vignette, two single-parent homes were used to meet the needs of a sibling group.

Dolores was six, Larry was two, and Virginia was only six months old when they were taken into foster care on a charge of neglect. Their father, who was in jail at the time, had brought the charge against their mother. This twenty-two-year-old woman had a history of instability. She had grown up in several foster homes, had run away, and had become pregnant. She broke off her relationship with Dolores's father soon after the baby's birth and a few years later married the man who was to be the father of Larry and Virginia. The marriage was not stable. After the children had been in foster care for three years, both parents agreed to surrender them.

Larry and Virginia, who had been placed together, had become very attached to their foster mother, who wanted to adopt them. Unfortunately, her husband did not agree. A home was found for them with a single male who had already adopted three boys and who wanted a little girl. His sister lived nearby and provided a good deal of mothering for the children. Although the placement was unusual, especially for a young girl, the agency studied the family and concluded that the home was stable and could meet the children's needs. Later this adoptive family was expanded to include more than one girl.

At first the agency had considered placing Dolores with her siblings, but there was some concern over whether her needs could be met in such a large sibling group. In foster care, Dolores had been separated from her younger siblings. A nervous child, she had benefited from the individual attention she had received in the foster home. An adoptive home was found for her with another single parent, a woman who was able to give Dolores the time and attention she needed.

Finding families for children in residential placement is often difficult, as illustrated in the vignette of Lennie, in Chapter 5. An innovative approach to this problem was developed by the Parsons Child and Family Center of Albany, New York, as a part of its continuum of child welfare services.

Potential adoptive parents often work as cottage volunteers. This can initiate a "chemical" matching process in which a natural attraction between a child and a new family can be allowed to develop. By entering the child's daily world, potential adoptive parents can become engaged in the child's grief process; get to know the child in realistic, as opposed to idealistic terms; and learn management skills that work well with the child. Thus, an artificial preselection process can be avoided, and children can be protected from entering into a series of preplacement visits that might end in their rejection by potential adoptive families. (*Case Record,* 1981, p. 4)

The process of selection and preparation often go on simultaneously. It is important for the family to understand what they want from a child, as well as what they have to offer that child.

Hartman's (1979) ecomap and genogram, referred to in Chapter 4, have been used effectively in the study of prospective adoptive families to help them identify their own supportive resources and to examine their expectations about the role that the adopted child will fill in the family. When the family includes other children, it is important that they be involved in the process of assessment and preparation. *Family sculpting* is a technique that has been used successfully for this purpose. Applied to a prospective adoptive family, this technique, developed by therapists to allow all family members to express their feelings, has proved particularly effective in permitting children to show how they perceive the relationships between the child to be adopted and other family members (Hartman, 1979).

Group techniques have been useful also in screening and preparing prospective adoptive parents. Some agencies use both group sessions and individual interviews. Groups can serve a screening function: participants who are not ready for the experience may screen themselves out when they become more aware of the realities they face. Films, slide presentations, and readings have been used in groups to stimulate discussion and enrich the parents' understanding of adoptive issues (Jarrett & Copher, 1980). Such meetings can be helpful if they do not focus only on information but allow for expression of the concerns and questions of participants. Learning that their feelings are shared by others often makes prospective parents more comfortable about participating freely and openly in the process (Hartman, 1979). Experienced adoptive parents often have a role in these sessions, first in clarifying expectations and later in providing support to those who have adopted.

Certain issues that are important when a childless couple is adopting an infant, such as feelings about infertility and telling the child about the adoption, are of no concern to families adopting older children. However, they need support in understanding the meaning of the behavior of the new family member; feelings must be worked out on both sides as new bonds are established and the new child becomes integrated into the family.

Long-term Foster Care as an Alternative to Adoption

Existing ties to parents or siblings may prove an obstacle to the adoption of older children. *Open adoption*, which does not cut off previous family ties, is sometimes considered in such cases. The other alternative is to arrange stable, long-term foster care. Some older children choose not to be adopted, preferring to remain in a guardianship arrangement with a relative or a familiar foster family. In such a situation, the agency has the responsibility to see that the child is prepared for independent living and to help the child maintain any positive family ties that remain. The following two vignettes illustrate such situations.

Gloria and Jean had been placed as small children in the same foster home. Their mother had agreed to surrender them for adoption, but their father, who was separated from her, refused to sign the surrender. He visited sporadically and made plans to take the girls to live with him, but something always interfered: he became ill, his marriage broke up, he lost his job. Gloria was fourteen and Jean was twelve when the agency finally decided to bring the case to court to ask for termination of parental rights. The plan was discussed with the girls, who had remained together in the same foster home during this period. They were happy that their foster mother wanted to adopt them, but they both felt a certain loyalty to their father. They decided to remain in foster care and to keep the relationship they had with their father. Eventually, both girls went to business school and became self-supporting. They continued to visit both their father and their foster mother after they became independent.

Pamela was eighteen when her mother died of cirrhosis of the liver. For several years she had assumed the role of mother for her three younger sisters, now aged sixteen, fourteen, and twelve, while their mother's health had deteriorated through alcoholism. The girls wanted to stay together. Although the youngest, Betsy, could have been adopted, she did not want to be separated from her sisters. A plan was worked out in which the two younger girls were placed together in a foster home, while the older two, Edna and Pamela, entered a group home. Pamela's goal was to make a home for her sisters as soon as she was able.

The planning in this case was directed toward preparing the girls for self-support and enabling them to keep in close touch with each other. As with all older children, it was important that they be involved in the decisions that had to be made among the options open to them.

Supportive Resources for Adoptive Families

Both adoptive workers and adoptive families have received help from regional *adoption resource centers*, which have been established with government funding. These centers disseminate information and promote support of programs that facilitate adoption for children who need it. Through conferences, training sessions, supportive networks of adoptive parents, and a variety of other methods, the centers have stimulated interest in, and drawn together groups with a concern for, adoption.

Summary

When a child needs a permanent substitute family, adoption is usually the first choice. In order to preserve continuity of relationships for the child, the possibility of adoption by a relative is one of the first options explored. If this solution is not possible, a nonrelative adoption is considered.

In the past, adoptions by nonrelatives most often involved children born out of wedlock. Agencies that specialized in adoption often provided services to pregnant young women thinking about surrendering their babies for adoption. Adoptive parents were screened, studied, and selected by agencies, and placements were supervised until legal approval of the adoption had been obtained.

While this process still occurs, the adoption field has undergone considerable change in a changing social climate. Now that more young mothers choose to keep their infants, the focus in adoption has shifted to finding homes for older children whose parents are unable to care for them adequately and for children with special needs. Standards for selection of adoptive parents that were set up to insure that an infant in need of adoption would have a stable home have been modified to accommodate the needs of older or handicapped children.

The adoption process involves a decision to sever a child's legal relationship to biological parents in order to establish a new legal relationship with substitute parents. This decision may be voluntary or involuntary. With an infant, the decision is more likely to be voluntary, although a parent may need help in resolving ambivalence. Involuntary decisions more often involve older children whose parents have neglected or abused them. An agency that seeks court ordered termination of parental rights must be able to document its efforts to locate absent parents or to help parents fulfill their roles adequately. Some knowledge of legal procedures is necessary in this process.

Special techniques have been developed to find families for older children and those with special needs. Adoption exchanges, on a statewide or national basis, have widened the pool of prospective adoptive parents for available children. Homes are recruited for specific children through audiovisual presentations, and successful adoptive parents help recruit others. Ethnic matching of recruiters and home study workers with the children to be placed has been effective in finding homes for many minority children.

Group methods are useful in the screening, preparation, and support of families interested in adoption. Groups can serve a dual function of providing information and allowing for an exchange of questions and concerns among participants. Those not prepared for the experience often screen themselves out in this process. For those who remain, the group sometimes becomes a source of ongoing support, especially when experienced adoptive parents are included.

Parents who adopt older children or those with special needs frequently require supportive services. Single parents have adopted successfully when they have had supportive resources. Subsidized adoption has enabled many families to adopt children who became integrated into their families after years in foster care. Regional adoption resource centers provide information and support programs to adoptive families and professional staff.

For an older child entering a new family, the ability to form new attachments will depend on working through feelings about previous attachments. Practitioners working with these children need to be sensitive to the meaning of behavior through which these feelings are expressed so that both the children and their adoptive families can be supported through the process of mourning past losses and testing new relationships.

Although no child is considered unadoptable today, some children do not choose to be adopted and others await appropriate homes. For these children, long-term foster care, designed to provide continuity and stability, may be the least detrimental alternative. Older children often need to be prepared for independent living.

CHAPTER 7

Other Specialists May Be Needed

MANY DISCIPLINES contribute to the welfare of children. Child welfare workers frequently need to consult with professionals in the fields of medicine, mental health, law, and education and with court personnel and probation officers. A variety of formal and informal relationships exist among these disciplines through which the needed services are provided. These may involve referrals for services, consultation regarding the needs of a client, or participation in planning conferences or multidisciplinary teams. Laws requiring professionals in all these disciplines to report suspected cases of child abuse or neglect have increased referrals and encouraged closer working relationships between child welfare practitioners and their colleagues in related fields. This chapter reviews some of the issues and problems that are of joint concern to the specialized fields serving children and their families, the related roles of professionals in these fields, and the methods that facilitate communication and service coordination.

Health and Medicine

Health problems of a parent or child can strain a family relationship to the point of breakdown. At the same time, the solution to a health problem may depend on the solution to a social or an emotional problem. Either situation would require joint efforts of medical and social work professionals to meet the need.

Hospital social workers are a frequent source of referral, especially when a hospitalized or convalescing parent needs child-care services. Examples can be found in Chapters 4 and 5 of referrals by hospital social workers in which the parent's ability to care for a child was in question. The mother's psychiatric condition (Mrs. Wu), drug addiction (Denise Evans), or alcoholism (the mother of the boy with sickle cell anemia) are frequent reasons for such referrals.Chapter 6 focused on referrals that were related to a parent's wish to surrender a child for adoption.

Child welfare practitioners also call on health professionals for a variety of specialized services. Doctors may be needed to verify evidence of abuse or neglect. Many hospitals have child abuse teams that provide consultation in such cases. When supplemental or substitute care is needed for children because of the chronic illness of their mother, a medical diagnosis is an important part of the assessment.

Cooperation between social workers in the medical and child welfare fields is important in planning for the discharge of hospitalized mothers. Medical social workers can make a valuable contribution to the assessment of a family's needs by interpreting medical information or by apprising doctors and nurses of social problems that affect health needs so that an adequate plan can be made.

Public health nurses, another frequent source of referral, also play a vital role in instructing mothers in the care of their children. They often visit mothers whose children have special health needs to insure that medical directions are being followed correctly. In Great Britain, *health visitors* follow up every new mother as part of an effort to reduce infant mortality. In this country, public health nurses are more likely to be utilized in this role when a mother lacks other resources for learning about baby care or when she needs added supports.

Mrs. Perry, cited in Chapter 4 as an example of the use of day-care services to keep a family together, received additional support from a student nurse, who counseled her on her children's health needs. The public health nurse who visited Mrs. Caldwell to follow up on her own medical needs was sensitive to the relationship she observed between mother and children and made a referral to a social agency, which was able to provide this mother with needed support during a critical period. The joint therapy provided to the O'Connell family by a psychiatric social worker and a psychiatrically trained public health nurse is an unusual example of cooperative services.

Historically, the child welfare and health fields have been closely related. Concern for maternal and child health was one of the major forces that gave impetus to the development of the child welfare field. The Children's Bureau, created in 1912 "to investigate and report . . . upon all matters pertaining to the welfare of children and child life among all classes of our people," (Andrews, 1977, p. 76) devoted much attention initially to reducing the infant death rate. The bureau sought to promote both the registration of all births, so that accurate statistics could be compiled, and the dissemination of information on prenatal and infant care to many mothers who did not have access to good medical care (Andrews, 1977). In 1921, when the Federal Maternity and Infancy Act (known as the Sheppard-Towner Act) was passed over strong opposition, the Children's Bureau was given responsibility for administering this statute. Title V of the Social Security Act of 1935 built upon this foundation, setting up a federal-state partnership in the fields of maternal and child health and providing medical care for handicapped children through grants to the states for approved programs. This act also set up a special fund, administered by the Children's Bureau, to demonstrate effective ways of offering maternal and child health and crippled children's services. The Children's Bureau continued to administer Title V programs until 1969, when most of them were transferred to the Public Health Service (Andrews, 1977).

The high proportion of selective service rejections in World War II had focused attention on the importance of early health care (Fink, 1963). The Emergency Maternity and Infant Care program (EMIC), which provided health services to the families of World War II servicemen, had a significant impact in reducing the infant death rate to its lowest point in U.S. history (Andrews, 1977). In the 1960s legislation was passed to encourage the early identification of health problems in children. The federal program was known as Early and Periodic Screening, Diagnosis, and Treatment (EPSDT). States that took advantage of EPSDT developed their own programs. The program in New York State, known as the Child Health Assurance Program (CHAP), is administered by public social service departments and makes financial assistance available to eligible low-income families for medical examinations for children and the treatment of conditions discovered in these examinations.

In addition to the early detection and treatment of a family's health problems, early identification of families at risk can protect against breakdown. Their contact with pregnant women in prenatal clinics, with new mothers on maternity wards, and with mothers who bring their children to health clinics places medical professionals in a crucial position to observe early signs of stress, which may lead to later difficulties in parent-child relationships. Those who are sensitive to these signs may be able to encourage families to take advantage of available services before problems become serious. Some efforts have been made by social workers attached to hospitals or clinics to develop criteria for identifying families at risk that can assist doctors and nurses in recognizing those who might benefit from referrals for help at an early stage in the development of a problem.

Unless the supports of an extended family are available, certain family constellations can be assumed to be at risk, such as single parents with large families, mothers whose children are closely spaced, and teenage parents. Premature birth, serious health problems of one or more children, or other handicapping conditions are likely also to increase risk. It may be evident from a mother's behavior with her child or her own physical or emotional condition that she will have difficulty giving adequate care to a child.

One of the most effective points for early intervention to strengthen families is the birth of a child, especially the first child. This is one of the areas in which medical and child welfare professionals can cooperate most effectively. Teenage parents are a particularly vulnerable group because frequently they must take on the tasks of parenthood before they have completed the task of becoming adults. A number of programs have attempted to offer comprehensive services to this population. Based often in hospitals or clinics, such programs generally offer a variety of services to these mothers in prenatal and postpartum periods.

Studies have shown varying degrees of success for such programs. One study of two programs that offered coordinated medical, social, and educational services to pregnant teenagers concluded that the hospital based program attracted a larger proportion of the eligible population than did the school based program. Both programs "had a positive impact . . . for more than one year post-partum in the areas of the infant's health, the mother's education and child-spacing" (Klerman & Jekel, 1973, p. 129). This impact tended to decline over time. A five-year study of teenage mothers served by an adolescent family clinic in Baltimore found also that comprehensive services could help to overcome the adverse effects of an early unplanned pregnancy for many individuals (Furstenberg, 1976). While the report noted many individual differences in the study group that contradicted popular stereotypes, the children of these teenage parents were found, on the whole, to be developmentally disadvantaged when compared to controls. Although these disadvantages related more to the economic circumstances of the family than to the mother's age, these factors were interrelated. This study found that comprehensive services that related the medical and health services required by teenage parents to their need for a variety of social and education services were more effective than medical services alone in preventing additional unwanted or unplanned pregnancies.

Some of the observations made in a comparison of the teenage mothers with a control group of their classmates who did not become pregnant illustrate vividly the need for a close working relationship between the professionals providing medical and health services and those providing other social services to this population.

We anticipated that child bearing in adolescence would deprive the young mother of the necessary training, material resources, and social support that might have been forthcoming had she managed to delay the transition to motherhood.

This supposition was fairly well supported by the results of our investigation. We discovered a sharp and regular pattern of differences in the marital, childbearing, educational, and occupational careers of the adolescent mothers and their classmates. The young mothers consistently experienced greater difficulty in realizing life plans; a gaping disparity existed between the goals they articulated in the first interview and their experiences following delivery. In contrast, we found that the classmates, especially those who did not become pregnant premaritally during the five years of our study, had a far better record of achieving their immediate objectives in life. . . .

The similarity in the backgrounds of the young mothers and the classmates seemed to support the inference that the career patterns of the young mothers and their classmates diverged primarily as a result of unplanned pregnancy. . . . even at the end of the study, the two samples held basically identical values and views about the desirability of marriage, ideal family size, educational attainment, economic independence, and childrearing. Given these similarities, it seems implausible that the unplanned birth was the by-product of initial cultural or personality differences between the young mothers and their classmates. . . .

We were able to show how the early pregnancy created a distinct set of problems for the adolescent parent that forced a redirection of her intended life course. . . . we established a number of links connecting early childbearing to complications in marriage, to disruption of schooling, to economic problems, and to some extent to problems in family size regulation and childrearing as well. . . .

Despite the fact that virtually all the participants in the study were low-income black females in their midteens who were premaritally pregnant for the first time, the outcome at the five-year follow-up was enormously varied.

Some women had been able to repair the disorder created by an untimely pregnancy by hastily marrying the father of the child. When these marriages were successful the situation of the young mothers closely resembled that of the former classmates who had delayed marriage and the childbearing until their early twenties. Other young mothers developed innovative styles of coping with the problems created by early parenthood. Rather than repair their family careers, they rearranged them, putting off marriage indefinitely and resuming their education. When able to restrict further childbearing and make care arrangements, these women often managed to achieve economic independence by the time the study ended. Still other participants were not so successful in coping with the problems caused by precipitate parenthood. Their prospects of achieving a stable marriage were damaged by the early pregnancy, and they were having great difficulty supporting a family on their own. Poorly educated, unskilled, often burdened by several small children, many of these women at age 20 or 21 had become resigned to a life of economic deprivation. (Furstenberg, 1976, pp. 217–219)

Furstenberg (1976) concluded that differences in outcome could be attributed partly to initial differences within the population. Some young women were able to overcome obstacles because they were "more capable and committed." Chance events also played a part: "A second child swiftly and effectively removed the young mother from the school system or the labor market, drastically altering her chances of economic independence at least for a time" (p. 222). Finally, women who had natural helping networks or better access to the limited resources available were at an advantage.

While medical and family planning services were important, if ongoing services were not provided to help the young mothers overcome the obstacles that arose in the attainment of both career and family planning goals, the results were apt to be disappointing: "The formerly firm decision not to have a second child may weaken when she enters a new relationship, loses her job, or merely has difficulty practicing contraception" (Furstenberg, 1976, p. 224). The study stressed the importance of continuing comprehensive services as long as needed and illustrated the benefits gained through this approach.

The birth of a child with special needs is another area in which a close working relationship among doctors, nurses, medical social workers, and/or child welfare workers can make it possible for parents to provide adequate care. Support groups have frequently been very helpful to parents whose children have certain handicapping conditions, such as Down's syndrome or cerebral palsy. The opportunity to share feelings and experiences with other parents under professional guidance has enabled many parents to cope more successfully with these conditions, to accept their children, and to help them develop (Murphy, Pueschel, Schneider, 1973).

The support group described by Murphy and her colleagues (1973) was sponsored by a hospital and led by a medical social worker.

The pediatrician joined the group for the last half hour to answer questions on Down's syndrome, expected development, medical complications, and genetics. . . . The function of the social worker was to facilitate introductions, assist the group in identifying topics for discussion, and encourage participation by the more reserved members while limiting the more aggressive ones. When individuals denied negative feelings or worries which might have been appropriate, the worker verbalized these for the group, allowing others to bring such topics into the discussion. She also assisted the group in exploring fears and questions at a somewhat deeper level than they might have done spontaneously and in functioning as a resource person in terms of information about the diagnosis and clinic and community programs. [One member of the group described the support the group provided.] "I look forward to coming; it must be like psychotherapy. I don't feel so alone. It recharges me so I feel strong enough to continue. . . . If I couldn't come here, I would get depressed and then it might affect my baby's development and I would not be able to give to him in the way that I should." (P. 116)

Programs that provide a variety of diagnostic and evaluation services to parents of young children with special needs represent another joint effort between the social work and health professions. These may be associated with a hospital or located in a community agency. Some of these programs have been very effective in teaching parents how to help their own children, rather than rely on professionals to provide all the services required. The Institutes for the Achievement of Human Potential and associated clinics in Philadelphia pioneered in teaching parents how to work with their brain injured children. Their philosophy is that parents are the solution to the problem, not its cause (Doman, 1974).

Multidisciplinary teams are becoming one of the most widely accepted models for coordinating the varied services needed to deal effectively with many of the problems encountered in the field of child welfare. Teams dealing with problems of child abuse and neglect are often hospital based. Medical personnel are an important component of these teams, whether they are located in a hospital, a community agency, or a residential treatment facility.

Mental Health

The importance of mental health professionals to the child welfare field is indicated by the fact that mental illness was the main reason for placement of the children in 26 percent of the cases in the Columbia University foster care study (Jenkins & Norman, 1972). Mental health professionals often call on child welfare agencies when there is a need to hospitalize a parent and there are no resources for care of the children. Referrals come also when a parent is being discharged from a psychiatric facility and will need supplemental or supportive services to insure that children will receive adequate care. A mental health center working with a family may make a referral when homemaker services are needed or placement of children must be considered.

The services provided to Mr. and Mrs. Wu, described in Chapter 5, are a good example of cooperation between mental health and social work professionals. The referral came to the social agency from the psychiatric division of the hospital from which Mrs. Wu was being discharged. Later the case manager from the social agency enlisted the professional services of the hospital's outpatient psychiatric department to provide therapy for the parents and to evaluate their ability to assume full parenting responsibilities.

Child welfare agencies depend heavily on the mental health field for resources to support parents in performing their roles or to meet the special needs of children. Evaluations by psychiatrists, psychologists, or psychiatric social workers are often an important part of the assessment of a family's needs. Such evaluations may be requested by the court in cases in which removal of a child from the home, termination of parental rights, or the return of children from court ordered foster care is being considered. They are also a usual part of the intake process when residential placement is needed for children.

Many family courts have clinics associated with them that can provide evaluation and treatment services requested by the court. Typically, these clinics provide psychiatric evaluation, psychological testing, and psychosocial assessments. Through a conference of the professionals who have interviewed one or more family members, the observations are summarized and recommendations developed, which are submitted to the court or to the agency requesting the evaluation. As a vignette in Chapter 5 illustrated, this was the process followed when John and Mary were placed in foster care; evaluations of family members were required by the court in arriving at the decision to remove the children from the home and to terminate parental rights. Such an evaluation was utilized also in arranging for John's residential placement when that became necessary.

Since there is usually limited time available for the interviews on which these evaluations are based, the background material supplied by the child welfare agency can be significant in focusing the evaluation on the areas in which decisions are needed. In situations such as John's, that is, in which there is some question as to the seriousness of a child's disturbance, a residential diagnostic program can provide a more in-depth evaluation, which includes observation of the child's interaction with others over a period of time. A therapeutic milieu in which multi-disciplinary services are provided as the evaluation takes place may contribute, as it did for John, to the child's growth during the process.

Parents and children are frequently referred by child welfare agencies to community mental health or child guidance clinics for individual, group, or family therapy. These services may be needed to avoid placement of children or to enable children to return home. While such referrals are utilized successfully by many families, a recurrent problem has been the difficulty of engaging families in treatment, especially in cases in which protective services are involved. This problem was illustrated in Chapters 4 and 5. Mrs. Dalton was unwilling to see a psychiatrist until she had developed a relationship with a therapist in a less threatening group situation. Jane, in Chapter 5, found it difficult to travel to the clinic to keep appointments with her therapist, but she responded when the therapist was willing to come to her home.

A study in California found that mental health services had been recommended for 58 percent of the protective services cases studied but accepted by only 43 percent of the cases in which they had been recommended (Giovannoni & Bercerra, 1979). Lack of availability was not the problem since the services were available in 99 percent of the cases.

Another study, in New York State, found that although therapy had been recommended for 62 percent of the protective services clients in the sample, 78 percent of this group never initiated therapy or did not complete it (Aronson, 1980). This study, which was concerned with factors that contribute to engagement in therapy, found that 40 percent of those recommended for therapy initiated it, 38 percent initiated but did not complete therapy, and 22 percent completed therapy. While these dropout rates are not significantly different from the dropout rates found in studies of psychiatric clinics and group therapy, they reveal a problem frequently encountered in relationships between the mental health and the child welfare field: overcoming the barriers that prevent families from using available resources. One of the solutions increasingly aimed at this problem is the use of multidisciplinary teams or multiservice centers offering a range of services. This approach has been found to increase the effectiveness of any one service offered.

Two studies previously cited provide some support for this point of view. Aronson (1980) found that twice as many ancillary services were recommended in cases for which therapy was recommended and that three of these were "significantly related to the recommendation for therapy: Legal Services, Debt and Budget Management, and Employment Related Services" (p. 120). Giovannoni and Bercerra (1979) found that concrete services, such as housing, employment, increased income, and child care, were acceptable to more of the families for whom they were recommended than were most therapeutic or educational services but were often much less available.

Some multiservice programs find that families are more willing to accept mental health services when concrete needs can also be addressed. When the Family Service Association of Nassau County established its Parent and Child Training Project (PACT) with family life education groups as the vehicle for outreach, 90 percent of the participants in the parent groups requested counseling and advocacy assistance with crisis problems (Ambrosino, 1979).

Parents and children may be more receptive to mental health services when these are available in the context of advocacy, medical, educational, and recreational services. This approach reassures clients that they need not be "sick" to participate. The Miller family, described in Chapter 4, illustrates the way a multiservice center can facilitate engagement of the entire family in the treatment process. While mental health centers also provide family therapy, it is often more difficult to engage a disorganized family in a mental health setting.

Residential treatment programs for children usually provide mental health services as part of a multidisciplinary program. Assessment and a treatment plan are developed jointly by the members of the team, and then each carries out an aspect of the treatment program, meeting periodically to review progress and revise the plan as needed. Programs based on a therapeutic milieu require a particularly close working relationship between mental health and child-care staff, with consultation readily available. John, the boy placed in a diagnostic residential setting, periodically saw a psychiatrist, who monitored his medication; the primary treatment in John's case was provided by the psychiatric social worker on the team. Frequent consultation with the child-care staff was important in observing and guiding John's progress.

Education

Family problems often have an effect on a child's school performance. Equally common, a child who is having difficulty in school can become a source of stress in a family, creating problems or exacerbating those that already exist. Teachers, school workers, and other educational professionals have a key role in the early identification of family problems. Their role is of equal significance as that of the health field. While health professionals may have earlier contact, school personnel have an opportunity to observe children over a longer period of time and in interaction with each other. Symptoms such as listlessness, inattention, an increase in aggressive behavior, or a decrease in the quality of work signal to a sensitive teacher that something may be wrong at home. School social workers can become a link to the home and perform the specialized function of relating a child's learning problems to their social context. Mental health resources may be drawn on through referral to a school psychologist or a community agency. Some of the examples in Chapter 4 illustrated the types of problems that may be referred by schools to a child guidance center or an agency that provides family counseling. Leon's refusal to go to school and Richard Miller's disruptive behavior in school both responded to family therapy.

Educational neglect may be charged when parents fail to cooperate with the efforts of school personnel to insure a child's school attendance. Such a report may be cause for intervention by protective services.

A child welfare worker concerned with the needs of a particular child is sometimes in the position of becoming an advocate for the child in relation to a school system that is not aware of those needs. This role is often important in the supervision of foster children. A working relationship with teachers and administrators that enables them to understand the special needs of a foster child can make the difference between educational success and failure for that child. When Mary, the child who had been sexually abused, was placed in foster care, careful preparation of the personnel in the school she would be attending was an important part of the planning process.

Since placement of children in residential schools frequently results from their inability to function in a community school, the ability of a school system to deal with a child's special needs can have a significant impact on the necessity for intervention by a child welfare specialist. This relationship has been recognized in New York State by the establishment of committees for the handicapped in each school district. Before a child is placed because of educational needs, the situation must be evaluated by the committee. If a placement subsidy is involved, it is paid through educational funds. This system was designed to encourage school districts to provide as adequately as possible for special needs of local children.

For children who do need residential placement, such settings offer an opportunity for particularly close cooperation between educational and social work professionals, who serve together as members of the treatment team for each child. The individualized school and treatment programs developed for Kevin and Marion in their residential placements, described in Chapter 5, illustrate the gains that are possible when the professionals providing academic, social, and psychological services work together.

Courts and Corrections

Child welfare practitioners frequently are involved with the legal and judicial professions. Whenever society intrudes into the parent-child relationship, it must resort to the courts, the institution established to insure that the rights of all parties involved in such an action are protected. The rights of children, as separate from those of their parents, have been the focus of attention in recent years. Some of the difficulties faced by the courts in deciding what is in a child's best interests have been explored by Goldstein, Freud, and Solnit (1973, 1979) in their efforts to clarify the meaning of the legal phrase the "best interests of the child." The interdependence of law, mental health, and social work is revealed clearly in the guidelines and criteria for decisionmaking recommended by this team, with backgrounds in law, psychiatry, and child development. Insights from these fields have been brought together by these authors to determine when the state is justified in intervening in family life and how a child's growth and development can be protected when such intervention is necessary. An awareness of their views is important to child welfare practitioners who are faced with such decisions.

> Whether the protective shell of the family is already broken before the state intrudes, or breaks as a result of it, the goal of intervention must be to create or re-create a family for the child as quickly as possible. That conviction is expressed in our preference for *making a child's interests paramount* once his care has become a legitimate matter for the state to decide.
>
> So long as a child is a member of a functioning family his paramount interest lies in the preservation of his family. (Goldstein, Freud, & Solnit, 1979, p. 5)

The grounds proposed by these experts as justification for intervention include a parental request for the state to decide custody or to take custody; the need for protection of familial bonds that have developed between children and longtime caretakers who are not their parents; and gross failures of parental care. The latter would cover

> the death or disappearance of both parents, the only parent or the custodial parent—when coupled with their failure to make provision for their child's custody and care. . . . Conviction, or acquittal by reason of insanity, of a sexual offense against one's child. . . . Serious bodily injury inflicted by parents upon their child, an attempt to inflict such injury, or the repeated failure of parents to prevent their child from suffering such injury. (P. vi)

Intervention may rest also on the refusal by parents to authorize lifesaving medical care under certain circumstances and a child's need for legal assistance. Grounds for the appointment of a lawyer to represent the child would be based on a request by parents who are unable to obtain legal assistance for their children, an adjudication on any ground for modifying or terminating parent-child relationships, or an emergency placement pending adjudication.

When intervention is necessary, the guidelines for placement decisions proposed in *Beyond the Best Interests of the Child* (Goldstein, Freud, & Solnit, 1973) are intended to protect the child's growth and development.

> [These] should safeguard the child's need for continuity of relationships . . . should reflect the child's, not the adult's, sense of time [and] must take into account the law's incapacity to supervise interpersonal relationships and the limits of knowledge to make long-range predictions. . . .
>
> The least detrimental alternative . . . is that specific placement and procedure for placement which maximizes, in accord with the child's sense of time and on the basis of short-term predictions given the limitations of knowledge, his or her opportunity for being wanted and for maintaining on a continuous basis a relationship with at least one adult who is or will become his psychological parent. (P. 6)

These grounds for intervention and guides for placement decisions cover most of the situations that bring child welfare workers into court. Court approval must be obtained whenever children are removed from their families without the consent of the parents, as frequently happens in protective services. If the relationship between parents and children is to be terminated, whether the request is voluntary, as in a surrender for adoption, or involuntary, as when an agency petitions for termination of parental rights in cases of abuse, neglect, or abandonment, court approval is necessary. In the areas of protective services, foster care, and adoption, workers must be familiar with legal and court procedures (Jones & Biesecker, 1977; Lindner, 1978; Pike et al., 1977).

Some states require periodic court review of all foster care placements. The intent of these laws is to insure that children not remain in foster care indefinitely without plans for their permanent status. One study of the impact of the New York State laws requiring eighteen- and twenty four-month reviews of foster care placements concluded that the court reviews had "the effect of moving the agencies toward more expeditious, systematic planning for children" (Kadushin, 1980, p. 385). Court reviews have been used also to motivate ambivalent or reluctant parents to arrive at a decision regarding their willingness to assume responsibility for their children. In Chapter 6 we saw that the court review helped Louise resolve her ambivalence about surrendering her child for adoption; in Dorothy's case, court review enabled the agency to replace a destructive parental relationship with a supportive one.

It requires considerable experience and skill for a child welfare worker to utilize legal and court procedures constructively to protect the interests of children and to involve the parents in this process. A worker needs to know how to summarize the important facts of a case in a petition, what information is significant in preparing a case, how to gather and record such information, and how to behave in court. When a child has been abandoned, the process of freeing that child for adoption may involve a search for the missing parents that will satisfy the courts. Any request to terminate parental rights must be documented with evidence of the agency's efforts to work with the parents toward achieving adequate care of their children. Even the decision of whether or when to bring a case to court needs to be based on awareness of the role the courts can play.

Members of the legal profession are frequently called on to prepare caseworkers for their role as witnesses in court. Clear outlines of the important points to be observed have been included in some of the training manuals developed for permanency planning (Jones & Biesecker, 1977; Lindner, 1978; Pike et al., 1977). Lawyers usually emphasize the adversarial nature of a court proceeding. Often, social workers are advised to leave their social work role behind when they enter the courtroom and to recognize the limitations of their expertise. Rather than offer a diagnosis of alcoholism or mental illness, a social worker should describe factually the behavior or conditions that have been observed. A good rule of thumb is be well informed, stick to the facts, and answer only what is asked.

Another area of protective services that requires a close relationship between child welfare workers and the courts is court ordered supervision of children in their own homes. Such supervision may be required in cases in which there is some doubt as to the parents' willingness or ability to correct a problem situation. This may give parents an opportunity to make the changes necessary to prevent removal of the children; supervision also may give added protection to a child being returned from foster care to a somewhat questionable home situation. The responsibility for supervision is often accompanied by specific court orders concerning actions to be taken or avoided by the parents, such as attendance at therapy, participation in a mutual aid group, or acceptance of a homemaker. The court may also issue specific directions to keep living quarters clean, to take children for regular health examinations, or to insure their attendance at school. This procedure was followed in a vignette in Chapter 5: since the court's authority had been effective initially in motivating Jane to work toward the return of her twin children, the agency requested its continued backing for the plan developed with Jane for the services that would be needed when she took on full responsibility for the children.

Some judges have the option of assigning supervisory responsibility either to a probation department or to a social agency. If they exercise the latter option, the agency becomes responsible, as would the probation department, for informing the court about the family's compliance with its orders. Such responsibility brings child welfare workers into an area that overlaps with corrections. There has been some controversy over the effectiveness of this practice. In discussing cases of children killed by their parents, Goldstein, Freud, and Solnit (1979) stated: "No amount of supervision from outside can counteract what happens within the privacy of a family" (p. 186). This observation, however, pertains to parents who have inflicted or attempted to inflict severe bodily injury upon their children. According to Goldstein, Freud, and Solnit, cases of neglect should be handled voluntarily, through offering of services to the parents, but should not be grounds for state intervention. This view expresses their "preference for minimum coercive intervention by the state" (p. 29). In relation to this point, they criticized mandatory reporting laws, stating that these

> have contributed little to protecting children. . . . Mandatory reporting has swelled the number of complaints for neglect and abuse that must be investi-

gated by the state. In most states a third or more of these complaints are for alleged neglect that does not involve imminent risk of serious bodily injury. Investigations in such cases frequently constitute an unwarranted intrusion into family privacy, weakening the integrity of the families involved. . . . The overbroad and vague base for mandatory reporting and inquiry has led to overreporting, to unnecessary demands on services that are inadequate even for those children at greatest risk of serious bodily injury. Thus, those already at serious risk are put at greater risk, and damaging coercive intrusion is encouraged into families of children whose needs, if real, can best be served—and perhaps can only be served—by a range of voluntary services that would be available, accessible, and attractive to families who are or tend to be disorganized. (P. 71)

On the other side, the authors quoted a finding by Ruth S. and C. Henry Kempe (1978), according to whom the great increase in reporting in many states between 1968 and 1972 indicated "that families are being helped sooner. In Denver, the number of hospitalized abused children who die from their injuries has dropped from 20 a year (between 1960 and 1975) to less than one a year" (quoted in Goldstein, Freud, & Solnit, 1979, p. 243).

Unfortunately, the desirable "range of voluntary services" is not always available, while current legislation and procedures require child welfare practitioners to fulfill, as best they can, the role of protecting the welfare of children in or out of their own families. And this responsibility often involves legal and judicial procedures.

Probation

Probation departments, as an arm of the courts, are involved with child welfare agencies primarily in two areas. In protective services, they may be required to conduct additional investigations when a case is brought to court on a petition. The probation departments of family courts are involved also when a child or youth is brought to court for behavior that threatens the welfare of society in some way.

The differing but related responsibilities of social agencies and legal or correctional institutions in handling infractions of law by minors have been the subject of considerable controversy for a number of years. The concept of the juvenile court and family court system developed along with the child guidance movement, reflecting the view that although families are primarily responsible for the socialization of their children and control of their behavior, parents often need help with this process. The juvenile justice system was established to put the emphasis on rehabilitation rather than punishment. To achieve this purpose, more informal legal procedures were used, and the focus was on social assessment of the problems and involvement of the child and family in treatment, if needed. Before long these courts were swamped with cases "variously labeled 'Person/Child/Minor/Juvenile in Need of Supervision (PINS, CHINS, MINS, or JINS)' . . . so called status offenses" (Goldstein, Freud, & Solnit, 1979, p. 28). These authors noted that "ungovernability statues are almost invariably impermissibly vague in wording and overbroad in scope" (p. 214). Although these laws have a very early precedent in the Massachusetts Stubborn Child Law of 1654, it has been observed that in such laws "the child is subject to sanction and the parent who shares responsibility for the child's behavior is untouched by the law" (Goldstein, Freud, & Solnit, 1979, p. 214).

Considerable government funding was invested in the late seventies to develop alternatives for handling these cases outside the juvenile justice system. Programs offering community services to youths at risk, that could divert them from the courts and provide alternatives to secure detention were financed through grants from the Law Enforcement Assistance Administration (LEAA). Social agencies, rather than probation departments, were encouraged to develop such programs, reflecting the emphasis on avoiding the labeling process set in motion when a youth enters the juvenile justice system. At the same time, pressure developed to institute more formal legal procedures in these courts for two opposing reasons. One was to protect the rights of the child, as in the well-publicized *Gault* case in which a child's right to legal representation was affirmed. The other was to protect the rights of society, a reflection of the growing concern about violent crimes committed by minors and the apparent inability of the juvenile court process to cope with this phenomenon.

As a result of these pressures, the tendency has been for courts to turn more so-called ungovernability cases over to social agencies, which may have few resources for dealing with them. Laws have been passed in some states forbidding the mixing of young people with these types of charges in the same residential facilities that house youths charged with juvenile delinquency or offenses that would be crimes if committed by an adult. A twenty-five-state survey of child welfare programs by the Children's Bureau and the Child Welfare League of America noted that "services for children and youth involved with the courts are increasingly being provided by the public child welfare agency" (U.S. Department of Health, Education, and Welfare, 1976, p. ix).

The placement of young people in residential schools or institutions is another area of child welfare shared by social services and probation departments. Some residential programs accept children placed by probation departments through the courts, as well as children placed voluntarily by their parents or through social agencies. The problems of the children may not differ much whether they enter placement through a social agency or through the courts. In general, the parents feel unable to cope with their children's behavior. Whether they turn to a social agency or the courts for assistance may depend on attitudes or on questions of eligibility or accessibility.

Most probation departments have intake workers whose function is to screen cases and determine whether they are appropriate for the courts. Those that are not may be referred to social agencies in the community if the parents are eligible for, and willing to accept, such help. On the other hand, if a child in the custody of a social agency is brought to court on a charge of juvenile delinquency, responsibility may shift from the agency to the probation department. Sandra, in Chapter 5, is the kind of child who is frequently found in this position. When Sandra's mother brought her to court, the judge placed Sandra in the custody of a social agency for foster home placement. Her second appearance in court, on a shoplifting charge, could have resulted in a finding of juvenile delinquency, which would have made subsequent placement more difficult. In view of the circumstances, the delinquency charge was dropped and another home was found for Sandra. If she had continued to act out more seriously, or if matters had reached the point at which the agency could no longer find a suitable placement and her mother would not take her home, it is quite possible that Sandra would have been put on probation and placed by the court in a residential school. Child welfare practitioners often need a working relationship with their counterparts in probation departments in such cases.

Because of the complex relationships among the various agencies responsible for the placement of children, computerized information systems have been developed as a means of keeping track of all children in placement, whether they are placed through social service agencies, the courts, or educational systems. These information systems have had varying success since their effectiveness depends on the accuracy of the data fed into them. The task of training the staff of multiple agencies to utilize such a system correctly is a major effort.

Summary

Children are served most effectively when professionals in the fields of child welfare, medicine, mental health, education, the courts, and probation work together closely. Medical personnel play a significant role in preventive and supportive services and in the diagnosis and treatment of cases of child abuse or neglect. Mental health professionals are involved in all types of family counseling and therapy, including preventive or supportive services, the diagnosis and treatment of child abuse and neglect, and the treatment of children's behavior problems.

Through their ongoing contact with all children, professionals in the field of education are in a unique position to contribute to the early identification of problems. Teachers, school social workers, or guidance counselors who recognize the existence of a problem or an incipient problem through changes in a child's behavior can encourage a family to get help. Conversely, obtaining appropriate educational services for a child can be an important factor in strengthening a family and keeping it together, and child welfare workers often need to work closely with school personnel in interpreting the special needs of a child. Identification of situations requiring protective services is another important role of school personnel.

The courts and professionals in the fields of law and corrections get involved in child welfare when it becomes necessary for the state to intervene in family life to protect children. Judicial action may be initiated at the request of a parent or a social agency. It may involve removal of children from their home or supervision in the home, termination of a parent-child relationship, or court approval of a substitute parent relationship for a child.

Probation departments are frequently involved in the placement of young people in residential schools. The problems of these children and the services they receive are often similar to those of children placed by departments of social services. In general, probation departments are involved with adolescents and older children whose behavior has become a problem to their communities. Many of the children who go through the court system do so because their acting-out behavior cannot be tolerated by the usual placement facilities of the child welfare system.

One means of establishing close working relationships among the many professions active in helping children is through the medium of multidisciplinary teams that assess needs, plan treatment, and evaluate progress. Such teams are sometimes established in connection with protective services programs, hospitals, or community agencies. Most residential treatment centers for children utilize such teams, and day treatment centers and some community based multiservice programs have access to them.

Computerized information systems are another means used to coordinate services and track children placed in out-of-home care through social services, the courts, and educational systems.

It must be recognized, in spite of the potential for meeting the needs of children more effectively through the cooperative efforts of professionals from varied disciplines, that the needed linkages between systems do not always exist in reality. Inadequate resources, lack of funding, and other restrictions sometimes prevent agencies from working with the whole family when that approach would be most effective.

CHAPTER 8

What Do We Still Need to Learn?

RESEARCH IN THE FIELD of child welfare spans more than half a century. In spite of its volume, which probably exceeds that of any other specialized field of social work, as research it is still in its infancy. Those who have attempted to evaluate or summarize this research have pointed out many problems of measurement and methodology, which often make valid generalizations impossible. One of these problems is the lack of a conceptual framework and clear definitions that would make it possible to compare the findings of one study with those of another.

For the student or practitioner interested in benefiting from the knowledge gained through research, this situation is apt to be confusing. Summaries or reviews of research may be of more use to the researcher than to the practitioner, who is usually looking for practical help or for principles that can be applied in the field. Kadushin found little in the research he reviewed in 1978 "that would enable the practitioner to make the awesome decisions which need to be made with any increased degree of confidence" (1978c, p. 124).

In spite of the questions that have been raised about the validity and value of much of this research, there is no doubt that it has had a significant impact on the field, not only on policy decisions but also on practice. Reference has been made in many of the preceding chapters to research findings as they have been applied to practice. This chapter is intended to give the reader a broad view of the areas of research that are related to child welfare, to point to some of the limitations and benefits of research that has been done, to suggest areas in which further research is needed, and to acquaint students and practitioners with sources through which they may keep up to date on research findings.

Before entering into this discussion it might be well to consider some of the uses of research. Those who look to reviews of research for definitive answers to the questions that trouble them in their daily practice will inevitably emerge confused and frustrated. If such answers could be provided by research and fed into a computer, there might be some hope of utilizing computers as an aid to decisionmaking. Some investigators are currently exploring this possibility. Whatever the outcome of their efforts, it is clear that computers will always depend on human beings to feed them correct information and to apply the information they have processed to an individual situation. Likewise, research findings have value only as they are processed and applied by the practitioner. Their value is not in providing answers but in increasing our awareness of the complexities that must be taken into account in constantly changing human situations and in providing some objective standards against which our subjective reactions can be tested. The questions that remain unanswered are an antidote to the feeling of omniscience, which has been called the occupational disease of social workers.

With this caveat, it may be possible to assess more realistically what has been and can be learned from research. Much child welfare research has been undertaken to answer questions about the kind of substitute care that is best for children when their own parents cannot care for them. Foster family care, institutional care, and adoption have frequently come under the scrutiny of researchers attempting to measure their effects on children, to identify characteristics of caretakers or methods that lead to success, or to determine the relative impact of inherited and environmental influences on children removed from their biological families. The emphasis has shifted in recent years to a greater concern with the processes of entrance into and exit from foster care. This broader view takes in the treatment modalities and service delivery systems that support families at risk, the criteria and tools for making appropriate placement decisions, and the development of service delivery models that relate the foster care field more closely to that of adoption in the concept of permanency planning for children in need of substitute families. Expanded government funding has made much of this research possible.

While some studies have taken a broad view of the field, much research continues to be specialized. Protective services for children is one specialized area that has received increased attention. Studies have attempted to determine the incidence of abuse and neglect, to identify the characteristics of families in which children have been abused or neglected, to study the effects of abuse and neglect on children, and to evaluate the effectiveness of various treatment modalities on parents and children.

Specialized research in adoption continues to reflect the traditional concern with the outcome of infant adoptions, as well as the more recent concern with the adoptability of children formerly considered not adoptable. The emotional problems manifested by adopted children compared to those in the general population represent another area still being explored. Research related to the issue of adoptability has included both data analysis of decisionmaking based on record reviews and demonstration projects of new methods of recruiting and supporting adoptive families for children with special needs.

Research in child development is in an area that must not be overlooked, even though most studies have been done within the mental health field. This area has always been of concern to child welfare professionals, but the field has been criticized in the past for failing "adequately to connect itself with the research done by psychologists in child development and human development" (Kahn, 1977, p. 111). The principles of child development have been called the stock-in-trade of the child welfare practitioner, suggesting the importance of this connection.

Research in each of these specialized areas will be reviewed briefly, primarily to highlight the questions that need further exploration. Bear in mind that these are highly interrelated in practice.

Child Development

Concern about the developmental retardation observed in many infants and young children raised in institutional settings stimulated study of the effects of maternal deprivation on the very young. The separation of children from their families that occurred as a result of World War II provided a basis and impetus for much of this research. Many of these studies, from the 1930s on, were reviewed, analyzed, and synthesized by Bronfenbrenner (1979). From them he drew hypotheses as to the conditions that are necessary for normal human development. His conclusions are expressed as hypotheses so that they can provide a framework for further exploration, even though he assembled an impressive amount of evidence for some of them.

Although Bronfenbrenner's (1979) framework is expressed in research terms, it has much to offer the practitioner confronted with the need to assess a mother's ability to nurture her children or a caretaker's ability to provide an environment conducive to a child's development. Since research language is often a barrier to practitioners, who are more interested in practical applications than in theoretical formulations, a few highlights from the wealth of material presented by Bronfenbrenner will be cited to illustrate its potential value in broadening the base of understanding upon which daily decisions are made.

MOTHER-INFANT RELATIONSHIPS

Not the least of Bronfenbrenner's (1979) contributions was his elucidation of the impact and interaction of the various organizational levels of our society upon the developing individual, from the microsystem of the immediate family to the macrosystem of the nation. Seeing the importance of the dyad, or two-person system, as "a critical context for development [and] the basic building block . . . of larger interpersonal structures" (p. 56), Bronfenbrenner outlined the qualities of a dyadic relationship that contribute to development. Dyads "that meet the optimal conditions . . . of reciprocity, progressively increasing complexity, mutuality of positive feeling and gradual shift in balance of power" are referred to as "developmental dyads" (p. 60). In support of these hypotheses, Bronfenbrenner cited a "series of experiments and follow-up studies" by Klaus, Kennell, and their colleagues at the Case Western Reserve School of Medicine in the 1970s that "dramatically document[ed] the motivating power and long-range developmental effect of the dyad as a context for development" (p. 61). These experiments involved modifying the hospital practices "to permit mothers to have their naked infants with them for about an hour shortly after delivery and for several hours daily thereafter" (p. 61). Follow-up studies after a month, a year, and two years revealed patterns of more affectionate interaction between mothers and children who were allowed this extended-contact. These studies were replicated by Hales, Kennell, and Susa in 1976 with a larger sample in a different cultural context. To determine whether immediate or extended contact was more important, two early-contact groups were introduced, "one limited to forty-five minutes immediately after delivery and the second for an equal interval but beginning twelve hours after the infant's birth. The results were unequivocal" (p. 63). Mothers who had immediate contact were reported to show significantly more affectionate behavior when compared to the mothers in delayed and control groups (Bronfenbrenner, 1979).

Follow-up data reported by Ringler (1977) on the children's developmental status at age five showed that "in comparison to controls the five-year-olds of the early contact mothers had significantly higher IQ's, understood language as measured by a receptive language test significantly better and comprehended significantly more phrases with two critical elements. The IQ difference was approximately 7 points (cited in Bronfenbrenner, 1979, p. 64).

Bronfenbrenner (1979) pointed out that these studies concentrated on the behavior of one member of the dyad (the mother) and did not pay sufficient attention to the reciprocal effect of the behavior of the other member of the dyad (the infant). He suggested further studies to explore the dyad as a context for "reciprocal development" (p. 65). Nevertheless, these studies have significance not only for the area of primary prevention, in which their impact on hospital maternity procedures has already begun to be felt, but also for foster care and adoption planning.

CHILDREN RAISED IN INSTITUTIONAL SETTINGS

Another group of studies analyzed by Bronfenbrenner (1979) compared infants raised in both "impoverished" and "enriched" institutional settings with those raised by their own or foster parents. These studies questioned whether the critical factor in a child's development is the relationship with the mother or the amount and kind of stimulation provided by the environment. Bronfenbrenner concluded that both elements are important but that the first year of a child's life is a particularly sensitive period for developing attachments. These studies indicated that "the infant's attachment to and dependence on the primary caretaker typically reaches its greates intensity" in the second six months of life (p. 143). Infants separated from their mothers and placed in an impoverished institutional environment during this period could be expected to experience more "immediate disruptive impact" but to have a greater probability of recovery from developmentally retarding effects if later placed in a more favorable environment. "The more severe and enduring effects are most likely to occur among infants institutionalized during the first six months of life, before the child is capable of developing a strong emotional attachment to a parent or other caregiver" (p. 150). The conditions needed to avert or reverse such damage to development are

> a physical setting that offers opportunities for locomotion, and contains objects that the child can utilize in spontaneous activity, the availability of caretakers to interact with the child in a variety of activities, and the availability of a parent figure with whom the child can develop a close attachment. (P. 144)

In one study, young children who had had a poor relationship with their mothers experienced less severe reactions to separation than did those whose relationships had been more positive. For those with positive emotional attachments, an enriched environment did not compensate for the loss, but return of the mother reversed the developmental damage.

These findings and hypotheses suggest that foster care and adoption workers need to be particularly aware of the opportunities for emotional attachment provided to children whose caretakers must be changed during the first year of life. Before the age of six months, an infant is likely to make the transition more easily, so long as a primary caretaker is provided with whom emotional attachment can develop. When such an emotional attachment has already begun to develop with a caretaker whom the child distinguishes from others, more emphasis needs to be given to considerations of continuity. These principles of vulnerable periods have been taken into account by Goldstein, Freud, and Solnit (1973) in developing their placement guidelines and the concepts of psychological parents and a child's sense of time.

The properties that enhance the developmental potential of any setting, as specified by Bronfenbrenner (1979), can be applied as well to a family, foster home, or group care setting.

> For example, the stipulation that an environment for young children offer opportunities for caretaker-child activity, permit locomotion, and contain objects that the child can use in spontaneous activity . . . pertains as much to a day care setting or a hospital ward as to an institution caring for children on a long-term basis. (P. 163)

Many residential programs for children have modified or enriched their environments in keeping with the findings of these studies. Among the most promising developments are the efforts of some institutions to relate their programs more directly to the environment of the family. Some of these were described in Chapter 5. These are examples of what Bronfenbrenner (1979) called "transforming experiments," which "introduce experimental modifications that represent a restructuring of established institutional forms and values" (p. 41). He pointed to a need for more exploration of this direction.

It is not possible within the scope of this book to cover all the research in child development which is applicable to the child welfare field. Bronfenbrenner's synthesis has been cited because of the many useful insights it provides.

Another area of psychological research which should not be overlooked is the understanding of human behavior gained from studies of animal behavior. One particularly interesting observation was made by Ronald Nadler, a psychologist at the Yerkes Regional Primate Research Center in Atlanta, Georgia, in studies of mother–infant relationships among gorillas in captivity. Under conditions of isolation gorilla mothers tended to abuse their infants, while in a natural social setting, with a male and experienced mothers present, they learned quickly to handle their young competently. Reports on these observations have drawn comparisons to the effects of isolation on human parents who abuse their children and suggest that the problem of overcoming or preventing child abuse may be profitably approached through the development of social support systems for parents (Rock, 1978).

Foster Care

Research in foster family care and institutional care will be dealt with together under this heading since some studies encompass both areas. The need for a continuum of resources for different levels of substitute care has often been pointed out, and children frequently move from one type of care to another and sometimes back again. Some studies that attempt to distinguish the effects of different types of care include adoptive homes, as well.

It may be useful before reviewing the areas of current research to look at a few of the major research studies in their historical context. Since research in human services cannot be done under laboratory conditions, it is impossible to divorce such studies from the social and political influences with which they interact.

The earliest studies, perhaps stimulated by the desire of foster care agencies to justify their programs, focused on the effects on children. In his 1966 review of foster care research, Fanshel cited "a classic follow-up study" undertaken by Theis for the New York State Charities Aid Association, which had placed some three thousand children in foster homes in the years 1898–1922. In an effort to survey all those who had reached the age of eighteen or over and had spent at least a year in foster care, Theis succeeded in locating 650 of them and rated more than 77 percent as functioning capably.

> [A] major finding of the study was that three out of four of all the subjects who had lived in foster care were found to be able to manage their own affairs with "average common sense," to keep pace economically with their neighbors, and to earn the respect and good will of their communities. In other words these subjects had "made good". (Quoted in Fanshel, 1966a, p. 102)

It is interesting to note the standards by which these young people were rated.

> Those who supported themselves honestly and adequately, worked steadily, were law-abiding, who lived in accordance with the better standards of their community and had good social and personal ethics were rated *capable*. Those who failed to get on either because of irresponsibility or lack of general ability were . . . *incapable*. (Theis, 1924, pp. 22–23)

The 22.8 percent classified incapable included eighty-nine individuals regarded as "harmless," forty-seven described as "harmful," twenty-six considered "on trial," and twenty in institutions. Those labeled harmless were described as "irresponsible or shiftless individuals of inferior capacity or inferior character, or those who are incapacitated but who are not antisocial" (p. 43). The group considered harmful included nineteen who had been in conflict with the law and fourteen who had had illegitimate children, the rest of the forty-seven having been so classified "because of their general misbehavior and inferior traits of character" (p. 43). This study determined that

> 50 percent of the children had satisfactory relationships with their foster parents and formed ties that were described as firm and lasting . . . hardly distinguishable from the natural relationship of parent and child. The study also found that the younger the child at placement the more apt he was to make a satisfactory social adjustment and to grow up without serious personal difficulty. (Quoted in Fanshel, 1966a)

During the next three decades interest in, and controversy over, the developmental effects of different types of substitute care continued. Many of the child development studies already discussed were done during this period. They focused on infants in foundling homes and young children in institutions for the retarded. Their findings had a significant impact on the field of child welfare, leading to increased emphasis on placement in family homes and a shift in the structure of residential programs toward more enriched environments and familylike living arrangements.

A major study in the child welfare field was published in 1959 by Maas and Engler. Two research teams, each composed of a child welfare worker and a sociologist, studied nine communities across the country (rural, small urban, and metropolitan areas and big cities) "with respect to the kinds of organizational arrangements that had been developed locally for the care of dependent and neglected children" (Fanshel, 1966a, p. 89). Maas and Engler found great variation in arrangements and outcomes. Few children in the rural communities either returned to their families or were adopted. One of the small urban communities had 90 percent of its dependent and neglected children in institutional care, while another had 85 percent in foster family care. The metropolitan areas showed a similar contrast: in one 64 percent of the children were in institutions, 30 percent in foster families, and 6 percent in adoptive homes; another had 20 percent in institutions, 58 percent in foster families, and 22 percent in adoptive homes. The authors emphasized that *time* was perhaps the most important factor in the movement of children out of foster care: "Once a child is in care beyond one and one-half years, his chances of being adopted or returned to his biological family greatly decrease" (p. 351).

This widely quoted finding spurred an increased research effort, supported by government funds, to develop ways of moving children out of temporary care. From the widespread concern over children adrift in foster care, the concept of permanency planning was born. At the same time, the families of children in care began to receive attention.

Further analysis by Fanshel and Maas (1962) of the data collected by Maas and Engler (1959) showed some of the factors contributing to lack of movement out of foster care: Those children who returned home tended to be the ones who were placed because of parental illness or a parent's death or children in large families where there were affectionate relationships with siblings and where parent-child relationships were maintained. Adoptive home placements tended to be infants born out of wedlock. Children who remained in foster or institutional care were those from strife-ridden or broken homes in which the mother had serious problems or was living with a mate other than the father (Fanshel and Maas, 1962).

DEMONSTRATION PROJECTS TO REDUCE FOSTER CARE

These findings were addressed by a number of government financed research projects that undertook to demonstrate effective methods of moving children out of foster care more quickly. Some of these focused on preventing entrance into care. In California, a joint project between the Children's Home Society of Oakland and the Alameda County Foster Care Department offered intensive casework services, emphasizing the use of behavioral contracts, by the voluntary agency to an experimental group of parents, while the public agency provided its usual services to children in foster care and a control group of parents. A major finding was that the experimental group had a rate of exodus from foster care that was double that of the control group (Wiltse, 1979).

Although under half the sixty families in the experimental group had been willing to sign contracts, the response of those who did was reported to be "overwhelmingly positive" (Wiltse, 1979, p. 14), yet these were largely involuntary clients whose children had been placed by the courts. A significantly higher percentage of those who signed contracts had their children returned. Stein, Gambrill, and Wiltse (1977) suggested that these encouraging results be tested further "in different settings and with different client populations" (p. 149). They also pointed to the need for "uniform guidelines for contract writing" (p. 149) and for definitions of the variables studied so that the results could be compared meaningfully. (Long-term foster care has been defined in some studies as beginning after three months; in others, after six months, or a year.)

A smaller study in Hartford, Connecticut, also tested the use of contracts. In a follow-up of twenty-nine youngsters who had been discharged from foster care within a one-year period with the use of contracts, "at the median period, between 19 and 24 months, 19 youngsters (66 percent) were still at the location to which they had been discharged.

The 66 percent who were considered to have a stable placement were distributed fairly evenly among natural parents and adoptive parents" (Fein, Davis, & Knight, 1979, p. 157). This finding encouraged the staff to "feel more optimistic about the possibility of permanence when children are returned to natural parents than they were before when adoptive placement seemed to be the more stable alternative" (p. 157). The small sample suggests that more research be done to test these findings, as Fein and co-workers noted. When studies can be made comparable, even small samples can contribute to an overall result.

The project that probably has done most to disseminate the concept of permanency planning was undertaken in Oregon in 1973. This statewide effort of the Children's Services Division of the Oregon State Department of Human Resources involved some five hundred children from nearly half the state's counties. Children selected for the project, Freeing Children for Permanent Placement, had been in foster care for a year or more, were considered unlikely to return home, and were considered adoptable. Through limited caseloads of twenty-five children per worker, a concentrated effort was made to locate absent parents and to assess parental capacity to care for their children. If the primary goal of reuniting the family could not be accomplished, steps were taken to terminate parental rights and to arrange for adoption. At the end of the three-year project, 26 percent of the children had returned to their own families, 36 percent had been freed for adoption and placed in adoptive homes, 3 percent were living with relatives, and 7 percent were in formalized long-term foster care arrangements. Only 9 percent of the cases had not been satisfactorily resolved, and the other 19 percent were still in process, most to be adopted (Pike, 1976). The project used a variety of methods to accomplish its objective, including contracts with the parents, but it put a strong emphasis on legal procedures. The concepts and techniques of permanency planning developed through this and other projects have been disseminated nationwide through guides, handbooks, and other resource materials. (Case Record; Jones & Biesecker, 1977; Pike et al., 1977)

EFFECTS OF FOSTER CARE ON CHILDREN AND FAMILIES: A LONGITUDINAL STUDY

One of the most comprehensive research studies funded during this period was a five-year longitudinal investigation of foster care in New York City (Fanshel & Shinn, 1978). This study, conducted under the auspices of Columbia University, was based on the systematic collection and analysis of data on more than six hundred children who entered foster care in 1966. Similar data was collected at four points in time over a five-year period. Separate teams collected information on the families of the children and on the agency services provided to both the families and the children (Jenkins & Norman, 1972, 1975; Shapiro, 1975).

This study, which presents a complex picture of the effects of foster care on children and their families, illustrates both the benefits and the limitations of research. While analysis of the data gives many tantalizing glimpses into possibilities needing further exploration, the generalizations that can be made, based on the data, are limited and subject to interpretation.

One of the major recommendations of this study was that data be collected routinely through a computerized information system. This information could then be analyzed in a number of ways without a major data collection effort. Fanshel and Shinn (1978) suggested "development of a multicausal statistical model appropriate for analysis of discharge from foster care" (p. 502) and proposed a long list of variables to be included in such a model, covering characteristics of the child, the family, the mother, the father, and agency services. Work on this model has been continuing since publication of the report.

The breadth of this study makes it difficult to select even a few highlights to suggest what it has to offer the practitioner. Findings of the effects of foster care on children tended to confirm findings from a number of previous studies. Kadushin (1978c) noted that the studies he had reviewed "found the physical, intellectual and emotional adjustment of most children in long term foster care to be satisfactory" (p. 102). However, contradictory findings on emotional adjustment required cautious interpretation.

> The rigorousness and specificity of definitions of "emotional adjustment" and the objectivity and measurability of data on which such assessments were made vary in the studies cited. Most frequently, determination of emotional adjustment was made by the worker on the basis of limited knowledge of the child's feelings and behavior. (Kadushin, 1978c, p. 102)

Although the methods used by Fanshel and Shinn (1978) provided the desired rigor, specificity, objectivity, and measurability, their carefully documented observations underlined the complexity of their subjects. Baseline data collected "on the children's social, emotional, and cognitive functioning on entrance into care" were compared with periodic assessments based on a health status index, an emotional problems indicator, and a developmental problems index that had been developed to document the children's biopsychosocial functioning. These instruments were supplemented with standard intelligence tests, followed by a clinical assessment of emotional functioning. Behavioral assessments of the children were also obtained periodically from both caseworkers and foster parents. Finally, a rating scale for pupil adjustment was used to collect information from teachers.

Cognitive Functioning. The most positive results were found in the area of cognitive functioning: "When we considered the full five-year span . . . length of time in care . . . was positively related to enhancement in IQ" (Fanshel & Shinn, 1978, p. 490). During the first two and a half years of the study, the children who remained in care "fared significantly better than the children who returned home. No such differentiation was found for the second two-and-one-half-year period" (p. 490).

The differences in school performance were not as significant.

> We found no major difference in school performance when we compared children remaining in foster care for five years . . . to those discharged for a period of three to five years. A sizable number of children showed improvement in performance toward the latter part of our study. (Fanshel & Shinn, 1978, p. 500)

The number "performing below their age-appropriate level" had dropped from 59 percent following entry into care to 53 percent at the end of five years (p. 500).

Emotional Adjustment. Fanshel and Shinn (1978) were more cautious in drawing conclusions about the emotional adjustment of the children they studied. They observed that "continued tenure in foster care is not demonstrably deleterious with respect to . . . the measures of emotional adjustment that we employed" (p. 491). However, they warned that in attempting "to assess the children's self-image through direct interviews . . . and such devices as the sentence-completion test . . . our subjects were apparently quite well defended in this area, and we were only able to catch a glimpse of the underlying feelings" (p. 479).

The associated study of foster care agencies also reported on the children's emotional well-being.

> Workers perceived the condition of the children they are responsible for as generally good for the first three to four years of placement. After that, the number of children whose emotional state was seen as deteriorating was greater than those seen as improving.
>
> Workers question the necessity for placement in relatively few cases. Nevertheless, for those who remained in placement for the full period covered, the experience was seen as damaging to one child in four and to every third or fourth mother. (Shapiro, 1975, p. 195)

Although the mental health of the children in foster care was found not to differ significantly from that of a comparable population not in care, these findings led the researchers to note the importance of special attention to the mental health of children in care (Fanshel & Shinn, 1978).

Prediction of Outcome: Parental Visiting as a Factor. In relation to outcome, the data analysis raised many interesting questions suggesting areas for further research but provided few reliable predictors. The authors placed particular emphasis on "the phenomenon of parental visiting" as deserving of "more intense research" (Fanshel & Shinn, 1978, p. 485). At the end of the five-year study, 56.1 percent of the sample had been discharged, 36.4 percent were still in care, 4.6 percent had been placed in adoptive homes, and 2.9 percent had been transferred to mental institutions or training schools. Noting that 57 percent of the children who remained in care "were unvisited by their parents, essentially abandoned," the researchers suggested that

> the well-being of the children is influenced by patterns of parental visit-ing. . . . parental visiting is the best variable we found . . . regarding the discharge of children from foster care. . . .
>
> We were impressed with the fact that parental visiting was linked to the amount of casework activity invested in a case and that such activity ex-plained a significant amount of unique variance in parental visiting. . . .
>
> Our finding that the caseworker's evaluation of the mother was a signifi-cant predictor of visiting behavior suggests that we need to know more profoundly how individuals relate to their parental responsibilities. . . . There is a very pressing need to determine whether undeveloped or damaged parental functioning—as evidenced by the request for placement and in the early failure to visit—is amenable to casework and other methods of influence and treatment. (Pp. 483, 485–486)

While these findings emphasize the importance of visits between par-ents and their children in foster care, Fanshel and Shinn (1978) recog-nized the complexity of the factors involved. A variety of reasons were given by the mothers interviewed for not visiting.

> Only one-fourth of all mothers said that they had no problems visiting their children. . . . Of those with problems about half . . . said their own illness prevented them from visiting as much as they would have liked. . . . over one-third of all mothers mentioned the distance from the child and the lack of travel money as creating problems. The foster care establishment was blamed for setting inconvenient visiting times by about 20 percent . . . and the same percentage accused agencies of trying to keep the mothers away. Eleven percent of the mothers blamed the foster parents themselves for making visiting difficult. . . . one-third of the mothers felt that visiting was upsetting emotionally for themselves and one-fourth said that it was disturb-ing for the child. (P. 485)

The related study of filial deprivation noted that

for about half of all parents, feelings tended to change after some months in placement, and most of the parents whose feelings changed reported reduction in anxiety. This may be a possible gain for parents, but it is also a warning to agencies that the sense of loss may diminish over time. Long separations may become unnecessarily prolonged. Less urgency for discharge was expressed by parents the longer the child was in care. The importance of acting quickly to expedite reunion is thus emphasized.

Visits to children while in care need to be analyzed in terms of parental initiative and mobility, as well as agency policies which may discourage rather than encourage parent-child contact. The fact that the youngest children, the black children, and the poorest children were visited least frequently speaks for the irrationality of the system. There is a need to examine visiting policies in relation to maintenance of family communication and interaction. (Jenkins & Norman, 1972, pp. 270–271)

Prediction of Outcome: Agency Services as a Factor. The study of agencies and foster children related one variable in particular to outcome.

The workers' evaluation of the mother predicted the child's discharge from care. Unlike all other variables examined, it contributed significantly to the discharge rate each time. It was superseded in importance only in the third year of placement, when the mother's determination to remove the children from care was stronger than other factors contributing to discharge. . . .

Over time, families with children in foster care have less contact with agency workers. These contacts are increasingly limited to the mother only and these mothers are increasingly likely to be seen in an unfavorable light, accompanied by decreasing optimism about their ability to make homes for their children. Whatever the problem that precipitates placement, the difficulty encountered by the workers in assessing maternal adequacy is the key reason for continuing placement. (Shapiro, 1975, pp. 195–196; italics added)

Shapiro recommended a study in greater depth of the criteria by which these assessments are made.

Shapiro (1975) reported that agency services did make a difference, especially during the first two years after placement, and that children placed for reasons of behavior were more likely to benefit from the system than were children placed because of family problems.

Although this study was not focused directly on the quality of the casework involved, it tested some of the basic assumptions related to casework and *demonstrated that at least one goal—the return of children in foster care to their families—could be achieved given conditions conducive to good casework.* It is especially noteworthy that such successes are achieved largely by BA workers with two to three years of experience. (P. 198; italics added)

On the negative side, a worker turnover rate of 25 percent and a high rate of replacement for the children indicated that foster care frequently did not provide the stability for the children that was intended.

Fully 42 percent of the children in the study had more than the two placements, usually imposed by the system. Shinn's analysis of replacement patterns indicated that most were for negative reasons. They were most likely to
be the result of unsuitable foster home placements or problems in the foster
family or agency requirements (religious matching, age limitations, program
closings, etc.). Few changes came about because of anticipated benefits to the
child. (P. 206)

A general conclusion of this study was that children placed for reasons of behavior (who tended to be from the higher socioeconomic
group) "were treated intensively in settings with high professional standards for a period of two or three years, at the end of which they were
discharged to their families in an improved condition" (Shapiro, 1975, p.
211). The mothers in this group tended to be satisfied with the services
they received and to perceive them as helpful (Jenkins & Norman, 1975).
"All other children . . . whose emotional problems were overshadowed
by the more visible disturbances of their parents, shared equally in the
deficiencies and inadequacies of the system" (Shapiro, 1975, p. 211). The
higher proportion of minority children in the group remaining in care
was at least partly a reflection of the larger number of children from the
higher socioeconomic group, placed for reasons of behavior, who returned home after treatment.

RECOMMENDATIONS FOR FUTURE RESEARCH
IN FOSTER CARE

Fanshel and Shinn (1978) recommended that in future research the
population be divided according to type (infants born out of wedlock,
children placed because of abuse or neglect, acting-out teenagers, etc.).
This would make it possible to differentiate factors affecting outcome for
the various groups.

They recommended also that greater attention be given to the "mac-
roscopic scale . . . the complex interplay of forces . . . affecting discharge" (pp. 503, 505). For example, the interfacing of child welfare
agencies with other systems, such as health care, may have a significant
effect on outcome. This approach is in line with Bronfenbrenner's (1979)
proposed framework, which takes into account the interrelationships of
systems on all levels.

In a subsequent analysis of data from the Child Welfare Information
System, Fanshel gathered information on 386 children who had been in
their current foster care placement for at least 12 months. They averaged
9.1 years of age and had been in care an average of 5.7 years. Less than
50 percent had seen either of their parents in 6 months. Seventy-five
percent of the children were reported to be deeply integrated into their
foster families; 77.9 percent of the foster parents in the sample had been

approached by the agencies about adopting the children in their care; 52.9 percent were very positive about the prospect; and an additional 19.5 percent were somewhat positive (Fanshel, 1979). It has been suggested that future research efforts should be extended to the foster children themselves.

FOSTER PARENTS

Considerable research has been directed toward the third element in the foster care triad—the foster parents. To a large extent this has been an effort to identify characteristics of successful foster parents. Again, the complexity of the situation has made it difficult to associate any specific characteristics with success, but these studies do provide insight into the factors that may be involved in successful interactions between foster parents and the children placed in their care.

Recommendations for improving satisfaction with, and quality of, foster care, based on interviews with thirty-four foster mothers, were made by Hampson and Tavormina in 1980. Although the sample was small, the mothers were interviewed by independent researchers, rather than by their caseworkers. The findings were compatible with findings in earlier studies by Fanshel (1966b) and Kraus (1971). Mothers who had had children in placement for more than two years had a significantly higher proportion of "social" motivation, which Fanshel had found to be associated with a preference for older children. The mothers who had had stable, long-term placements reported no regrets or problems with the job. Mothers with shorter placements reported more "private" motives, such as wanting a child to care for or companionship for self or for a child. Kraus's 1971 study also had found such motives to be associated with less stable placements. Hampson and Tavormina (1980) recommended more careful matching of the needs of the child to the abilities and motivation of the parents, better training in group sessions for foster parents, more support from caseworkers or from paraprofessionals such as experienced foster parents, and a more professional status for foster parents.

Most of the foster parents in the Fanshel and Shinn (1978) study were rated positively by the social workers. The physical care they provided was rated excellent to good, and 85 percent were rated warm and affectionate. One of the surprising and interesting findings of this study was the observed effect foster parents had on the children's developmental gains.

> Foster parent qualities played a role in IQ gain and behavioral change— although not in the expected ways. The style of discipline (democratic permissiveness) was significantly correlated with non-verbal IQ gains [while

the] intellectual climate developed by the foster parents [was] a significant predictor of changes in several areas of observed behavior. (P. 498)

These researchers speculated that a more relaxed style of discipline "loosened up" the child and allowed development to take place.

Similarly, in studying the effects of child-care workers in institutions on their charges, Fanshel and Shinn (1978) noted that exposure to younger, inexperienced workers had a more positive effect on both IQ and behavioral change than did exposure to older, more experienced staff. To explain this pattern, they "conjectured that the younger child care counselors served as a source of intellectual stimulation," whereas the older counselors may have become "institutionalized" in their attitudes and therefore provided less stimulation (p. 498).

RESIDENTIAL PROGRAMS

Specialized research on institutional programs has been concerned with many of the same areas addressed by general research in foster care: the developmental effects on children and the processes of entrance into and exit from care.

Reviews of the literature on criteria for placement decisions have yielded little agreement. One such review concluded: "The decision to place a child in residential treatment is presently a highly individualized matter based on a complex set of idiosyncratic factors defying categorization" (Maluccio & Marlow, 1972, p. 239). Kadushin (1978c) observed in his later summary of the research that while there was some "consensus in the field regarding which kind of children belong in which kind of facility" (p. 127), the available resources did not always permit an appropriate decision. However, he cited a number of studies showing that decisions to place in residential programs were made only after the failure of extensive efforts to provide alternative services in the child's home or in the community. According to a 1975 study by Bedford and Hybertson, although the services required to prevent placement were expensive, they still cost less than a residential treatment program.

Some outcome studies reviewed by Kadushin (1978c) looked at factors contributing to successful discharge; others examined the effects of programs on the behavior of youngsters in residence. The findings of some of these studies appear contradictory because of differences in the institutional programs. For example, opposite conclusions were drawn from two similar follow-up studies of discharge from two residential treatment programs for boys. A study by Taylor and Alpert (1973)

of 75 children discharged from Children's Village, a residential treatment facility for children that provides child and family services in Connecticut, showed that the single most important factor associated with postdischarge adaptation was the child's perception of family support after discharge and the continuity of such support before, during, and after institutionalization. Both family support and the continuity of such support were essential. They were more important for postdischarge adjustment than the degree of change achieved by the child during residential treatment. (Kadushin, 1978c, p. 129)

In a study of seventy boys discharged from a residential treatment center in California, "a strong positive association was found between the boys' functioning at discharge and the functioning at follow-up," but there was no "statistically significant association . . . between adjustment at follow-up and a scale of environmental support" (Oxley, 1977, p. 496; quoted in Kadushin, 1978c, p. 130).

> The researchers attributed the difference between their findings and those of other studies to the fact that this residential treatment center was oriented to ongoing, active participation by the parents in the program. . . . The support system of the family was available to the children throughout their experience, and this carried through after discharge. (Kadushin, 1978c, p. 130)

Such findings have contributed to a greater emphasis on involving families in residential treatment programs and have prompted some of the demonstration projects that are currently adding to the body of research in this area.

Evaluative studies, which attempt to measure the effects of a program on residents, can have a significant impact on the staff of an institution. Mayer (1965) described the effects of a series of four research studies undertaken in Bellefaire, a residential treatment program for boys in Cleveland. The involvement of the staff in the research influenced their attitudes both toward their own work and toward the research, which in turn affected the outcome of the investigation. In a study at Children's Village, a hundred residents were rated by staff members over a one-year period. This group of boys showed significant changes in many areas of behavior: "According to staff ratings the deviant behavior of a group of preadolescent boys in residential treatment tended to show slow, steady and often significant improvement" (Schaffer & Millman, 1973, p. 160).

In recent years a number of demonstration projects have been developed to expand the continuum of services available to disturbed children and their families. Some of these were described in Chapter 5. Whittaker (1980) suggested, "The residential center can and should be conceived of as a family support system, rather than as a substitute form of care that treats the child in isolation from his family and home community" (p. 2). Whittaker (1980) cited several innovative programs that attempt to combine the advantages of family foster care and residential treatment. One is a small, multifunction residential care facility operated as a support services unit by the Casey Family Program in Seattle; this agency specializes in long-term foster care services. Another is a parent therapist program which serves "emotionally disturbed children in a service model that falls somewhere between specialized foster care and residential treatment" (Whittaker, 1980, p. 2). A third is "a behaviorally-oriented, family style group home," known as Achievement Place, which uses so-called teaching parents in a program geared to delinquents (p. 2). Such programs should be a promising direction for research in the area of residential treatment.

Adoption

Specialized research in adoption has addressed such areas as statistical trends, placement of children with special needs, effects of subsidized adoptions, comparisons of independent and agency adoptions, follow-up, the role of genetic versus environmental factors in child development, and prediction of outcome. Studies prior to 1977 were reviewed extensively by Kadushin (1978b). This period saw a distinct change in the types of children available for adoption. Surveys for the period 1970–1977 showed a downward trend in adoption of infants, which function was handled largely through voluntary agencies. During the same period there was a slight increase in the number of children accepted for adoptive placement by public agencies; most of this group were over the age of one year and a third were handicapped.

Finding placements for children with special needs is difficult but possible and usually such placements are successful. The "work of specialized agencies, extension of adoption subsidies, and widening the pool of applicants through nontraditional and transracial families have increased possibilities of placement for such children" (Kadushin, 1978b, p. 56).

Concern about the adoption of children with special needs predated the shortage of adoptable infants. In 1958 Boehm concluded that "the most effective service to a 'hard-to-place' child is to prevent his becoming hard-to-place"; she added that "placement in foster care for a period of more than two years is the factor which discriminates most highly against adoptability" (p. 28).

In a follow-up study of adopted children, Jaffee and Fanshel (1970) concluded that characteristics of the adoptive parents were more related to outcome than were characteristics of the child. The question of whether child characteristics are a barrier to adoption was explored by the Citizens' Committee for Children of New York, Inc. in 1981. The data analyzed had been collected in 1978–1979 on a sample of one thousand of the approximately 6000 children in the New York City foster care system who have the goal of adoption, 63 percent of all the children surveyed had no intellectual, physical or psychological problems reported. . . . Children spent an average of 7 years in the foster care system before they were adopted. The unadopted children had been in care an average of 8 years already and are still waiting. . . . Children remained in foster care for an average of 5.2 years before they were legally available (freed) for adoption. . . . The characteristics of the children waiting to be adopted did not appear to be substantially different from those of children who had already been adopted. (P. 2)

The report concluded: "The characteristics of the children themselves do not constitute a barrier to their adoption within a reasonable time period" (p. 3). Recommendations were made on recruiting adoptive homes, including the selection of foster homes with a view toward adoption; changing administrative procedures; streamlining legal and court requirements; putting emphasis on goal setting; and altering reimbursement practices.

Kadushin (1978c) pointed out that changing social conditions need to be taken into account in evaluating the permanency planning recommendations made by some demonstration projects. He speculated that "the refusal of Medicaid to pay for abortion . . . might make a sufficiently large pool of healthy white infants available for adoption. In such a case, older nonwhite children once again would become much more difficult to place" (p. 114). In this context, he questioned the emphasis on termination of parental rights as a first step to freeing children for adoption. If the availability of adoptive families for these children is not taken into account at the outset, they could end up belonging neither to their own nor to substitute parents, but to the state.

It is possible that social conditions will change to create a greater need for research focused on the questions traditionally asked about the placement of infants—the relative contributions of genetic and environmental influences, the effect on the adopted child of the method of learning about the adoption, etc. Whether or not this shift occurs, the need to find permanent homes for youngsters of all ages, races, and conditions will continue to exist, and the services required to support such placements will need to be refined. The ecological perspective, which embraces the interaction of the many systems impinging on the family, appears to have much to offer in this search.

Protective Services

An expansion of specialized research in the area of the needs of children who have been abused or neglected has been supported since

1974 by government funding under the auspices of the National Center on Child Abuse and Neglect. Although this research has covered many aspects of the problem, from surveys of incidence to identification of characteristics of the population and evaluation of treatment methods, it has merely begun to scratch the surface of what needs to be known. Several of those who have reviewed research efforts in the field have concluded that very little can be stated with any certainty.

The problems encountered in evaluating research on child abuse and neglect are similar to those that must be dealt with in all human services research—the interpretation of statistics, the limitations of retrospective research, and the effects of investigator bias. Questioning the accuracy and interpretation of incidence studies, Dorman (1981) cited the experience of investigators contracted to do a study for the National Center on Child Abuse and Neglect. In data gathered from professionals mandated to report cases, they found that only a third of the total number of cases had been reported. Noting that central registries can give an accurate count of reported cases, Dorman questioned the interpretation of these figures: "Does a rise in the number of reported cases reflect a rise in incidence or simply mean that more people are reporting because of the ease of reporting, greater availability of services, or media campaigns?" (p. 1). Are poor people disproportionately represented in such reports? If they are, does this reflect the occurrence of more abuse in lower income families or merely their greater susceptibility to being reported?

> Pelton . . . in *The Social Context of Child Abuse and Neglect* . . . stresses the distinction between stating that CAN happens in families of all classes and stating that it occurs with equal frequency in all classes. . . . the composition of the total population of child abusers is an unknown, and we must be cautious in regarding the population reported as a representative group. (Dorman, 1981, p. 1)

In regard to the limitations of retrospective research, Dorman (1981) quoted a study by Hunter that compared abusive and nonabusive parents who had been abused as children.

> [A] widely agreed-upon finding of retrospective research is that abusive parents are very likely to have been abused children. An equally important issue is obscured by studying this abusive sample: how many abused children grow up and *do not* abuse their children and, most important, what factors make the difference? (P. 2)

One of the most striking findings in the Hunter study was the "richer network of social connections" in the nonabusive group.

> It is justified, based on current findings, to conclude that being abused in childhood increases one's chances of becoming abusive. With further re-

search, it would be encouraging also to be able to state that certain other factors increase the likelihood that the abused child will not become abusive, helping us to encourage successes instead of predicting failures. (Dorman, 1981, p. 2)

The effects of bias are most apparent in research on causal theories. The researcher's viewpoint is shaped by the training of a particular discipline. For example, a bibliography on child abuse and neglect by Kalish divides causative factors into "sociological/cultural causes, psychological causes, dynamics of pregnancy and the neonatal period, and family dysfunction" (Dorman, 1981, p. 2).

Another review of research in protective services noted that

investigators have tended to study only one variable and to follow one of the three theoretical approaches to the problem: (1) the *mental health model* (also known as the psychiatric model) stresses the etiology and the personality characteristics of the one who is responsible for the maltreatment; (2) the *sociological model* examines the societal and family situational factors which are hypothesized to impact on the problem; and (3) the *victim-centered approach,* in which the characteristics of the child are studied and the part the child might play in causing abuse is analyzed. (Aronson, 1980, p. 22)

PROBLEMS OF DEFINITION

Many research reviews have pointed out differences in the definitions of abuse and neglect used in many studies. There are two aspects to this problem.

One aspect concerns the definitions used by protective services workers on which their decisions and actions in a case are based. Giovannoni and Bercerra (1979) addressed this problem and found "a high level of agreement among professionals and the general population in their perceptions of child mistreatment, agreement that indicates a very high potential for consensus with respect to the social definitions of mistreatment" (p. 208). However, within this consensus there were many differences between professionals and the general population and between specific professional groups and specific ethnic groups in the population as to the seriousness with which certain types of mistreatment were regarded.

The other aspect of the problem of definition concerns research. The term "abuse" may be used to include both abuse and neglect, or abuse may be defined as only the intentional infliction of serious and lasting injury on a child, while all other kinds of maltreatment (including lacerations and bruises or excessive corporal punishment) may be lumped together under the heading "neglect." Aronson (1980) found, in analyzing a sample of 341 cases from the New York State Central Registry, that only 10 percent were cases of abuse (the battered child syndrome) while 90 percent were considered neglect (including all other types of maltreatment). In her review of the literature, she found only one major study that focused on neglect: Polansky's 1975 survey of research and studies on neglect. He defined child neglect

> as a condition in which a caretaker responsible for the child either deliberately or by extraordinary inattentiveness permits the child to experience avoidable present suffering and/or fails to provide one or more of the ingredients generally deemed essential for developing a person's physical, intellectual, and emotional capacities. (Polansky, Hally, & Polansky, 1975, p. 5)

There might be some question as to whether there is general agreement on the essential "ingredients."

STUDIES OF CAUSAL FACTORS

In addition to studies concerned with incidence and reporting, many studies have attempted to identify causal factors and/or the characteristics of parents who abuse or neglect. Kempe and Helfer (1972) found the parent, the child, and the situation to be major contributing variables. Garbarino (1976) noted that economic stress was the best predictor of reported abuse rates in New York State. Gelles (1976), reviewing studies of physical abuse, reported that "only four of nineteen personality traits found in studies to characterize abusers have been cited by two or more researchers, i.e., impulsivity, immaturity, depression, and a lack of ego-strength" (quoted in Aronson, 1980, p. 26). A study of neglectful mothers by Polansky, Borgman, and Desaix in 1972 identified the most prevalent problems as chronic depression, borderline schizophrenia, and mental retardation. Several studies found isolation to be associated with abuse or maltreatment. Elmer (1967) reported that abusive mothers had fewer associations and scored higher on an index of social isolation than did two control groups. Likewise, Garbarino (1977) found social isolation to be positively associated with maltreatment in every study that considered it as a factor (Aronson, 1980).

A number of studies have identified factors that put children at high risk for abuse: prematurity, low birth weight, illegitimacy, congenital malformation, being a twin, conception during a mother's depressive illness, and being the child of a woman with frequent pregnancies and excessive work demands (Aronson, 1980; Elmer, 1967; Elmer & Gregg, 1967; Fontana, 1971; Justice & Justice, 1976; Klein & Stern, 1971).

A study in Texas (Coombes, McCormack, Chipley, & Archer, 1978) attempted to develop an index of factors that could be used in the identification of cases of abuse and neglect. Factors found to be present in common in cases of abuse and neglect were unemployment, unstable family composition, unstable home environment, chronic marital problems, alcoholism, impulsive or inconsistent parents, manipulative or hostile parents, lack of home routine, parents unable to offer explanations, and parents unable to accept severity of problem.

STUDIES OF TREATMENT MODALITIES

Studies of methods of practice used with families in protective and preventive services were reviewed by Jones, Magura, and Shyne in 1981. They noted the use of multiservice family centers, short-term and long-term intensive casework services, multidisciplinary teams, comprehensive services combined with outreach and advocacy, group services, lay services, parent education, and various types of contracting. The findings were drawn from a variety of demonstration projects and many would bear further testing (some of these findings were quoted in earlier chapters).

Prospects for Future Research

Further research is needed in all the areas outlined in this discussion. With the prospect of reduced government funding for such research, there is some question as to the sources of support that can be found.

Certainly, the computerized tracking systems that have been developed in many states will provide data that can be analyzed to add to the knowledge in the field. As noted earlier, the usefulness of these data will depend on the accuracy with which they are provided by the practitioners who feed these systems.

Indeed, practitioners can greatly assist the total research effort in the child welfare area. Findings need to be tested in the field, and the practitioner who takes a scientific approach and tests promising findings of the course of daily practice can make a valuable contribution by keeping an organized record of results through conference papers and publications.

Summary

While there has been a great deal of useful research in various aspects of the child welfare field, the value of many investigations is limited by the lack of an adequate theoretical framework that would allow findings to be compared and validated by replication. The practitioner needs to be aware of research in child development, which is basic to the field, as well as the findings of specialized research in the areas of foster care, adoption, and protective services. Much of the specialized research is interrelated since a family in need of child welfare services may require, at one time or another, preventive or protective services, foster family care or institutional care, or adoption services.

Computerized information systems present an opportunity for more systematized data collection and analysis, but the effectiveness of these systems for research will depend on the accuracy with which individual practitioners feed into them the necessary information. This, in turn, will depend on the experience that practitioners gain in utilizing information available through these systems either for practical purposes or for increased understanding of the complex factors with which they must deal in their daily work.

Every practioner has the opportunity to make some contribution to research by testing promising findings in an organized way and by recording the results in order to share them with others.

CHAPTER 9

Future Trends

THE IMPACT of a rapidly changing society on the American family and the child welfare services that support and supplement the family has caused concern about the future of these two social institutions. As they both try to adapt to the changes around them, their futures are intertwined. The shape each will take must depend, to a large extent, on the solutions found to the problems of the society of which they are a part.

Practitioners working to prevent family breakdown are acutely aware of the stresses that unemployment, poor housing, and inadequate health care place on parents. They recognize their own limitations in dealing with these factors and the effects of governmental decisions on the well-being of the families they are trying to serve. The family policy issues dealt with at the 1980 White House Conference on Families reflected these concerns.

A study that compared the economic status of families in the advanced industrial countries drew the conclusion that "most other countries are far more generous than the U.S. to families with children—particularly those in modest circumstances" (Kamerman & Kahn, 1981). Assistance largely takes the form of child or family allowances in other industrialized nations.

The history of child welfare services in the United States reflects many contradictory forces operating in a free society. This society has been accused both of being too child centered and of failing to show enough concern for the needs of all children. Likewise, the quality and extensiveness of U.S. child welfare services have been both praised and criticized. There is praise for the spirit of volunteerism that characterizes much of American social work and that has provided leadership in developing resources for substitute care and/or family supports. There is criticism of the tendency to place more emphasis on service to the child than on services to strengthen the family and of the tendency of systems of substitute care, once established, to perpetuate themselves without regard to the changing needs of those they are supposed to serve.

Many of the advances made in the field have been marked by bitter legislative battles (Andrews, 1977). In the past, religious leaders and groups were often at the forefront of efforts to ameliorate the effects upon the family of stresses created by a fast-growing industrial society. As the public conscience was touched, legislative action was taken and resources expanded through public funding. During periods of affluence, these programs grew. When economic downturns caused competition over funds, the effectiveness of these programs was questioned closely. This sometimes had a healthy effect in stimulating innovation and forcing institutions to adapt to new situations. It also brought about legislative struggles of the kind seen in the 1981 Congress. Hard-won legislation to provide child welfare resources designed with an emphasis on strengthening families and providing permanent homes for children was threatened with repeal before it could be implemented. The conflicting views in evidence at the 1980 White House Conference on Families were another example of this process in operation.

In a period of such rapid change it is difficult to foresee the future either of the family as an institution or of the services that will be needed to assure all children adequate parental care. Despite this uncertainty, some hopeful signs and trends can be seen. The solutions people find to their own problems may be guideposts to the future; perhaps only timely encouragement and support are necessary to bring about the requisite changes.

In the midst of a massive breakdown of families, individuals and groups have spontaneously banded together to support each other in unrelated extended families or small communities. This recognition of the value of informal support systems in strengthening families or supplying needed substitute care for children has been utilized by social agencies that have developed programs based on mutual aid networks and self-help groups. Some of these programs were described in earlier chapters. They often expand limited financial and professional manpower resources through a partnership of professionals and lay people to which each makes a unique contribution.

Unfortunately, such innovative programs are often the first to suffer when funds are cut, even though they may be cost-effective in the long run. It can be hoped that the experience gained through these programs will not be lost and that models that have demonstrated success will continue to be applied in a variety of communities and situations.

Another model that has proved its value through widespread replication is the team concept for coordinating, and increasing the effectiveness of, services. Teams are generally made up of professionals, but they also promote the integration of professional training and expertise with the life experience of volunteers, aides, and sometimes the recipients of services. A number of models developed in response to varying needs and circumstances have been mentioned in the course of this book. They have in common the tying together of different disciplines and backgrounds in the service of finding a solution to the problems of a particular family.

Both the team and the mutual aid concept have been utilized in community based multiservice programs developed to meet the needs of a particular geographic area. These programs draw together the professional and the informal resources of a community through the use of all types of social work methods—casework, group work, and community organization—often combining one type of skill with another. The Center for Family Life in Sunset Park and the Lower East Side Family Union, both described in Chapter 4, are examples of such programs, differing in approach but offering the potential for successful prevention.

The extension of the collaborative process to include the recipient of services, as well as other professionals, is an area that bears further exploration. As a review of the literature on collaboration with social work clients observed:

> A major theme surfacing from this review . . . was the ability and willingness of clients to collaborate. They repeatedly told social workers that different kinds of human need call for different responses. Therefore, the relationship and interventions must be shaped accordingly. Accomplishing this requires ongoing research, with client participation in problem identification, design, and interpretation of feelings. (Carroll, 1980, p. 416)

Many of the program models already discussed—mutual aid groups, teams, and community based multiservice centers—have been successful in promoting such collaboration. In some of these programs, families are attracted by informal activities and request professional help after a trusting relationship has been established. In others, the experience of meeting with a team of concerned individuals who are ready to offer assistance with professional and personal problems convinces parents that help is possible and enables them to face and accept their need, reassured that their views will be taken seriously. When an intensive one-to-one relationship is needed, the shared responsibility can support this relationship and make it more endurable for all the parties concerned.

Including clients in case conferences and encouraging their participation in the choice of foster care are methods being used by some traditional agencies to develop such collaboration. In a study that explored outcomes of foster care, youngsters who had had an opportunity to participate in their placement decision were significantly more satisfied than were those who did not (Bush, Gordon, & LeBailly, 1977). Hartman's ecomap and genogram (1978, 1979) also have been used by some agencies to enhance the collaborative process.

The changes affecting the family have had an impact on the resources for substitute care, as well. Some agencies find it more difficult to recruit foster homes now than in the past, both because more women are entering the labor market and because of the greater demands made on foster parents by the population in need of such care today. The effort to keep as many children as possible in their homes and in the community means that the children who require substitute care are apt to be those who are more disturbed, as a result of serious abuse or neglect. Many of these children can succeed in carefully selected foster homes, with parents who have the abilities or skills that are needed and who receive adequate support services.

One direction that holds promise as a solution to this problem is a trend toward granting more professional status to foster parents. This may be achieved through additional training or through participation with professional staff as members of a team. In some cases, couples become salaried foster parents employed by an agency. A few agencies have experimented with treatment homes in which foster parents function as members of a multidisciplinary team. Residential programs have established group foster homes, with the residential professional staff as a backup to the foster parents; such partnerships enhance the contributions of both partners. The trend in group care toward provision of a continuum of services and greater integration of parents into the process is another promising direction for healing damaged children and their families.

The children in need of care today present a challenge to those on whom they are dependent for services. Practitioners have to understand both normal and pathological child development and family dynamics in order to serve these children effectively and to help foster parents and other child-care workers cope with them. This training must be provided not only to students in schools of social work but also to those already in the field.

Practitioners need also to understand more fully the cultural and ethnic backgrounds of the families and children they serve. The gap in understanding that often still exists between the "typical middle-class, white woman" who is attracted to the field of child welfare and the minority families at the bottom of the economic rung whom she is frequently called upon to serve must be filled both by training of existing personnel and by expanding avenues through which minorities can enter the field.

The generic training now being offered in many schools of social work is an excellent framework for developing the specialized skills needed for the child welfare field. Translating this training into direct service requires an opportunity to practice these skills. Too often those who have acquired such training become enmeshed in administrative responsibilities, which leave little time for the sharing of skills and knowledge with direct service staff who have not had the benefit of this training. This is a particular problem in public agencies, in which large caseloads and complex accountability procedures tend to absorb a good deal of the time and energy of supervisors. There has been some experimentation with having supervisors share direct service functions, either in the intake process or in more difficult cases. Such efforts need strong administrative support if they are to succeed, but they can enrich the experience of both supervisors and their staffs. Consultation with experts in related fields and the availability of support groups, such as those described in Chapter 3, can contribute a great deal to the efforts of administrators and supervisors to provide ongoing training to direct service staff.

The regional training and resource centers, located at universities throughout the country, are a valuable source of such training. The materials they have developed and distributed, which have been quoted throughout this book, need to be more widely known and applied.

Training opportunities, which have been dependent in the past largely on funding sources, may depend more in the future on a creative collaboration between schools and service agencies to make maximum use of existing resources. Many of the emerging concepts and programs that have been mentioned—teams, multiservice centers, mutual aid networks, and other forms of partnership among professionals, paraprofessionals, and those who need their services—offer possibilities for extending the knowledge and skills of the practitioners who participate in them. Specialized training is needed, but much can be gained through the interaction among specialists and generalists that these programs promote.

At the same time that creative use of existing resources is emphasized, the potential benefits offered by advanced technology cannot be overlooked. The application of computer technology to human services is still in an experimental stage. In child welfare, more than perhaps any other field of social work, the application of techniques that have been used successfully to manage large businesses appears to offer a means of improving accountability and planning. Certainly, the government funding on both national and state levels that has been invested in the development of information systems has been based on this premise. Many statewide tracking systems have such goals as insuring that realistic plans are made for all children as quickly as possible after they enter care, facilitating achievement of these plans at the earliest possible time, identifying areas for program improvement, and providing a base for social service and fiscal planning (Madison, 1977). Sobey (1977) observed, "The more that programs and fields grow, differentiating and specializing from one another, the more they need mechanisms of integration" (p. 21). In many states in which separate systems grew up for the placement of children through the courts and through local social service agencies, information systems can help coordinate this process.

As the development of data systems continues, more and more practitioners are affected by them. The systems depend for their effectiveness on the accuracy of the information fed into them, and this in turn depends on the training of large numbers of practitioners in the necessary tasks. These tasks are frequently felt as burdensome and time-consuming by practitioners. Most information systems contribute more to planning and management decisions than to the case decisions that must be made by practitioners. Although some efforts are being made to develop computerized systems that will be useful to protective services workers in making the decisions their jobs require, the practical value of such systems has yet to be demonstrated. At best, they can probably provide limited aid to decisionmaking, but they should never be expected to replace human judgment.

It is not surprising that many practitioners regard computer information systems with suspicion, if not downright hostility. Computer technology now penetrates people's lives to such a degree that the experience of its advantages and its limitations can hardly be escaped. Much of the suspicion and hostility comes from the difficulty of mastering these systems and a lack of understanding of what can realistically be expected of them. In order to function, they require a uniformity of definition that our desire for individuality resists. Some standardization is necessary in the operation of large organizations, but it is important, too, to preserve the flexibility that makes creative solutions possible. Those responsible for developing data systems need to be aware of the effect they have on the daily activity of practitioners if a balanced solution is to be found to this problem.

Whatever their individual views, practitioners in the field of child welfare will need to learn to deal with computer technology, to understand what it can do for them, and to learn how they can contribute to its effective use. This is one of the challenges of the future—to insure that our technological capability serves us rather than becomes the master of our lives.

The field of child welfare will need to continue in the future, as it has in the past, to adapt to a rapidly changing society. Its role as a support to the institution of the family will have to be regarded both critically and creatively if it is to influence, as well as to adjust to, these changes.

In an era of shrinking funding, creative solutions that make better use of existing resources are one promising direction. A partnership between those with professional backgrounds and those with life experience is possible through the expansion of mutual aid groups and networks, multidisciplinary teams, community based multiservice programs, a more professional status for foster parents, and increased collaboration with users of services. The specialized training for the field must equip practitioners to provide effective services to the extremely damaged children and families who frequently become their responsibility. Ways must be found also to bridge the differences in cultural and ethnic background that continue to exist between the majority of practitioners and large numbers of the families and children they serve.

Another direction that cannot be avoided is the use of computer technology in making planning and management decisions. This requires joint efforts by those who develop the systems and those who use them to insure that, in fact, they serve the intended purposes.

APPENDIX A

The Protective Services Casework Process*

Introduction

Technical jobs always have prescribed ways of doing things. Because CPS [Child Protective Services] casework is a technical job, this is true of CPS casework. The CPS process has beginning, middle and concluding aspects which are applied to helping people solve specific problems.

A. The Person Who Employs the Process
1. You, the CPS worker, operationalize that which is commonplace into a systematic helping approach. For instance, your impressions are systematized into a diagnosis of your client's problems.
2. You have specific methods for helping clients.
3. Your involvement is purposeful and conscious.
4. You know what to do, say and how to behave.
5. You have a process which you employ to help the client.

B. The CPS Casework Process
1. Understanding the total CPS casework process is important.
   a. Understanding this process will enable you to understand your job precisely.
   b. Understanding the overall process will provide you with a

* From Holder, Mouzakitis, Romero, Sahd, and Salisbury (1980, pp. 6–8).

structure and, therefore, will increase your comfort in doing your job.

   c. This overall structure can be shared with the client.

   d. Understanding the process enables you to evaluate your performance; that is, you can determine if you are doing what should be done.

   e. Understanding the process is important because the process works!

2. The casework process in CPS is based on several principles.

   a. It uses a unified approach, based on step-by-step procedures.

   b. There is interconnectedness between the steps of the process based on progression.

     (1) The process is progressive in that each step builds on previous steps.

     (2) Later steps depend on first accomplishing the initial steps.

   c. Flexibility allows you to respond spontaneously to the client's needs.

     (1) It is important that you be flexible enough to back up and start over.

     (2) Flexibility is based on the dynamic nature of your interaction with the client. It is always subject to change.

   d. It is critical that you have control in managing crises (emergencies) and recognize that dealing with CPS related problems takes time.

   e. The CPS casework method is based on an analytical model for problem solving which includes:

     (1) Studying the problem situation.

     (2) Assessing the risk to the child in the family.

     (3) Estimating the probability of further risk to the child and the likelihood of successful treatment strategies.

     (4) Choosing among alternative treatment strategies.

     (5) Continuously evaluating the effectiveness of the selected strategies.

3. Process can be defined by its many elements.

   a. Process employs particular methods or techniques.

   b. Process is grounded in planning or preparation.

   c. Process suggests moving a client from problems to solutions.

   d. All that occurs in the process is designed to effect a particular desirable outcome or result.

   e. Helping permeates the process from beginning to end.

4. The CPS casework process consists of seven basic steps.

   a. *Intake* is the first step in the process. It includes:

     (1) Receiving the referral.

     (2) Possibly making collateral contacts and checking records.

(3) Exploring the appropriateness of the referral.

(4) Deciding to commit the agency to the referral as a report of abuse or neglect.

(5) Documenting the record.

b. *Initial assessment* (investigation) is the second step. It includes:

(1) Making initial contact with the child and family.

(2) Making subsequent assessment visits.

(3) Assessing the damage to the child.

(4) Assessing the potential for continuing risk to the child.

(5) Evaluating the family indicators of abuse or neglect.

(6) Determining if abuse or neglect exists and continuing the case as open.

(7) Determining the need to invoke the authority of the family court.

(8) Providing emergency services as needed.

(9) Providing feedback to appropriate persons.

(10) Documenting the record.

c. The study of the problem and people—*the diagnostic assessment*—is the third step. It includes:

(1) Studying the family problems in more depth from a causal perspective.

(2) Individualizing family members.

(3) Assessing strengths and areas for improvement.

(4) Determining resources available to and needed by the family.

(5) Specifying assessment conclusions (diagnostic assessment).

d. *Case planning* is the fourth basic step. It includes:

(1) Specifying the changes which need to occur to assure the child's continued safety (setting the goals).

(2) Deciding on the potential for goal attainment and estimating when goals will be attained (prognostic assessment).

(3) Deciding what services will be given: to whom, by whom, how often and for how long.

(4) Establishing dates for review.

(5) Documenting the case plan.

e. *Service provision* (treatment) is the fifth step. It includes:

(1) Involving and advising the client on the plan to assure that it is understood.

(2) Arranging for and coordinating non-direct services.

(3) Providing direct services.

(4) Documenting the progress of all services.

f. *Case plan evaluation* is the sixth step. It includes:

(1) Evaluating client progress.

(2) Updating the assessment.

    (3) Making decisions to continue the plan, revise the plan or terminate the plan.

  g. *Termination* of the case plan is the seventh step. It includes:

    (1) Evaluating goal attainment.

    (2) Analyzing the potential for the case remaining stable.

    (3) Examining the need for referral to other services.

    (4) Advising and preparing the client for termination.

    (5) Advising other agencies or involved persons.

    (6) Documenting the record with the rationale for termination (case closure).

5. The CPS casework process can be charted to demonstrate the interdependence of the steps and its dynamic nature.

  a. There are five critical decision points in the process represented on the following chart by diamonds.

  b. The dynamic nature of the process is illustrated by the forward and return vectors which show that the worker may go back to previous steps in the process and repeat them.

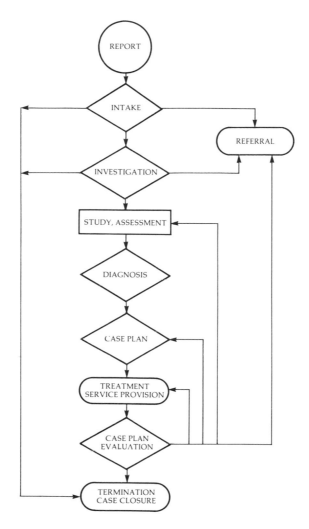

APPENDIX B

Permanency Planning*

Assessment

Agency intervention into a family is made necessary by parental or child problems in one of the following three basic categories:

1. Absence
2. Condition
3. Conduct

Regardless of the service plan, an assessment of family functioning with regard to these areas is a necessary prerequisite. Begin by defining what the parental or child's problems are, in one or more area, then look at services which will help to alleviate the problems.

ABSENCE

> *Parental Absence*—This refers to the lack of consistent contact between the parent and child over a period of time.
> *Examples:*
> Parents may be separated and the non-custodial parent seldom visits, or visits erratically.
> Parents may leave child unattended or with neighbors for long periods of time without returning as planned.
> Parent may have left child with relative or in foster home and left the area with no fowarding address.

* From Jones and Biesecker (1977, pp. 4–5, 21–24).

Child's Absence—This refers to behavior on the part of the child resulting in his being away from and without a home.
Example:
Child runs away from home either regularly or for an extended period of time.

CONDITION

Parental Condition—This refers to qualities within the parent which
prevent adequate nurturing. These qualities should have a dig-
nosis and prognosis.
Examples:
Parent may be mentally retarded, assessed as trainable, without the
capability of providing for a child's basic needs.
Parent may have physical illness which requires hospitalization or
full time nursing care.
Parent may be mentally ill to the extent that he is out of touch with
reality and/or dangerous to himself or others.
Child's Condition—This refers to qualities within the child which prevent him from receiving the care and nurturing he needs in his
home. These qualities should have a diganosis and prognosis.
Examples:
A child may have a physical major handicap requiring special treatment which the parent does not know how to provide.
A child may be emotionally disturbed and need special education
classes and the family special counseling to learn to help him.
A child may be mentally retarded requiring 24 hour specialized supervision, which a single parent cannot provide.

CONDUCT

Parental Conduct—This refers to parental behavior which is detrimen-
tal to the child.
Examples:
Parent's housekeeping may be so poor as to endanger the child's
health and safety.
Parent may abuse the child frequently.
Parent may fail to provide supervision to the child so as to endanger
the child's safety.
Child's Conduct—This refers to a child's behavior which is disruptive
to the family.

Examples:

A child may be hyperactive, sleep little at night and have trouble following rules necessary for his safety.

A child may run away from home, refuse to go to school and openly disobey parental discipline.

A child may be abusive to people or destructive to property.

ASSESSMENT

To assess the home situation:

1. Decide which categories apply to the parent and child.
2. Define in clear language which the problem is.
3. Define strengths and resources the family has to work with.
4. List possible plans for solving the problem *and* maintaining security and permanence for the child.

Adoption

This refers to the situation where the rights and responsibilities of a biological parent to a child are terminated and assumed by another individual who becomes the child's legal parent.

WHEN TO SELECT THIS GOAL

Adoption is the permanent plan offering the most stability to the child who cannot return home to his parents. It is also the most traumatic to the family since it generally involves permanent separation of child and family. All reasonable efforts should be made to reunite the family before moving to adoption. The goal of adoption should be considered under the following circumstances:

- The goal of return home has been ruled out.
- The parents through words or action have shown an inability or unwillingness to care for the child for a period of at least 6 months, and the biological parents will not be able to provide for the child's health and safety within a reasonable period of time (6 months).
- The parent wants the child to be adopted, or parental rights have been terminated.
- An adoptive home is available or can be found within a reasonable period of time (1 year).
- The child wants to be adopted.

HOW TO IMPLEMENT THIS GOAL

The goal of adoption involves permanent separation of child and family, and this will require considerable work by the agency. There are three basic steps in the adoptive process:

1. Freeing the child for adoption.
2. Finding an adoptive home.
3. Developing a plan for placement.

Freeing the Child for Adoption

The release of a child for adoption is a legal procedure. Before continuing with adoption plans, consult with your agency attorney, court or another attorney familiar with adoption laws in your state and get the following information:

1. What statutes in your state pertain to adoption.
2. What procedures must be followed if a parent wants to voluntarily relinquish his parental rights.
3. What are the grounds necessary to terminate a parent's rights when [he] will not release the child voluntarily.

Many statutes permit termination of parental rights based upon:

Absence—Abandonment of the child for a long time or a series of shorter periods of abandonment

Condition—A parental condition which can be diagnosed as precluding parent ability to care for the child adequately

Conduct—Parental behavior which has demonstrated the parents' unwillingness or inability to provide adequately for the child's health and safety

Best interest of the child—The child has formed strong ties with another family and/or will be damaged by a return to the biological parents

4. What factual evidence is necessary and admissible in court if parental rights arc to be terminated.
5. What if one parent will release the child and the other won't, or you cannot locate one parent.
6. What is the appeal process.

PREPARE YOUR CASE

Review your case record, your notes, all letters and correspondence with the child's parent. Develop a chronology of your information for termination of parental rights.

List in chronological order the following information for both parents:

1. Reason, date and plan for placement. Note court orders, etc. that document these items.
2. Visits between child and parent including dates, who made the arrangements, where the visit occurred and how the child and parent behaved.
3. Gifts given to the child—include cards and letters. Note appropriateness, whether one child in a family was left out, dates gifts were given and who gave them.
4. Financial support for child. Who paid what and when, was there court order requiring payment.
5. Parental involvement in casework plan for child's return. Document plans developed, note success and failures at goal achievement.
6. Document parental conditions which necessitate termination of parental rights.
7. Agency service provision to the family to help in rehabilitation. Include dates of contacts, document services provided.
8. Periods of abandonment and agency attempts to locate missing parents.
9. Child's reaction and preference.

Review your chronological record with regard to state statutes for termination of parental rights.

If you believe you have a strong case, meet with your attorney to plan to take your case to court.

If your case is weak, begin *NOW* to collect the information you need. If the agency has failed to provide adequate services, you may need to plan for return home with a clear casework plan. Should that plan fail you will then have a clear documentation for termination at a future time.

When you have determined that you are ready to go to court, prepare the parents for what is to happen. This applies to voluntary as well as involuntary plans for adoption.

1. Explain clearly to parents the nature of the court proceedings which will occur.
2. Explain clearly to parents their rights to counsel.
3. Explain to the child, if he is to be involved in this process, what is going to happen in the court proceedings.

PRESENT YOUR CASE

When presenting your case in court, there are certain things which will enhance your case and minimize your anxiety:

1. Be prepared, review your chronology with your attorney and know what he will ask and what you plan to say.
2. Dress neatly and appropriately for the courtroom.
3. Tell the truth and don't exaggerate.
4. Listen carefully to questions asked. Answer *only* the question asked and ask for it to be repeated if you are unsure what the question was.
5. Speak slowly, in a loud voice and use clear, simple language.
6. Give only factual answers unless you are *specifically* asked for your opinion.

Once your case has been presented in court, your attorney should advise you of the procedure for decision-making by the Judge, and what the appeal process might do to plans for adoptive placement of the child. If he does not tell you, ask him.

APPENDIX C

Sample Written Agreement*

I, (Client), have stated my interest in regaining custody of (Child), and in order to work toward that goal, I agree to the following conditions:

1. I agree to visit (Child), every Wednesday from 1:00 P.M. to 3:00 P.M. in the (Child Welfare Agency) office.
2. I agree to meet with (Caseworker), every Wednesday at 3:00 P.M. in the (Child Welfare Agency) office to discuss my visits with my child, to review planning concerning my child, and to discuss changes in my situation as well as any other relevant matters.
3. I agree to participate in weekly meetings with a counselor from the County Mental Health Clinic.
4. I agree to keep (Caseworker) of (Child Welfare Agency) informed at all times of my whereabouts and home address.

I, (Client), understand that failure to meet the terms of this agreement may result in a petition for termination of parental rights to my child, (Child).

_____(signed)_____ _____(date)_____
(Client)

I, (Caseworker), acting on behalf of (Child Welfare Agency), agree to assist (Client) in her efforts to regain custody of her child, (Child), and, in order to work toward that goal, agree to the following conditions:

1. I agree to have (Child) at the (Child Welfare Agency) office every Wednesday at 1:00 P.M. for visit with her mother, (Client).

* From Pike, Downs, Emlen, Downs, & Case (1977, pp. 50–51).

200

2. I agree to meet with (Client) each Wednesday at 3:00 P.M. in the (Child Welfare Agency) office.
3. I agree to arrange transportation, upon request, for (Client) so that she can attend weekly meetings with the mental health clinic counselor.
4. I agree to maintain (Child) in foster care until a permanent plan can be accomplished for her.
5. I agree to keep (Client) informed of any significant matters relating to her child, (Child), such as illnesses, school progress, etc.

<u>   (signed)   </u>   <u>   (date)   </u>
(Caseworker)

It is jointly understood and agreed between (Client) and (Caseworker) that this agreement will continue in effect for a period of ninety days (unless jointly modified) and will be reviewed by (date), to evaluate progress toward meeting the stated goals.

References

ADOPTION RESOURCE CENTER, 1980. *The Adoption Resource,* The Information Bulletin of Region II, Fall 1980.

AMBROSINO, S., 1979. "Integrating Counseling, Family Life Education, and Family Advocacy." In *Social Casework,* 60(10): 579–585.

AMERICAN PUBLIC WELFARE ASSOCIATION, 1975. *Standards for Foster Care.* Chicago: American Public Welfare Association.

ANDREWS, D., 1977. "Two Hundred Years of Child Health in America." In *Two Hundred Years of Children,* ed. E. Grotberg, (OHD)77–30103. Washington, D.C.: U.S. Government Printing Office.

ARONSON, D., 1980. "A Study of Selected "Protective Service" Factors Which May Contribute to Client Recommendation and Engagement in Therapy." Doctoral dissertation, Hofstra University.

BANDOLI, L., 1977. "Leaderless Support Groups in Child Protective Services," *Social Work* 22(2): 22–35.

BECK, B., 1979. *The Lower East Side Family Union: A Social Invention.* New York: Foundation for Child Development.

BEDFORD, L., and L. HYBERTSON, 1975. "Emotionally Disturbed Children: A Program of Alternatives to Residential Treatment," *Child Welfare* 54 (2): 109–115.

BERNSTEIN, B., D. SNIDER, and W. MEEZAN, 1975. *Foster Care Needs and Alternatives to Placement.* New York State Board of Social Welfare.

BLACKWELL, G., and R. GOULD, 1952. *Future Citizens All.* Chicago: American Public Welfare Association.

BOEHM, B., 1958. *Deterrents to the Adoption of Children in Foster Care.* New York: Child Welfare League of America.

BRONFENBRENNER, U., 1979. *The Ecology of Human Development: Experiments by Nature and Design.* Cambridge: Harvard University Press.

BUSH, M., A. GORDON, and R. LeBAILLY, 1977. "Evaluating Child Welfare Services: A Contribution from the Clients," *Social Service Review* 51(3): 492–494.

BUSH, S., 1977. "A Family-Help Program That Really Works," *Psychology Today*, May 1977, 48, 50, 84–88.

CARROLL, M., 1980. "Collaboration with Social Work Clients: A Review of the Literature," *Child Welfare* 59(7): 407–417.

Case Record, 1981, 5(3): 3–5.

CATALANO, R., J. HOWARD, and A. ROSS, 1974. *Foster Care of Children in New York State*. New York State Department of Social Services.

CHILDREN'S DEFENSE FUND 1978. *Children Without Homes*. Washington, D.C.: Children's Defense Fund.

CITIZENS' COMMITTEE FOR CHILDREN OF NEW YORK, 1971. *A Dream Deferred: Child Welfare in New York City*. New York: Citizens' Committee for Children of New York, Inc.

—————, 1978. *Social Services—Short Shrift for 600,000 Children*. New York: Citizens' Committee for Children of New York, Inc.

—————, 1981. *Myth and Reality: A New Look at Children Available for Adoption*. New York: Citizens' Committee for Children of New York, Inc.

COOMBES, P., M. MCCORMACK, M. CHIPLEY, and B. ARCHER, 1978. "The INCAD-EX Approach to Identifying Problems and Evaluating Impact in Child Protective Services," *Child Welfare* 57(1): 35–44.

COPANS, S., H. KRELL, J. GRUNDY, J. ROGAN, and F. FIELD, 1979. "The Stresses of Treating Child Abuse," *Children Today* 8(1): 22–35.

DAVOREN, E., 1975. "Working with Abusive Parents: A Social Worker's View," *Children Today* 4(3): 2, 38–43.

DOMAN, G., 1974. *What to Do about Your Brain-injured Child*. New York: Doubleday.

DORMAN, R., 1981. "Evaluating CAN Research." In *Family Life Developments*. Ithaca: Region II Child Abuse and Neglect Resource Center, Cornell University.

DRYDYK, J., B. MENDEVILLE, and L. BENDER, 1980. "Foster Parenting a Retarded Child: The Arizona Story," *Children Today* 9(4): 10, 24–25.

DUKETTE, R., R. BORN, B. GAGEL, and M. HENDRICKS, 1978. *Structured Assessment: A Decision-making Guide for Child Welfare*. Chicago: U.S. Department of Health, Education, and Welfare, Region V.

DUNU, M., and M. CLAY, 1978. "Family Union Keeps Families Together," *Practice Digest* 1(1): 22–23.

ELMER, E., 1967. *Children in Jeopardy*. Pittsburgh: University of Pittsburgh Press.

————— and G. GREGG, 1967. "Developmental Characteristics of Abused Children," *Pediatrics, 40,* 596.

FAMILY SERVICE ASSOCIATION OF AMERICA, 1969. "Summary of Family Advocacy Program, November 26, 1969." New York: Family Service Association of America. Mimeo.

FANSHEL, D., 1966. "Child Welfare." In *Five Fields of Social Service: Reviews of Research*, ed. H. Maas. New York: National Association of Social Workers. (a)

—————, 1966. *Foster Parenthood: A Role Analysis*. Minneapolis: University of Minnesota Press. (b)

—————, 1979. *Computerized Information for Child Welfare: Foster Children and Their Foster Parents*. New York: Columbia School of Social Work.

—————— and H. MAAS, 1962. "Factorial Dimensions of the Characteristics of Children in Placement and Their Families," *Child Development 33*(1): 123–144.

——————, and E. SHINN, 1978. *Children in Foster Care: A Longitudinal Investigation.* New York: Columbia University Press.

FEIN, E., L. DAVIS, and G. KNIGHT, 1979. "Placement Stability in Foster Care," *Social Work 24*(3): 156–157.

FINK, A., E. WILSON, and M. CONOVER, 1963. *The Field of Social Work.* New York: Holt, Rinehart & Winston.

FINKELSTEIN, N., 1980. "Family-centered Group Care," *Child Welfare 59*(1): 33–41.

FONTANA, V., 1971. "Which Parents Abuse Children," *Medical Insight 3*(10): 16–21.

——————, 1976. *Somewhere a Child Is Crying: Maltreatment Causes and Prevention.* New York: American Library.

——————, and E. ROBISON, 1976. "A Multidisciplinary Approach to the Treatment of Child Abuse," *Pediatrics 57:* 760–764.

FREUDENBERGER, H., C. MASLACH, A. PINES, M. REED, and B. SUTTON, 1977. "Stress and Burn-out in Child Care," *Child Care Quarterly 6*(2): 88–137.

FRY, A. R., 1974. "The Children's Migration," *American Heritage 26*(1): 5–10, 79–81.

FURSTENBERG, F., JR. 1976. *Unplanned Parenthood.* New York: Free Press.

GARBARINO, J., 1976. "A Preliminary Study of Some Ecological Correlates of Child Abuse: The Impact of Socio-economic Stress on Mothers," *Child Development,* 1976, pp. 47, 178.

GARBARINO, J., 1977. "The Human Ecology of Child Maltreatment: A Conceptual Model for Research." Society for Research in Child Development, New Orleans.

GELLES, R., 1976. "Demythologizing Child Abuse," *Family Coordinator 25,* 135–141.

GERMAIN, C., 1973. "An Ecological Perspective in Casework Practice," *Social Casework 54*(6): 323–330.

——————, (ed.), 1980. *The Ecological Perspective in Social Work Practice: People and Environments.* New York: Columbia University Press.

GIOVANNONI, J., and R. BERCERRA, 1979. *Defining Child Abuse.* New York: Free Press.

GOLDSTEIN, J., A. FREUD, and A. SOLNIT, 1973. *Beyond the Best Interests of the Child.* New York: Free Press.

——————, 1979. *Before the Best Interests of the Child.* New York: Free Press.

HALES, D., J. KENNELL, and R. SUSA, 1976. "How Early is Early Contact: Defining the Limits of the Sensitive Period." Report to the Foundation for Child Development on the Ecology of Human Development Program. New York: Foundation for Child Development.

HAMPSON, R., and J. TAVORMINA, 1980. "Feedback from the Experts: A Study of Foster Mothers," *Social Work 25*(2): 108–113.

HARING, B., 1975. *1975 Census of Requests for Child Welfare Services.* New York: Child Welfare League of America.

HARLING, P., and J. HAINES, 1980. "Specialized Foster Homes for Severely Mistreated Children," *Children Today 9*(4): 16–18.

HARTMAN, A., 1978. "Diagrammatic Assessment of Family Relationships," *Social Casework* 59(8): 465–476.

——————, 1979. *Finding Families*. Beverly Hills: Sage.

HOLDER, W., C. MOUZAKITIS, M. ROMERO, D. SAHD, and O. SALISBURY, 1980. In *Helping in Child Protective Services: A Casework Handbook*, "The Protective Services Casework Process." ed. W. Holder and C. Mohr. Denver, Colorado: American Humane Association.

HUNTER, R., 1980. "Parents Who Break with an Abusive Past: Lessons for Prevention," *Caring* 6(4): 1, 4, 6.

INTERFACE 1980. *An Ounce of Prevention: A Survey of Preventive Services Programs Contracted by New York City Special Services for Children*. New York: Interface.

JAFFEE, B., and D. FANSHEL, 1970. *How They Fared in Adoption: A Follow-up Study*. New York: Columbia University Press.

JANCHILL, SISTER MARY PAUL, 1975. *Criteria for Foster Care Placement and Alternatives to Foster Care*. New York: New York State Board of Social Welfare.

—— ——————, 1980. *Guidelines for Decision-making in Child Welfare*. New York: Human Services Workshops.

JARRET, J., and M. COPHER, 1980. "Five Couples Look at Adoption," *Children Today* 9(4): 12–15.

JENKINS, S., and E. NORMAN, 1972. *Filial Deprivation and Foster Care*. New York: Columbia University Press.

——————, 1975. *Beyond Placement: Mothers View Foster Care*. New York: Columbia University Press.

JEWETT, C., 1978. *Adopting the Older Child*. Cambridge: Harvard Common Press.

JONES, M., and J. BIESECKER, 1977. *Permanent Planning Guide for Children and Youth Services*. Millersville, Pa.: Millersville State College.

JONES, M., S. MAGURA, and A. SHYNE, 1981. "Effective Practice with Families in Protective and Preventive Services: What Works?" *Child Welfare* 60(2): 67–80.

JUSTICE, B., and R. JUSTICE, 1976. *The Abusing Family*. New York: Human Sciences.

KADUSHIN, A., 1978. "Child Welfare Strategy in the Coming Years: An Overview." In *Child Welfare Strategy in the Coming Years*. HEW pub. no. (OHD) 78-30158. Washington, D.C.: U.S. Children's Bureau. (a)

——————, 1978. "Children in Adoptive Homes." In *Social Service Research: Reviews of Studies*, ed. H. Maas. New York: National Association of Social Workers. (b)

——————, 1978. "Children in Foster Families and Institutions." In *Social Service Research: Reviews of Studies*, ed. H. Maas. New York: National Association of Social Workers. (c)

——————, 1980, *Child Welfare Services*. New York: Macmillan.

KAHN, A., 1976. "Service Delivery at the Neighborhood Level: Experience, Theory, and Fads," *Social Service Review* 50(1): 23–56.

——————, 1977. "Child Welfare." *Social Work Encyclopedia*, 16th ed., J. R. Morris, ed. New York: National Association of Social Workers.

KALISCH, B., 1978. *Child Abuse and Neglect: An Annotated Bibliography*. Westport, Conn.: Greenwood Press.

KAMERMAN, S. and A. KAHN, 1981. *Child Care, Family Benefits, and Working Parents*. New York: Columbia University Press.

KEMPE, C., 1962. "The Battered Child Syndrome," *Journal of the American Medical Association 181:* 17–24.

——————, and R. HELFER, 1972. *Helping the Battered Child and His Family.* Philadelphia: Lippincott.

KEMPE, R., and C. KEMPE, 1978. *Child Abuse,* Developing Child Series. Cambridge, Massachusetts: Harvard University Press.

KLEIN, M., and L. STERN, 1971. "Low Birth Weight and the Battered Child Syndrome," *American Journal of Diseases of Childhood 122*(15).

KLERMAN, L., and J. JEKEL, 1973. *School-age Mothers: Problems, Programs, and Policy.* Handen, Conn.: Shoe String.

KOCHMAN, A., and D. GAINES, 1977. *Evaluation Report: Parent and Child Training Project.* New York: Family Service Association of Nassau County.

——————, 1978. "Involving the Parents of Children at Risk." Paper presented at the Family Service Association of America North American Symposium on Family Practice, New York City.

KRAUS, J., 1971. "Predicting Success of Foster Placements for School-age Children," *Social Work 16*(1): 63–71.

LAIRD, J., 1980. "An Ecological Approach to Child Welfare: Issues of Family Identity and Continuity." In *The Ecological Perspective in Social Work Practice: People and Environments,* ed. C. Germain. New York: Columbia University Press.

LINDNER, C., 1978. *In the Best Interests of the Child: Social Work in the Family Court.* New York: Federation of Protestant Welfare Agencies.

MAAS, H., and R. ENGLER, 1959. *Children in Need of Parents.* New York: Columbia University Press.

MADISON, B., 1977. "Child Welfare Services." In *Changing Roles in Social Work Practice,* ed. F. Sobey. New York: University Book Service.

MALUCCIO, A., and W. MARLOW, 1972. "Residential Treatment of Emotionally Disturbed Children: A Review of the Literature," *Social Service Review 46*(2): 230–250.

MARR, P., 1981. "Foster Care Teamwork Comes to Kansas," *Case Record 5*(1): 1–2.

MAYER, M., 1965. "A Research Attempt in a Residential Treatment Center: An Administrative Case History." In *The Known and Unknown in Child Welfare Research,* ed. M. Norris and B. Wallace. New York: National Association of Social Workers.

MILLMAN, H., and C. SCHAFFER, 1975. "Behavioral Change: Program Evaluation and Staff Feedback," *Child Welfare, 54*(10): 692–702.

MURPHY, A., S. PUESCHEL, and J. SCHNEIDER, 1973. "Groupwork with Parents of Children with Down's Syndrome," *Social Casework 54*(2): 114–119.

NATIONAL COMMISSION FOR CHILDREN IN NEED OF PARENTS 1979. *Who Knows? Who Cares? Forgotten Children in Foster Care.* New York: National Commission for Children.

NORTH SHORE CHILD GUIDANCE ASSOCIATION, 1978–79. *Annual Report.* Nassau County, New York: North Shore Child Guidance Association.

NASSAU COUNTY DEPARTMENT OF SOCIAL SERVICES, 1977, 1978. *Operation Placement: Evaluation Reports, First and Second Years.* New York: Nassau County Department of Social Services.

O'DONNELL, E., and O. REID, 1972. "The Multiservice Neighborhood Center: Neighborhood Challenge and Center Response," *Welfare in Review* 10(3): 1–7.

OXLEY, G., 1977. "A Modified Form of Residential Treatment and Its Impact on Behavioral Adjustment," *Social Work* 22(6): 493–498.

PIKE, V. 1976. "Permanent Planning for Children in Foster Care: The Oregon Project," *Children Today* 5(6): 22–25, 41.

—————, S. DOWNS, A. EMLEN, G. DOWNS, and D. CASE, 1977. *Permanent Planning for Children in Foster Care: A Handbook for Social Workers* (OHDS) 77-30124. Washington, D.C.: U.S. Government Printing Office.

PISANI, J. 1975. *The Children of the State I: Preliminary Report of the Temporary State Commission on Child Welfare.* New York.

POLANSKY, N., R. BORGMAN, and D. DESAIX, 1972. *Roots of Fertility.* San Francisco: Jossey-Bass.

POLANSKY, N., C. HALLY, and N. F. POLANSKY, 1975. *Profile of Neglect: A Survey of the State of Knowledge of Child Neglect.* Washington, D.C.: U.S. Government Printing Office.

RADBILL, S. X., 1968. "A History of Child Abuse and Infanticide." In *The Battered Child,* ed. R. Helfer and E. Kempe. Chicago: University of Chicago Press.

RADOWITZ, S., 1979. *Community Based and Supported Parents' Centers for High-risk Parents.* New York: Published privately.

REGIONAL RESEARCH INSTITUTE FOR HUMAN SERVICES, 1981. *Case Record* 5(3), Summer.

Report on Provision of Child Welfare Services in New York State (1974–1975). New York State Department of Social Services.

RINGLER, N., 1977. "Mother's Speech to Her Two-Year-Old Child: Its Effect on Speech and Language Comprehension at Five Years." Paper presented at the annual meeting of the Pediatric Research Society, St. Louis.

ROCK, M., 1978. "Gorilla Mothers Need Some Help from Their Friends." *Smithsonian* 9(4): 58–62.

SCHAEFER, C., AND H. MILLMAN, 1973. "The Use of Behavior Ratings in Assessing the Effect of Residental Treatment with Latency-Age Boys," *Child Psychiatry and Human Development* 3.

SCHNEIDER, R., 1978. "Behavioral Outcomes for Administration Majors." *Journal of Education for Social Work* 14(1): 102–108.

SCHNEIGER, F., 1978. "The Worker Burnout Phenomenon: Implications of Current Research for the Child Protective System," *Research for Action* (newsletter suppl. 1). New York: Community Council of Greater New York.

SHAPIRO, D., 1975. *Agencies and Foster Children.* New York: Columbia University Press.

SHYNE, A., 1980. "Who Are the Children: A National Overview of Services," *Social Work Research and Abstracts* 16(1): 26–33.

SOBEY, F. (ed.), 1977. *Changing Roles in Social Work Practice.* New York: University Book Service.

SPECHT, H., 1981. "Professionalism: Weighed and Found Wanting? An Opinion by Harry Specht," *Public Welfare* 39(3): 8–9.

SPINELLI, L., and K. BARTON, 1980. "Home Management Services for Families with Emotionally Disturbed Children," *Child Welfare* 59(1): 43–52.

STEIN, T., and E. GAMBRILL, 1976. "Behavioral Techniques in Foster Care," *Social Work* 21(1): 34–39.

STEIN, T., E. GAMBRILL, and K. WILTSE, 1977. "Contracts and Outcome in Foster Care," *Social Work* 22(2): 148–149.

———, 1978. *Children in Foster Homes: Achieving Continuity of Care.* New York: Praeger.

STONE, H., 1980. "Foster Parenting a Retarded Child: The New Curriculum," *Children Today* 9(4): 11, 24–26.

STREAN, H., 1978. *Clinical Social Work: Theory and Practice.* New York: The Free Press.

———, 1981. "A Critique of Some of the Newer Treatment Modalities," *Clinical Social Work Journal* 9(3): 155–171.

SUNLEY, R., 1978. *Final Report: Parent–Child Project.* New York: Family Service Association of Nassau County.

TAYLOR, D., and S. ALPERT, 1973. *Continuity and Support following Residental Treatment.* New York: Child Welfare League of America.

THEIS, S., 1924. *How Foster Children Turn Out.* New York: State Charities Aid Association.

TURITZ, A., and R. SMITH, 1965. "Child Welfare." In *Encyclopedia of Social Work,* ed. H. Lurie. New York: National Association of Social Workers.

TURNER, C., 1980. "Resources for Help in Parenting," *Child Welfare* 59(3): 179–188.

U.S. DEPARTMENT OF HEALTH, EDUCATION, AND WELFARE, Children's Bureau, 1976. *Child Welfare in 25 States: An Overview* HEW pub. no. (OHD) 76-300090. Washington, D.C.: U.S. Government Printing Office.

WEISSMAN, H., 1978. *Integrating Services for Troubled Families.* San Francisco: Jossey-Bass.

WHITTAKER, J., 1980. "Family Involvement in Residential Treatment: A Support System for Parents." In *The Challenge of Partnership: Working with Parents of Children in Foster Care,* ed. A. Maluccio and P. Sinanoglu. Child Welfare League of America.

WILTSE, K., 1979. "Foster Care in the 1970's: A Decade of Change," *Children Today* 8(3): 10–14.

WITHEY, V., R. ANDERSON, and M. LAUDERDALE, 1980. "Volunteers as Mentors: A Natural Helping Relationship," *Child Welfare* 59(10): 637–644.

ZINMAN, D., 1977. "Depression Is the Root of Many Teen Troubles," *Newsday,* 19 September 1977.

Index